# Data Mining:
## Building Competitive Advantage

**Robert Groth**

ISBN 0-13-086271-1

**Prentice Hall PTR**
**Upper Saddle River, NJ 07458**
**www.phptr.com**

**Library of Congress Cataloging-in-Publication Data**

Groth, Robert.
  Data mining : building competitive advantage / Robert Groth.
    p. cm.
  ISBN 0-13-086271-1
  1. Data mining. I. Title.
QA76.9.D343G76   1999
658.4'038--dc21
                                          99-42508
                                            CIP

Production editor and compositor: *Vanessa Moore*
Cover design: *Anthony Gemmellaro*
Cover design director: *Jerry Votta*
Manufacturing manager: *Maura Goldstaub*
Marketing manager: *Bryan Gambrel*
Acquisitions editor: *Tim Moore*
Editorial assistant: *Julie Okulicz*
Project coordinator: *Anne Trowbridge*

©2000 Prentice Hall PTR
Prentice-Hall, Inc.
Upper Saddle River, New Jersey 07458

Prentice Hall books are widely used by corporations and government agencies for training, marketing, and resale.
The publisher offers discounts on this book when ordered in bulk quantities.
For more information, contact Corporate Sales Department, Phone: 800-382-3419;
Fax: 201-236-7141; E-mail: corpsales@prenhall.com
Or write: Prentice Hall PTR, Corp. Sales Dept., One Lake Street, Upper Saddle River, NJ 07458.

Product names mentioned herein are the trademarks or registered trademarks of their respective owners.

ISBN 0-13-086271-1

Printed in the United States of America

10  9  8  7  6  5  4  3  2  1

Prentice-Hall International (UK) Limited, *London*
Prentice-Hall of Australia Pty. Limited, *Sydney*
Prentice-Hall Canada Inc., *Toronto*
Prentice-Hall Hispanoamericana, S.A., *Mexico*
Prentice-Hall of India Private Limited, *New Delhi*
Prentice-Hall of Japan, Inc., *Tokyo*
Prentice-Hall (Singapore) Pte. Ltd., *Singapore*
Editora Prentice-Hall do Brasil, Ltda., *Rio de Janeiro*

*This book is dedicated to*
*Zachary Jerome Constantin Groth.*

# Contents

# List of Figures

# Preface

In the two short years since the first version of this book was published, the data-mining industry has progressed at nothing short of light speed. Just look at a few of the more significant events:

- SAS Institute releases Enterprise Miner.
- SPSS buys ISL and their Clementine data-mining software.
- Yahoo! buys HyperParallel, Inc.
- Aspen Technologies buys NeuralWorks.
- Oracle Corporation buys Thinking Machines.
- Many data mining vendors, like DataMind, remake themselves to apply data mining to industry applications.

Version One of this book emphasized all the attention data mining has recently received, citing many sources such as an article in *Bank Systems & Technology*, January 1996, which stated: "Data mining is the most important application in financial services in 1996." In a 1996 commercial by IBM, played during the SuperBowl, fashion models discuss the use and advantages of data mining. Finally, there was a graph from the META Group projecting the data-mining market to be a $800 million dollar market by the year 2000.

Data mining is still gaining momentum and the players are rapidly changing. A second version of this book was needed to update discussions on current players and industry trends. For example, there is a major push in today's industry to change from a tools-oriented focus to a more solution-oriented focus.

This version of the book greatly expands on how data mining solves business problems. You the reader want to understand not only the current trends in the industry, but also what data mining is and how it can be applied to provide competitive advantage. META Group made the comment: "The majority of global 2000 organizations will find data-mining technologies to be critical to their business success by the year 2000." While this is interesting, there are specific reasons why this statement is true. The burning questions you should be asking are: Why are global 2000 organizations finding data mining to be "critical"? What are the benefits of data mining, both to me and my business? How do I make the most of data mining?

## The Purpose of This Book

This text, *Data Mining: Building Competitive Advantage,* resulted from the revelation that data mining is becoming mainstream and that there are few books about data mining devoted to the business professional. It provides an innovative, easy approach to learning data mining for business professionals, students, and consultants. The CD-ROM at the back of the book makes learning data mining a hands-on activity. You can try out different software packages available for data mining and learn how these tools are being used to solve industry problems.

This book focuses on how knowledge discovery is used in different industries, and discusses several of the data-mining software products available. Sample studies are provided for specific industries, including retail, banking, insurance, and healthcare.

This text takes a different approach to introducing data mining than the academic books currently on the market. The focus of this book is on industry applications, discussions of specific business problems, and a hands-on teaching style to demonstrate how tools can be used to attain business benefit.

This book provides answers to the following basic questions:

- What is data mining?
- How is data mining used in industry today?
- Why use data mining?
- Which vendors are in the data-mining market?
- Where do you go to find information on data mining?
- How do you data mine?

### Industry Focus

Data mining is an evolving field, with great variety in terminology and methodology. To gain a reasonable understanding of data mining, you should have a broad perspective on how it is being used within the industry today. Data-mining tools currently on the market are also discussed, as well as how to get more information on the vendors and Web sites available to you.

This book covers industry applications of data mining in various industries, including:

- banking and finance
- retail and marketing
- telecommunications
- healthcare

This book broadens the scope of what is relevant to learning data mining. Not only should you learn the methodology and terminology needed to use data mining, you should also learn specific examples of how to achieve fast results in the corporate environment.

You never hear as much as you should about industry solutions of data mining. Most companies are reluctant to discuss findings that lead to dramatic returns on investment, for competitive reasons. Industry applications making use of data-mining technology drive competitive advantage. People use data-mining technology to predict outcomes: which customers are likely to respond to specific marketing campaigns, claims that are fraudulent, or products customers are most likely to buy. The more success a company has in predicting such outcomes, the more tight-lipped they are prone to become.

### Hands-On Teaching Style

This book also provides a hands-on approach to learning data mining. By devoting three hours of your time, you can use the enclosed CD-ROM to familiarize yourself with data mining's major processes.

Once we cover the concepts of data mining, we'll go directly to exercises that show the ease of turning data into information. The CD-ROM contains demonstrations of two data-mining tools: Angoss® KnowledgeSeeker™, and RightPoint® Software's DataCruncher.

## Audience

This book gives a general overview of data mining and is written for a broad-based audience. The book will be useful to:

### Business Professionals

Anyone in business who deals with large amounts of data should consider the data-mining tools and applications described in this book. Effort is made to provide industry examples as well as to make the use of data-mining products understandable.

### Database Administrators (DBAs)

Database administrators should be interested in this book, since it explains how end users can extract data from relational databases and data warehouses in order to mine data. Sample data structures are described for different industries. The data fields used in different types of data-mining studies are also discussed in detail.

### Marketing Analysts

Data mining is especially useful to marketing organizations, because it allows them to profile customers to a previously unavailable level. Some people refer to this as "one-to-one" marketing. In general, today's distributors of mass mailings use data-mining tools. In several years, data mining will be a mandatory strategic requirement of marketing organizations.

### Students

Students who desire a practical introduction to the basics of data mining and the current market can start with this book.

### Systems Analysts and Consultants

Consultants can benefit from the discussions of the vendors involved and by industry-specific examples.

## Scope of This Book

*Data Mining: Building Competitive Advantage* does not include detailed explanations of the algorithms used with data mining. If you want to learn more about the algorithms, I would suggest *Advances in Knowledge Discovery and Data Mining*, by Usama M. Fayyad, Gregory Piatestsky-Shapiro, Padhraic Smyth, and Ramasamy Uthurusam. This book, at over 550 pages, is the most comprehensive work available today on the technical approaches used in data mining.

This book is devoted to the business professional and targets an audience of professionals who do not necessarily have a statistics background and who want to learn about data-mining applications, or who wish to attempt data mining.

## Organization of This Book

*Data Mining: Building Competitive Advantage* is divided into three parts:

### Part 1   Starting Out

The first chapters introduce data mining, discuss the data-mining process, and cover vendors involved in this market.

Chapter 1, "Introduction to Data Mining," introduces basic concepts of data mining and explains why data mining is important.

Chapter 2, "Getting Started With Data Mining," discusses several of the approaches taken in data mining and their potential benefits.

Chapter 3, "The Data-Mining Process," covers the process of data mining and introduces different types of studies as well as data-preparation issues.

Chapter 4, "Data-Mining Algorithms," discusses the types of algorithms and technologies being used today.

Chapter 5, "The Data-Mining Marketplace," introduces vendors in the data-mining market today, and includes discussion of applications such as SAS Enterprise Miner and IBM's Intelligent Miner.

### Part 2    A Rapid Tutorial

Chapters 6 and 7 introduce two leading data-mining software products.

Chapter 6, "A Look at Angoss: KnowledgeSEEKER," covers the leading, commercial data-mining software product, which is based on a decision-tree model and is focused on end users. A business example for the healthcare industry is discussed.

Chapter 7, "A Look at RightPoint DataCruncher," covers an innovative commercial data-mining software product that is focused on marketing professionals. A business example for the telecommunications industry is discussed.

### Part 3    Industry Focus

Chapters 8 and 9 focus on specific industry uses of data mining. Examples for each study performed are provided, with tips on how these can be performed on corporate database systems.

Chapter 8, "Industry Applications of Data Mining," looks at types of data-mining studies in banking and finance, retail, healthcare, and the telecommunications industry. Examples of companies performing data mining are provided.

Chapter 9, "Enabling Data Mining Through Data Warehouses," looks at how data warehouses provide a methodology for helping perform data-mining studies. Four data-warehouse industry examples are provided to discuss the type of data that would be integrated and introduce how some data-mining studies could be performed using these data warehouses.

## CD-ROM Installation Requirements

The minimum system requirements for installing the CD-ROM included in this book are discussed in Appendix B. Each of the data-mining software products included in the CD-ROM have their own requirements.

The installed software enables you to run the CD-ROM-based tutorial included in this book. Additional files have been added specifically for this book beyond those provided by Angoss Software and RightPoint Software.

## Acknowledgments

This book would not have been completed without the help of many individuals. Many thanks to my wife, Michele Groth, for her review of the book, and to Leo Gelman who contributed greatly to the discussion on data warehousing in Chapter 8. Karen Thomas provided significant contributions to Chapter 7, discussing RightPoint's DataCruncher. Miguel A. Castro, from Dovetail Solutions®, is to be credited for the additions to this book in the area of market-basket analysis and assortment optimization.

Special thanks to Angoss Software, Belmont Research, Inc.®, RightPoint Software®, SAS Institute®, HNC Software Inc., MapInfo®, Neural Applications Corp®, NeuralWare®, Pilot Software®, and Silicon Graphics® for providing the use of images used in this book. Angoss Software and RightPoint Software contributed to the demo CD-ROM included at the back of the book.

Thanks to Penny Buckley at Angos Software, Patricia Campbell at HNC Software Inc., Craig Zielazny and Casey Klimasaus at NeuralWare, Karen Gobler at Pilot Software, Lisa Jacobsen at MapInfo, A.J. Brown, and Ram Srinivasan from RightPoint Software, Beverly Stockstill at SAS Institute, Tracy Timpson and Patricia Baumhart at Silicon Graphics, Jim Ong at Belmont Research, and Kurt Kimmerling at Neural Application Corporation. All products are trademarks or registered trademarks of their respective companies.

# Starting Out

These first five chapters provide an overview of the basic concepts of data mining, the approaches taken in applying data-mining technology, the process of data mining, some of the more popular data-mining algorithms, and, finally, an introduction to vendors in the data-mining market today.

# CHAPTER 1

# Introduction to Data Mining

$\mathbf{T}$his chapter examines two fundamental questions about data mining: What is data mining and why is it valuable?

The chapter is organized as follows:

- Section 1.1  What Is Data Mining?
- Section 1.2  Why Use Data Mining?
- Section 1.3  Case Studies of Implementing Data Mining
- Section 1.4  Successful Process of Using Data Mining
  for Competitive Advantage
- Section 1.5  A Note on Privacy Issues
- Section 1.6  Summary

## 1.1  What Is Data Mining?

Data mining is the process of finding trends and patterns in data. The objective of this process is to sort through large quantities of data and discover new information. The benefit of data mining is to turn this newfound knowledge into actionable results, such as increasing a customer's likelihood to buy, or decreasing the number of fraudulent claims.

The meaning of the term "data mining" is open to debate. Data mining has also been referred to as *KDD*, or *knowledge discovery in databases*. The difference between data mining and KDD varies, depending on the author you read or article you choose. Some argue that data mining is only the discovery component of the much loftier KDD process.

In this book, data mining is defined as a process of identifying hidden patterns and relationships within data. Data mining in this book is described in a functional manner with a specific goal: *This is a book about data mining for business professionals.*

Let's start with an example of how data mining is useful for a marketing professional. Marketers have learned, by astute observation, that new parents with cars will likely buy children's car seats. Since there happens to be a law requiring special car seats for children, the correlation between new parents with cars and the purchase of children's car seats is obvious (although one reviewer had to point out that they could always get a car seat from a friend or family member). You would not likely employ data-mining techniques to better understand this phenomenon because the link is well understood.

Now ask another question: What color of car seat would a parent prefer to buy for their child? This is a much more difficult question to answer and requires more variables to predict the likely outcome. Some variables might be the age, gender, income level of the parents, car color, and the gender of the child. Even the color of the child's hair might have an impact on what color car seat will be bought. There could be any number of pieces of information that could help us understand what color preference a parent might have. The benefit of data mining is that out of all the pieces of data that you may have, it will tell us what pieces of data are the most relevant for your desired outcome. Data mining becomes more useful as the amount of data and variables stored by an organization increases.

In business, there are many patterns that are difficult to understand. Yet a better understanding of these patterns can affect your company's competitive ability. Take a moment to consider a few of the typical questions a marketing department might ask:

- In addition to the products they already have, what products is my customer likely to buy?
- What are the characteristics of my most profitable customers?
- What are the variables that determine when my customer may jump to a competitor?

Not only can data mining help answer these types of questions, it is best suited for analysis of customer information as data becomes increasingly complex.

*Sure I want to know the answer, but why can't I just query a database and find out the answers for myself?*

End users are often confused about the differences between query tools, which allow end users to ask questions of database management systems (DBMS), and data-mining tools. Perhaps the best way to differentiate these tools is to use an example.

Assume you are playing the game of BattleShip™. The typical question you ask your opponent is:

**_Is there a battleship in row B, column 5?_**

This type of question, or query, asks if a battleship is in a specific location. This is similar to most queries performed on databases today. By asking this question, you are making an assumption about the location of what you are searching for.

With a data-mining tool, you would ask a question like:

**_What are the most likely positions where the opponent would place his or her battleship?_**

A data-mining tool discovers patterns in your opponent's battleship placement. It does not require any assumptions; it tries to discover relationships and hidden patterns that may not always be obvious. In order to work, data mining also requires some historical knowledge of what your opponent has done before, whereas a query tool requires no historical knowledge.

The process of finding your opponent's battleship through query or data mining contrast: by querying, you are using the equivalent of a flashlight to search; by data mining, you search and narrow the field with the equivalent of motion sensors.

Many analysts today use the query tool "flashlight" to locate interesting information in their data. While tools exist to query, access, and manipulate data, the user is left to point the flashlight where they may find useful trends and patterns. Data mining automates the process of discovering useful trends and patterns.

## 1.2  Why Use Data Mining?

Dr. Penzias, a Nobel Prize winner interviewed in ComputerWorld in January 1999, comments:

> _"Data mining will become much more important, and companies will throw away nothing about their customers because it will be so valuable. If you're not doing this, you're out of business."_

In business, there are clear reasons for investing in data mining. If data mining can provide actionable results that improve business processes, then data mining is a competitive weapon. For example, Table 1-1 examines three clear cases where data mining can directly affect a company's profitability.

Notice that in all three examples, the bottom line revenue of a company was affected by the quality of the intelligence gathered by data mining. Of course in some cases, such as the stock market, the predictions are much less certain than in other areas. In direct mail, for example, it is easy to identify the top 10% of the people most likely to respond to a campaign. These are only a few cases of using data mining to enhance a company's competitiveness.

**Table 1-1**    How Data Mining Affects Various Companies

| **Data Mining in Retail** | |
|---|---|
| Business Problem | Increase response rates on direct-mail campaigns. |
| Solution | Through data mining, marketers build predictive models that indicate who will most likely respond to a direct-mail campaign. |
| Benefit | Increase revenues by targeting campaigns to the right audience. |
| **Data Mining in Insurance** | |
| Business Problem | Decrease number of fraudulent claims. |
| Solution | Through data mining, marketers build predictive models that identify those claims that are most likely fraudulent. |
| Benefit | Increase profits by reducing costs. |
| **Data Mining in Financial Markets** | |
| Business Problem | Improve ability to predict the likely fluctuations in the market. |
| Solution | Through data mining, financial analysts build predictive models that identify patterns that have historically caused market fluctuations. |
| Benefit | Increase revenues by investing more intelligently. |

### 1.2.1   Examples of Using Data Mining

Here are a few areas in which data mining is being used for strategic benefit.

**Direct Marketing**

Data mining has been widely used in direct mail. The ability to predict who is most likely to respond to mail or most likely to buy certain products can save companies immense amounts in marketing expenditures. Direct-mail marketers employ various data-mining techniques to reduce expenditures; reaching fewer, better qualified potential customers can be more cost-effective than mailing to your entire mailing list. Users of such technology include Bank of America, People's Bank, Sundance, Equifax, Reader's Digest, Group 1, Marriott, and *The Washington Post.*

The use of data mining in marketing is, however, much broader than just direct marketing. In Figure 1-1, the chart summarizes the mainstream use of data mining in marketing. Marketers want to better understand how they can acquire new customers, grow the value of those customers, and retain them. Data mining can help in all three of these activities.

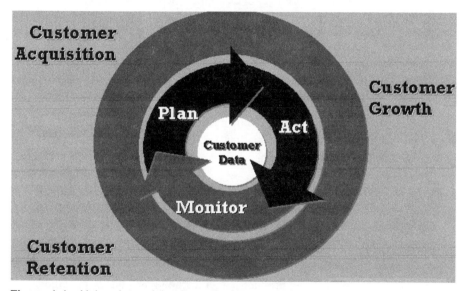

**Figure 1-1** Using data mining in marketing to acquire, grow the value of, and retain customers.

### Customer Acquisition

Customer acquisition is the number-one issue for small company marketers. As corporations increase budgets to attract and obtain new customers, data mining becomes a critical tool for profiling good customers, performing market segmentation, and improving the results of direct-marketing campaigns. In the past, these activities, if performed at all, were left in the hands of trained statisticians, or given out as projects to outside agencies. This has resulted in campaigns that are slow to market and often too late to be effective in highly competitive environments. In addition, the number of campaigns that can be managed in a given time period is often much lower than what the business demands. Data mining solves these problems by putting tools in the hands of the marketers driving these campaigns — it keeps control where the need is. As a result, marketers can be much more responsive to creating new campaigns and can implement a direct feedback loop to improve their efforts on a regular basis.

### Customer Retention

Customer retention is also a major issue for all businesses. One Harvard study suggests: "Reducing customer attrition by 5% can double a company's profits." Given the high cost of finding new customers, a key issue for many organizations is customer retention. Often referred to as *churn*, customer turnover is a difficult problem to manage because it usually occurs without warning. For example, when a customer calls their long-distance carrier to have their account closed in favor of a competitor, the telecommunications provider knows only at that moment that their valued customer is churning. Once they are predisposed to leave, it is unlikely that the customer can be convinced to stay. Data mining introduces a major paradigm shift to churn management by adding predictive capabilities. Data-mining tools can be used to model the patterns of past churning customers by examining billing histories, demographic information, and other customer data. Then, the same model can be used to predict other good customers who are likely to leave in the near future. Armed with this information, the marketer can proactively instigate campaigns to keep their customer, rather than fighting to get them back later.

### Cross-Selling

Growing a customer's value is yet another critical marketing function. The notion of increasing *customer share* is key to most organizations. Unlike increasing *market share*, which focuses on obtaining a greater number of customers, increasing customer share refers to getting more of the dollars each individual customer has to spend. Two common methods for this are customer-based product-launch campaigns, and cross-selling. Riddled with as much guesswork and gut instinct as they are today, these methods are often not as effective as they could be. Data-mining tools improve product launches to an installed base, as well as cross-selling activities by helping marketers understand which customers are most likely to purchase new products, and which products are typically purchased together. This results in a more focused effort to customers ready to spend additional dollars.

### Trend Analysis

Understanding trends in the marketplace is a strategic advantage, because it is useful in reducing costs and bringing products to market in a timely manner.

Financial institutions desire a quick way to recognize changes in customer deposit and withdrawal patterns. Retailers want to know what products people are likely to buy with others (market-basket analysis). Pharmaceutical companies ask why someone buys their product over another. Researchers want to understand patterns in natural processes. Wal-Mart and the University of Rochester Cancer Center are two of the many institutions using data mining for trend analysis.

### Fraud Detection

Data-mining techniques can model which insurance claims, cellular phone calls, or credit-card purchases are likely to be fraudulent. Most credit-card issuers use data-mining software to detect credit fraud. Citibank, the IRS, MasterCard, Dunn & Bradstreet, and Visa are a few of the companies who have been mentioned as users of such data-mining technology. Banks are among the earliest adopters of data mining, and include Chemical Bank, U.S. Bancorp, Bank of America, Wells Fargo Bank, and First USA Bank. One article estimated an industry-wide loss of $800 to 2 billion each year from cellular phone fraud. Every major telecommunications company has an effort underway to model and understand cellular phone fraud.

### Forecasting in Financial Markets

Data mining is used extensively to model financial markets. There are books on using neural networks for financial gain. Walkrich Investment Advisors, Daiwa Securities Company, and Carl & Associates, among others, use data-mining techniques to model the stock market.

## 1.3 Case Studies of Implementing Data Mining

The many articles in the mid-90s about data mining discuss it as an "emerging market," which is absolutely amazing considering how many companies use it. The best argument in favor of data mining's usefulness is the number of companies that are data mining today and refusing to talk about it. The list of companies that use data mining looks like a Fortune 500 *Who's Who*.

### 1.3.1 An Example of Data Mining at US WEST

US WEST, one of the nation's largest telecommunications companies, with more than 20 million customers, is using SAS Institute's Enterprise Miner™ software to further hone its already successful target-marketing strategies.

Like many other telecommunications companies, US WEST was experiencing a loss in market share due to deregulation. The vice president of relationship marketing sold the board of directors and CEO on a customer relationship management (CRM) business plan by asking a simple question: "How would you like to maximize customer profitability by optimizing the return on marketing investment in acquisitions and retention?" That exchange led, in 1998, to US WEST developing an enterprise-marketing strategy incorporating SAS Enterprise Miner as the data-mining platform.

Along with SAS Enterprise Miner, US WEST makes use of campaign-management software to allow marketing professionals to plan, build, execute, and assess targeted marketing campaigns. Integrating data-mining and campaign-management software eliminates the need for marketers to score entire customer databases (which is very time consuming), reduces manual intervention and human error, substantially shortens marketing cycles, and enables smaller, highly-targeted segmentations to generate a higher marketing ROI.

Marketers at US WEST invoke models generated by SAS Enterprise Miner, and dynamically score only the records needed for a specific campaign. The result: marketers can continually refine targeted campaigns for faster, better results (e.g., improved marketing ROI). "We will maximize rates of customer retention and cross-selling by quickly determining whether a campaign is working and quickly shifting gears. This is certainly a more intelligent basis for campaign management; it shortens the cycle time both for campaigns and for sophisticated analysis," says Dr. Jovan Barac, US WEST's director of decision-support systems. He has successfully transformed the US WEST modeling and scoring paradigm from a set of ad-hoc techniques into a unified environment. "We're now able to production-score more than 10 million customers," he continues. "A world-class decision-support system and its integration with customer service and network and billing systems provide a strong infrastructure for the CRMS system. But integrated data mining and campaign management are its brain and heart."

In Enterprise Miner software, the SAS Institute offers an automated analytic solution that quickly identifies hidden trends in data, saving decisionmakers time and delivering ROI. Other companies that have selected the SAS Institute's data-mining technology include major banks, telecommunications companies, retail stores, and direct marketers.

Business analysts use Enterprise Miner software to run predictive models on commercial customer information to identify the best customers as well as those who leave. Results are then used for targeted promotions. Analysts are building and testing different modeling techniques at record speed — in days as opposed to weeks. Plus, for the first time, they're able to visualize and compare different models' performances together on a single lift chart as shown in Figure 1-2.

Cross-industry customer base companies deploying Enterprise Miner software include Ameritech Services, a telecommunications company based in Chicago and one of the world's 100 largest companies; San Francisco-based Bank of America, the fifth-largest U.S. bank and a world leader in financial services; GE Capital Retailer Financial Services, based in Stamford, CT.; ICG Equipment Company, a telecommunications company based in Englewood, CO.; Integrated Marketing Partners Group in Rochester, NY; Nordstrom Inc., a Seattle-based retailer; People's Bank of Bridgeport, CT.; Royal Bank of Canada;

Toronto-Dominion Bank, Canada's fifth-largest bank; and US WEST, a Denver-based telecommunications company.

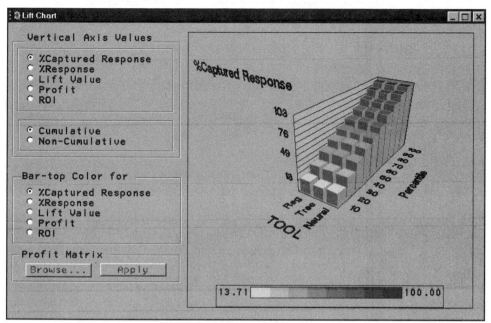

**Figure 1-2** Comparing different data-mining algorithms and their response rates for marketing, using SAS Institute's Enterprise Miner.

### 1.3.2 An Example of Data Mining at Bass Export

Bass Export, the United Kingdom's biggest exporter of beer, selected IBM's Intelligent Miner™ to create data-mining business solutions. Bass Export owns and operates nine breweries and distributes more than 60 ales and beers in more than 80 overseas markets. According to the IBM Quarterly, Bass Export realized that great brands and good service might not be enough to maintain its lead in the U.K. beer market. Mike Fisher, IS and change director at Bass Brewers, comments: "Each week, we deliver orders to 23,000 customers. It's vitally important that we understand the buying habits of each of them, the profitability of each individual account, and the profitability of each brand we deliver there."

IBM has deployed Intelligent Miner at many sites. IMS America uses Intelligent Miner for a number of pharmaceutical applications, including targeting and segmenting prescribers, evaluating promotional effectiveness, and building predictive behavior models. AIB Bank builds lasting customer relationships by better understanding the makeup of its customer population, anticipating customer needs, and predicting customer behavior. The Bank of Montreal uses Intelligent Miner for Data to understand its most profitable customer segments. Other customers include Bell Atlantic, The Health Insurance Commission (HIC) Australia, John Hancock Mutual Life Insurance Company, Mellon Bank, and Safeway.

### 1.3.3    A Data-Mining Example at Reuters

Reuters is a world leader in providing financial information, such as online price data for many financial applications in areas like the foreign exchange, commodities, and stock markets. The data Reuters uses comes from many outside sources and the possibility of data errors is a major business problem for them. It is extremely hard to differentiate data errors from market shifts.

Reuters makes use of Clementine, SPSS's data-mining workbench, to build data-mining models that increase the rate of error detection. Reuters has used Clementine to automate the data-quality process. Several errors that were previously unknown were discovered in the process of building these models.

Other customers using SPSS's Clementine include West Midlands Police Department, for crime prevention; Winterthur Insurance, for customer-relationship management; Unilever, for product-safety evaluation; Halfords Department Store, for siting retail outlets; and IAURIF, a French regional studies organization, for traffic-flow predictions.

## 1.4    A Process for Successfully Deploying Data Mining for Competitive Advantage

How do you translate the information discovered through data mining to competitive advantage? There are many examples of data mining being successfully used, and yet it should be noted that the act of building data-mining models does not, by itself, guarantee any business value. For data mining to be profitable, the information learned by data mining must be somehow deployed; some action must be taken.

A fundamental problem of discovering important trends and patterns in your data is that this information, to be used to your competitive advantage, must be acted upon. Although you may discover the traits that make someone more likely to buy a particular product, this information may be useless if you don't have the data required or the process in place to make such predictions on your customer base.

To be used as a competitive weapon, data mining must be part of a larger process that ensures that the information learned by data mining is transformed into actionable results. Below is a detailed example outlining a successful process employed by a telecommunications company to maximize their competitive advantage from the use of data-mining tools and technology. This process outlines five broad steps: problem definition, discovery, implementation, action, and monitoring results.

### 1.4.1   Problem Definition

In the following example, a telecommunications company is looking at two different product lines, voice mail and paging, and wishes to understand the separate customer bases for each product line.

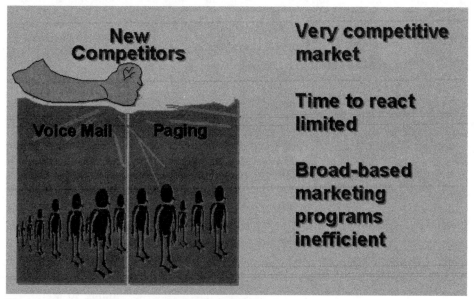

**Figure 1-3**   A problem for telecommunications.

As the telecommunications industry gets more competitive, it is becoming harder to retain customers using traditional broad-based methods. The company in this example used data mining to segment their customers, and to fine-tune their marketing message to reflect a better understanding of their customer base.

**Example.**   In this example, data mining was used for two specific purposes:

1. Identify profitable groups within their customer base and predict how to effectively retain these customers.
2. Identify profitable groups within their customer base and predict how to effectively cross-sell to these customers.

Customer retention is the number-one priority of many telecommunications companies. Once customers have been acquired, you want to retain their business. Keeping a customer is less expensive than replacing a customer, especially if the customer is a valuable one. A 1995 report from Digital Equipment Corporation estimates that the combined cost of marketing, advertising, and provisioning is $275 to $400 for each new subscriber. Assuming a churn rate common to the cellular industry of 30%, a 100,000 subscriber base costs $8.25 million to maintain ($100,000 \times 30\% \times 275$). Loyal, valuable customers provide ongoing revenue and excellent return on customer-acquisition costs.

Data mining provides a way to model traits and predict the likelihood of valuable customers who are likely to stop doing business with you. This modeling helps you identify signs of churning among good customers early enough to offer a compelling incentive to retain them.

Cross-selling to your customer base is the number-two priority in this industry. A customer's value increases as you acquire more of the dollars she or he has to spend. Customer growth means improving customer value by selling them more products and services.

Customer-growth campaigns need to deliver offers for products or bundles of products to the individuals most likely to be interested in them. RightPoint software campaigns help you spot customers especially suited to particular offers.

### 1.4.2    Discovery

The next step for this company is to begin data-mining analysis to discover more about their customers. In this case, the first process is to identify and segment high-valued customers in the customer base.

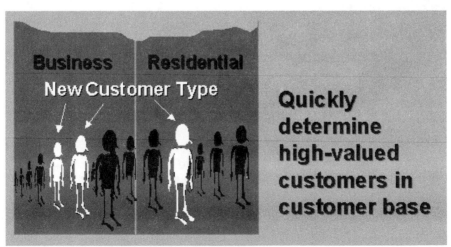

**Figure 1-4**    Identifying high-valued customers.

The first step was to quickly identify the customers they really wanted to protect — that is: Who are the most important, most profitable customers based on a *lifetime value* calculation?

In this case, a new user type was identified: They referred to them as "Power Users." The result was to find a set of customers who are heavy phone users, individuals who are constantly on the phone.

### 1.4.3    Implementation

Once this new group of Power Users is identified, what do you do with the information? Because the company's goal is to retain and increase the value of these customers, the next step of this process is to create marketing campaigns that provide compelling offers to these types of users.

Multiple offers may be made to this customer segment. Data mining can then be used to determine which of these offers are most effective for which types of people.

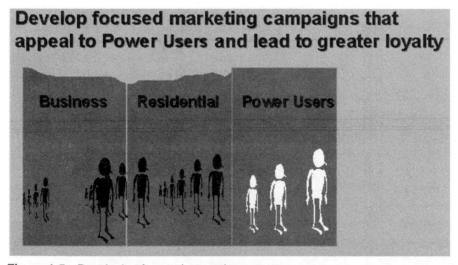

**Figure 1-5**   Developing focused campaigns.

Power Users are different from the masses. In this step, this customer segmentation is separated out from the pack. Power Users have special needs and issues and new marketing programs were developed to focus on retaining this segment. In this case, the provider is going to create a customer-loyalty program to retain as many of the Power Users as they can *before* they leave.

Developing focused campaigns is a difficult task. Offers need be based on timely information, so that campaign targeting stays accurate as human behavior and marketing conditions change.

Also, different offers are appropriate at different times for any individual. In this example, Power Users are more influenced by more expensive rate plans in months where they exceed their number of prepaid minutes. Also, a competitor's campaign may necessitate special offers during a particular time period. A customer's value, loyalty, or market segment might differ from month to month as a result of changing family or job profiles.

### 1.4.4   Taking Action

The next step is to make these campaigns actionable. Deploying the results of the predictive modeling seems straightforward, but, in reality, there are complications. In this example, the philosophy was taken that campaigns are best targeted at the time a customer contacts you. This is the point of contact: a call center or a Web site interaction, for example. Customers who initiate interactions have set aside the time to give you their attention. This means the data-mining models need to be integrated into customer touch points.

To integrate into the customer touch points, the provider chose to deliver the new campaign through call centers, so that when a Power User called in, aggressive phone interaction could be taken to retain this high-valued customer

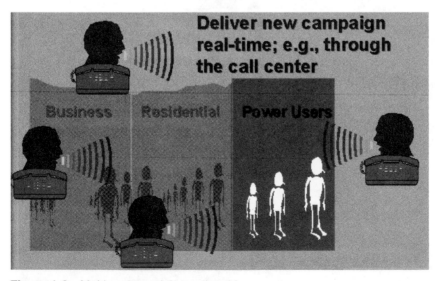

**Figure 1-6**   Making data mining actionable.

Here is an example of how predictive modeling can influence the process of a customer interaction:

1. A cellular phone subscriber calls his service provider to inquire about how to interpret a new billing format.
2. The operator enters the customer's account number in the call-center application, then retrieves information about the customer's bill.
3. While the operator is explaining the billing format to the customer, automated campaign targeting using the data-mining models is conducted behind the scenes, using the most up-to-date information available about the customer, the product line, and campaigns underway. When targeting is complete, information describing one or more customer-specific offers is displayed in the call-center application.
4. The campaign targeting in this example reveals through the data-mining models and business rules that the customer is valuable and may be a churn candidate. Offers displayed for the operator include two new product suggestions and a special discount incentive for this customer.
5. The products suggested and the special discount are tailored to the customer, acknowledging his particular needs and characteristics at the time of contact. The data-mining model showed that if the customer accepts additional products, he or she is less likely to change providers. Also, the special discount incentives are tied to agreeing to remain a customer for a set period of time.
6. The operator relays the offers to the customer, referring to a script displayed for each offer. The script wording is customized to complement both the customer's profile and the operator's skill level.

### 1.4.5   Monitoring the Results

The final step is to check the success of the marketing campaign. Because we are responding to a time-sensitive issue (competition), we need to know if the campaign is successful as quickly as possible . . . not six months into it.

The customer agrees to purchase one of the products, but declines the offer for the second product. The indication that one offer was accepted and another offer declined is captured and can be used for campaign refinement. Other information, such as reasons given by the customer for turning down an offer, can also be captured.

This information can be used to fine-tune which offers are being accepted and which are not. A marketer wants to know that 43 offers were made today and 22 were accepted. These metrics provide a way to guage whether or not the data-mining models are improving customer response over offers where no predictive technologies are used. This process usually involves several rounds of refinement to improve the response rates.

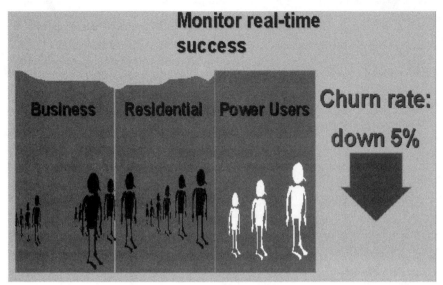

**Figure 1-7**   Monitoring the success of a campaign.

Several companies also have "dynamic learning" engines, which build data-mining models on-the-fly as customers accept and reject offers. This way, not only are you monitoring the success of a campaign, you are also getting smarter as you go along.

### 1.4.6   Discussion of the Process

The process just outlined was an example of a successful process that has been used in several large companies today to incorporate data mining into actionable results. This is by no means the only way to use data mining, but it does point out that there is a lot more involved in making data mining a strategic weapon than just building the model. For a more in-depth discussion of the process, see the case study of Halifax Bank (in Chapter 8), which used a process similar to the one described here.

This process of problem definition, discovery, implementation, taking action, and monitoring results involves much more than just building data-mining models. It involves:

- Integrating data mining with business strategies and marketing campaigns. Business rules would be used in this scenario along with predictive models. The marketing campaigns drive some "offer" that the customer is to receive.
- Integrating data-mining models with a decision-delivery mechanism into the call center.

- Creating a feedback loop to monitor the success of the campaigns. This is the only way to track results of the marketing campaigns (which use the data-mining models) to calculate return on investment.

The successful use of data mining will always require a clear process of how it is to be used. One retail company used data mining to find out that a particular brand of products was their most unprofitable brand. The action to take would seem to be: don't sell the brand line; however, a week later that same company had a strategic initiative for management to push that brand harder. The point is that no matter what data mining tells you, if the results are not part of your business process and not ultimately helping direct strategy, then the value of data mining is greatly diminished.

## 1.5   A Note on Privacy Issues

Data mining has made many people uneasy when considering its possible implications for privacy. For example, credit information for an individual allows you to learn a great deal about that individual. Medical records as well can say a lot about who you are. This information can be used for unethical purposes, like learning who to exclude for loans, credit cards, or health insurance.

The government has stepped in and provided regulations on what is allowed and what is not. For example, the European communities do not allow banks to combine their financial data with credit information, which is something still allowed in the United States. The U.S. government demands that banks explain why they extend or do not extend credit information. Certain variables, like gender, can get companies in a lot of hot water if they use them in their models to predict credit worthiness.

In another example, the Fair Credit Reporting Act requires that banks notify customers that information they provide to a bank can be used by their investment sales subsidiary. Many banks, like First Union and Mellon Bank, have privacy notifications on the Web concerning this issue; however, not all do.

The telecommunications industry has regulations on information that can not be used in their modeling processes. The use of Caller ID information has been heavily regulated. Also, much of the data a local phone provider has can not be used by the cellular side of the house.

Regulation in the data-mining industry has clearly just started, but it is likely to grow over time as people take advantage of the new products now available to mine data. Yahoo bought not just a data-mining tool, but a data-mining company to help it with understanding its customer base. Yahoo has also published a very clear privacy policy on its Web site. The advantages of data mining on the Web are clear, but the concerns over customer privacy issues continue to drive discussions on increased regulation and crackdown.

The most interesting thing about the tools discussed in this book when considering privacy issues is this: data-mining tools widely available to business professionals provide broad access to information that was largely in the hands of the Fortune 500 only a few years ago. Is this dangerous, or is it just broadening the playing field?

## 1.6  Summary

In this chapter, we looked at defining data mining, why it is used, and then provided examples of its use, as well as successful processes for implementing data mining. In Chapter 2, we will examine what data mining can accomplish in much further detail.

# Getting Started with Data Mining

There are many different ways to mine data. Finding hidden patterns and trends in data requires creativity and a plan of attack, just as the game of chess requires knowing many different strategies in order to master it. There are a few very specific "strategies" to the field of data mining that are well understood and are explored in this chapter.

The chapter is organized as follows:

- Section 2.1    Classification
- Section 2.2    Clustering
- Section 2.3    Visualization
- Section 2.4    Association
- Section 2.5    Assortment Optimization
- Section 2.6    Prediction
- Section 2.7    Estimation
- Section 2.8    Summary

## 2.1  Classification (Supervised Learning)

The *classification* or *supervised learning approach* to data mining is very common in the business world. The human mind naturally segments things into distinctive groups. For example, people can be lumped into the classifications of babies, children, teenagers, adults, and the elderly. Classification provides a mapping from attributes to specified groupings. For example, the attribute age *two years or younger* can be mapped to the category *babies*. Once data is classified, the traits of these specific groups can be summarized. The data-mining example below models customer churn rate, and is a classification study that attempts to separate customers into two groups: those who were loyal and those who left and never returned.

An analyst for a telecommunications company wants to understand why some customers remain loyal while others leave. Ultimately, the analyst wants to predict which customers his company is most likely to lose to competitors. With this goal in mind, the analyst can construct a model derived from historical data of loyal customers versus customers who have left. A good model enables you to better understand your customers and to predict which customers will stay and which will leave.

The example of modeling customer loyalty, or churn rate, illustrates the process of defining a *study*. Studies formulate the scope of a data-mining activity. A study will identify an overall goal and the data to be used. Having a goal in mind when data mining is not only useful, it helps define the data-mining process. Goals do not have to be specifically defined in data mining.

By defining a business problem, you have already started the process of data mining and have formulated a goal. You can easily state a goal in our example.

### 2.1.1  Goal

*I want to understand what makes customers more likely to stay with or leave my company.*

A goal differs from the process of asking a specific question, because you are not assuming any correlations. For example, you could have asked a question like: How many people whose line usage over six months is decreasing are no longer customers? This question assumes a link may exist between decreasing line usage and customers who are likely to leave. Query tools are able to ask specific questions; data-mining tools prioritize the importance of information linked to a definable goal.

### 2.1.2   Subject of the Study

Studies require a *subject*. For example, Table 2-1 shows a historical data set of customers. The data set has a field, *Cust_Type*, which indicates whether a customer is loyal or has left for a competitor. We can use such a data set as the subject of our study.

**Table 2-1**   Data Set for Customer Churn

| Column Name | Type of Data | Value | Description |
|---|---|---|---|
| Cust_ID | Numeric | Unique values | Unique identifier for a customer. |
| Time_Cust | Numeric | Integer values | Days a customer has been with company. |
| Line_Use | Character | Very high<br>High<br>Medium<br>Low<br>Very low | Minutes used by the customer in the last month. |
| Trend | Character | Increase<br>Varied-increase<br>Same<br>Varied-decrease<br>Decrease | An indicator of usage trends for a customer's last six months. |
| Status_Indicator | Character | Survey-high<br>Survey-fair<br>Survey-low<br>Unknown | Survey results on customer satisfaction. |
| Cust_Type | Character | Loyal<br>Lost | Is customer still with company (loyal) or no longer customer (lost)? |

Table 2-1 shows data elements that identify a customer, describe the customer, and indicate whether the customer is loyal or has left the company.

Note that building this model of customer churn requires knowledge of which customers have remained loyal and which have not. This type of mining is called supervised learning, because the training examples are labeled with the actual class (loyal or lost) that the model is supposed to predict.

The specific trait to be profiled from Table 2-1 is specified in column *Cust_Type*. This column specifies, row by row, whether a customer has historically been a loyal customer or has left for good (values: *loyal, lost*).

The column *Cust_Type* is defined as the *output* or *dependent variable* if it is used as the basis of the study, e.g., *the study profiles those who have historically been loyal customers and those who have left the company.*

In Chapters 6 and 7, where product examples of data mining are discussed, both studies are classification studies.

## 2.2  Clustering (Unsupervised Learning)

*Clustering* is a method of grouping rows of data that share similar trends and patterns. Clustering, or segmentation, is the process of dividing a data set into distinctive groups. For example, in the case of fraudulent claims, the records may naturally separate into two classes. One of the categories may correspond to normal claims and the other may correspond to fraudulent claims. Of course, there may be some legitimate claims that are mislabeled as fraudulent, and vice versa.

For example, in direct marketing you may want to examine market segments. If you have customer segments based on age ranges (ages 0–5, 6–10, 11–15, 16–20, 21–25, 26–30, 31–35, 36–40, etc.), it may be interesting to cluster the groups into coarser groups like babies, children, teenagers, etc. Clustering helps determine which groups should be together.

Clustering studies have no dependent variable. You are not profiling a specific trait as in classification studies. These studies are also referred to as *unsupervised* learning and/or *segmentation*.

> *Why is it that not having a dependent variable means the learning is unsupervised?*

For supervised learning, the model takes in the independent variables, produces a guess for the dependent variable that is compared with the actual dependent value, and an error-correction is made; hence, the study is "supervised." There is no such process in clustering because there is no outcome to compare it with; hence, the study is referred to as "unsupervised."

In the previous classification example, building the model of customer churn requires knowledge of which customers have remained loyal and which have not; the training examples are labeled with the actual outcome (loyal or lost). Clustering can also be based on historical patterns, but the outcome is not supplied with the training data.

### 2.2.1   A Clustering Example

Retailers want to know where similarities exist in their customer base so they can create and understand different groups to which they can sell and market. They will use a database with rows of customer information and attempt to create customer segments.

Clustering techniques try to look for similarities and differences within a data set and group similar rows together into clusters or segments. For example, a data set may contain many affluent customers with no children and also may have customers with lower incomes and one parent in the family. During the discovery process, this difference can be used to separate the data into two natural groupings. If more such similarities and differences exist, the data set could be further subdivided.

Figure 2-1 shows a sample clustering study that takes customer data and tries to divide it into different segments. These clusters are generated automatically.

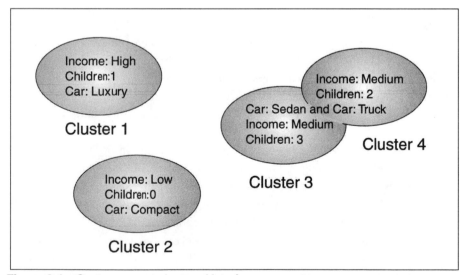

**Figure 2-1**   Customers are clustered into four segments.

A chart like this one attempts to gain knowledge about the groups of data within a data set. Once clusters have been identified, an analyst can try to understand the similari-

ties and differences in the clusters. In the example in Figure 2-1, four clusters are identified. Further investigation can show the reasons that these clusters appear different. For
example, Cluster 1 contains customers who drive luxury cars, Cluster 2 contains customers who have compact cars, and Clusters 3 and 4 four have customers who drive sedans
and trucks. The data in clusters sometimes overlap, and, in the case of Clusters 3 and 4,
there are as many similarities as differences.

There are three dimensions in the example in Figure 2-1 (income, number of children, and type of car). Each customer is represented by a "point" in these three dimensions, and clusters arise if there are many points (customers) close together.

One question often asked when clustering data is:

*Is there a way to optimally figure out how many groups, or clusters of data, exist
in a data set?*

Figure 2-1 automatically came up with four clusters, but you might have gone with
two or three. Today, many approaches to clustering allow the user to decide on the number
of clusters to create within a data set, whereas others try to come to a decision using one
algorithm or another. This is an area of continuing research.

## 2.3  Visualization

Visualization is simply the graphical presentation of data. Data can sometimes be best
understood by graphing it. For example, visualization techniques can easily show *outliers*. Outliers are values that are clearly not in the range of what is expected: consider a
data set where people may have incomes between $1,000 and $4,000 a month, but one
individual earns $44,000. Having one person with such an abnormal salary can skew a
model derived from such a data set.

The process of representing data graphically is used today in most query tools. In
fact, Microsoft Excel has graphing and mapping capabilities. Still, visualization can mean
much more than two-dimensional charts and maps.

Representing data graphically often brings out points that you would not normally
see. Consider the map in Figure 2-2 from MapInfo Corporation.

Figure 2-2 graphically analyzes census income and existing customer information to
help choose the right location for a new service center. The dots on the map indicate where
current customers are. The colors for the different geographies indicate income levels
based on census information, where the darker levels indicate higher income areas. The
visual interpretation of this information helps an analyst determine where a service center
should be placed.

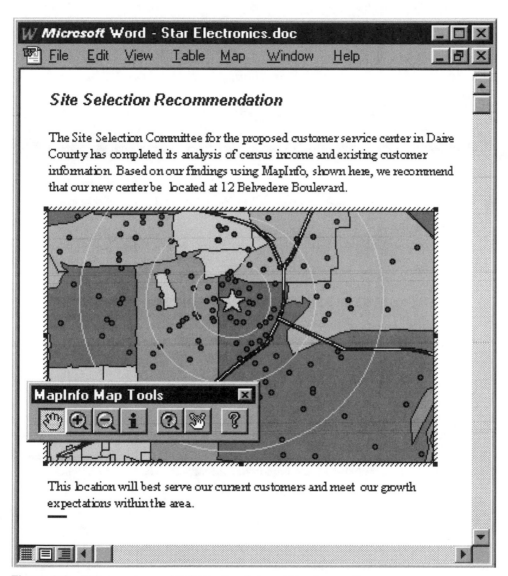

**Figure 2-2**   This map is used to help visualize good business sites.

Figure 2-3 is a multidimensional histogram that was generated by SAS Institute's Enterprise Miner. This diagram plots home value, yearly income, and dollars spent.

Looking at these variables in a three-dimensional way adds insight that you might not normally have. For example, Figure 2-3 shows that there was one case where Dollars Spent had the value 13295, which was highly unusual. A case like this is often regarded as an *outlier* and this graph easily shows that the vast majority of cases of Dollars Spent were in the 0–5812 range.

Silicon Graphics, a provider of a spectrum of data-mining tools, is a leader in visualization techniques for data mining, using their expertise in three-dimensional animation and rendering. Several data-visualization examples using Silicon Graphics tools are shown in Chapter 5.

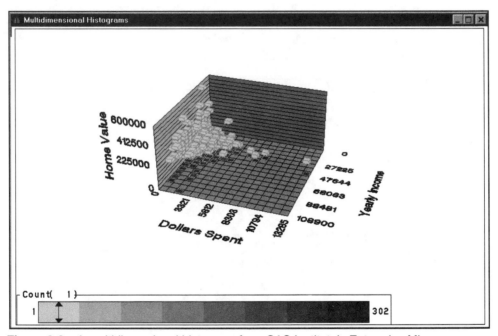

**Figure 2-3**   A multidimensional histogram from SAS Institute's Enterprise Miner.

## 2.4  Association (Market Basket)

Before starting this section, the author would like to note that the following sections on association and assortment optimization are provided by Dr. Miguel Castro of Dovetail Solutions. Dovetail Solutions specializes in data-mining applications and consulting for the retail and catalog industries.

Association or Market Basket (MB) Analysis refers to business-useful information that can be gleaned from aggregate associations among the different items sold in catalogs or at retail stores (be they physical or online). The input to MB analysis is point-of-sale (POS) transactional data. The output of MB analysis is information and recommendations that exploit product associations and customer-purchase behavior.

MB analysis turns transactional data into associations of the form: *"If customers buy product A they also tend to buy product B, x% of the time."* More generally, the "products" can be extended to represent attributes. These attributes could be demographic, promotional, seasonal, and include other relevant information, such as "the customer is a female between the ages of 30 and 35." They can also be extended to represent item "roll-ups" or taxonomies, such as "all dairy products" or "all products on sale in February." These can allow us to detect associations between, for example, product categories and the demographics of customers who purchase from those categories.

Applications of MB analysis include cross-marketing, store layout, catalog design, loss-leader analysis, product pricing and promotion. MB analysis allows us to infer customer preferences from their purchase patterns. However, today's MB analysis often fails to live up to its potential. Here's why.

### 2.4.1   The Trouble with Market-Basket Analysis

Suppose, for example, that when customers buy bread at a grocery store, 30% of the time they also buy milk. While this information could be interesting, it may not be very useful by itself. For instance, if 30% of all transactions in that store contain milk, the association between bread and milk is likely just random. However, if only 10% of all transactions contain milk, the 30% association between bread and milk may be meaningful (one might say that the products "lift" or "attract" each other). On the other hand, if milk is present in 50% of all baskets, one could argue that the products "repel" each other. The problem is that most MB analysis performed today does not distinguish between random and non-random item associations, even though this distinction is often crucial to extract meaningful information from transaction databases.

Most MB analysis performed today is based on what's known as the "Support-Confidence Framework." The goal is to extract associations of the form *"If A then B,"* meaning, "When customers buy A they often also buy B." In the support-confidence framework we search for rules with *support* and *confidence*.

*Support* is defined as the minimum percentage of transactions (or baskets) in the database containing items A and B. *Confidence* is defined as the minimum percentage of those baskets containing A that also contain B. For example, suppose the database contains 1 million transactions, and that 10,000 of those transactions contain both A and B. We can then say that the support of the association *if A then B* is $10,000 \div 1,000,000 = 1\%$. Likewise, if 50,000 of the transactions contain A and 10,000 out of those 50,000 also contain B then the association rule *if A then B* has a confidence of $\$10,000 \div 50,000 = 20\%$.

*Confidence* is just the conditional probability of B given A: *Confidence = Prob (B ÷ A)*. Note that confidence does not distinguish whether the association between A and B is random or not. In other words, confidence alone does not distinguish random associations from associations containing useful information. To reiterate our example, if milk occurs in 30% of all of the transactions in the grocery store, knowing that milk also occurs in 30% of all transactions containing bread does not tell us anything new. We are more interested in finding association rules between milk and other items where the occurrence of milk is different from what would be expected by random chance. For example, we would be more interested in finding that milk occurs in 50% of all baskets containing coffee, which represents a "lift" of 20% above the expected random occurrence of milk. This could suggest actionable strategies such as cross-marketing, product layout, etc. On the other hand, the random occurrence of milk in bread-containing baskets would likely not lead to actionable strategies.

Unlike confidence, support is a more interesting quantity, because it allows us to weed out very infrequent transactions. For example, if two items occur together in five out of 1,000,000 transactions, we may want to ignore the association between the items for two reasons. First, the sample size is so small that the association may not be statistically significant. Second, we may only wish to spend our time and marketing dollars on higher-volume associations.

Two criticisms are offered for the above justifications of using support. First, instead of using support as a proxy for statistical significance, we may as well use a direct measure of the statistical significance of product associations. Second, if we are concerned about spending marketing dollars wisely, we may as well define a "Dollar Support" measure to allow us to ignore associations where relatively few dollars are spent. In this way, we could capture transactions that occur rarely, but that involve high-revenue items such as big-screen TVs at department stores.

An even more fundamental criticism of the support measure is that transactions with low support could in fact be very significant. To illustrate, suppose that Coke® occurs in 50% of all transactions at a convenience store, and that Pepsi® also occurs in 50% of all transactions. By random chance, we would expect Coke and Pepsi to appear together in 25% of all of the transactions in the convenience store. Now, if we observe Coke and Pepsi together in only 0.01% of all transactions, we may be tempted to ignore this co-occurrence on the basis of low support. However, this small co-occurrence represents a large deviation from the random expectation of 25%. This could be an indication that either the two products compete in the same market, or that the two products address different market segments. Either way, this information can be extremely valuable from a marketing perspective, and could help marketers with product pricing, assortment, etc. Moreover, despite the low co-occurrence, this information would have high statistical significance if either item separately had high occurrence (as is likely the case in the Coke and Pepsi example).

In Chapter 4 when discussing algorithms used in data mining, Dovetail Solutions offers insight into better ways of discovering associations.

## 2.5  Assortment Optimization

Assortment optimization is the process of selecting the product mix that best achieves the retailer's business goals. These goals could include a combination of short-term profitability and long-run market share, or building loyalty or "customer equity." To achieve this we need more than just pricing and cost data. Among other things, we need to know how substitutable products are and to what extent they compete within the same market segment. We also need to know whether a given product stimulates the sales of other products. For example, a "loss leader" may not be profitable by itself, but if it generates substantial store traffic and stimulates the purchase of high-margin items, it may be very profitable, and thus should be included in the assortment. This information can be obtained from transactional data and the type of analysis that we mentioned above in the context of market basket, along with other techniques that we will cover in this section.

Studies show that "80/20 laws" are alive and well in retail product assortments (Swander and Pace, 1993). The top 20–30% of SKUs (Stock Keeping Units) generate the majority of revenues, while the rest generate less than 50% of revenues. Assortment optimization is increasingly recognized as an essential strategic tool for marketers in many sectors of the retail industry. This is because of the high costs of labor, distribution, and inventory, along with the low profit margins prevalent in the retail industry.

Usually, assortment optimization consists of examining a current category assortment and deciding whether to remove existing items or add new ones. A typical category contains on the order of 100 items, and the number of added or removed items rarely exceeds a dozen. However, because of the "80/20 laws," this can have a significant impact on cost reduction and increased profitability.

The process of assortment optimization can be divided into two parts. The first part is concerned with how sales volume changes when we add or subtract items from an existing assortment. The second part deals with how costs are affected when we change an assortment. In what follows, we consider how the combination of these parts can produce an optimal assortment.

### 2.5.1  Sales Volume: Variety versus Substitutability

When we remove an item from a category, part of the sales from the removed item get redistributed among the remaining category items, and part of the sales from the removed item may disappear. Likewise, if we add a new item to a category, part of the new item's sales will result from "cannibalizing" the sales of existing items in the assortment. Also, part of the new item's sales may come from new customers who have never purchased from that category before, or who buy the new item in addition to buying the existing items. In effect, there is a *tension* between variety and substitutability in every product assortment. The more variety a category has, the higher the category sales volume is likely to be. Because of item substitutability, however, the more variety a category has, the smaller the marginal impact on sales volume will be for each additional item. This is reflected in Figure 2-4, which shows the decreasing marginal return of sales volume as the number of category items increases.

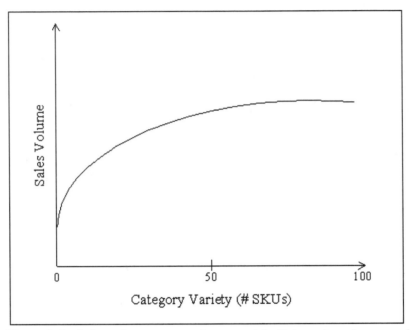

**Figure 2-4**    Sales volume versus category variety. Sales volume increases initially but then levels off as the number of SKUs in the category increases.

In short, demand for an item can be transferred to or from other items in the category because the items are similar or substitutable. In other cases, demand cannot be transferred because consumers are loyal to specific items and do not perceive them as substitutable.

A rough but straightforward way to estimate transferable demand is by using the variety curve of Figure 2-4. Variety curves are category specific, and can be obtained either from long in-house transactional histories, or from household panel data supplied by outside vendors. For example, suppose that we have an 80-item category and are trying to determine the effect of removing the 80th item from the assortment. To estimate transferable demand we can determine the change in category sales when going from 80 to 79 items by reading it off the variety curve. Let's say that the variety curve tells us that category sales change by 1% when decreasing the assortment from 80 to 79 items. If the category sales are $5,000 per week, this represents a decrease in category sales of 1% × $5,000 = $50 per week. Suppose also that item 80 sales are $200 per week. This means that $50 per week constitutes the *non-transferable demand*, while the remaining $150 would be the *transferable demand* of item 80. The non-transferable demand represents lost sales, while the transferable demand will be redistributed among the remaining items in the assortment. The argument for adding an item to the assortment (instead of removing it) is similar. In Chapter 4, concerning algorithms, we discuss improvements on the method of using variety curves to estimate changes in category sales to increase precision.

### 2.5.2   Costs: The Other Half of the Story

Now that we know how sales volume is affected by changing a category assortment, we must consider how costs are affected. We know that sales volume flattens out as we increase the number of items in an assortment. Costs always increase, however, with increasing assortment variety (see Figure 2-5).

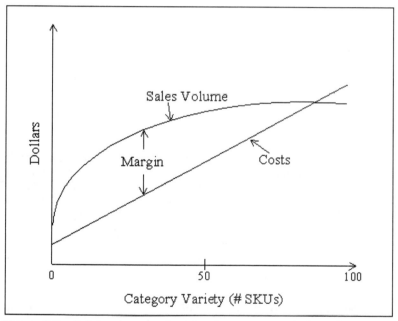

**Figure 2-5**   Sales volume and costs versus category variety. As in Figure 2-4, the sales volume increases rapidly at first and then levels off with the increasing number of SKUs in the category. The costs, on the other hand, continue to increase with increasing variety. The profit margin is the difference between these two curves.

The result of these two tendencies is that profitability increases with variety until it reaches a maximum, and then decreases. Consequently, there is an optimal assortment that maximizes profitability (see Figure 2-6). While profitability is not necessarily the only business goal of a retailer, it is an important one that points to the significance of understanding the effect of assortment variety on costs.

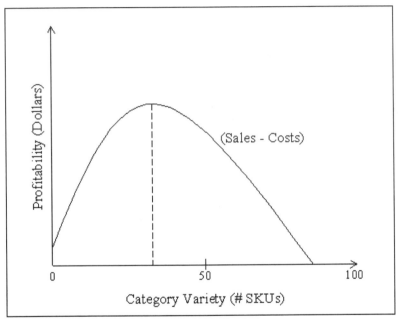

**Figure 2-6**  Profitability versus category variety. Profit margin (or profitability) is the difference between sales volume and costs (in dollars), as in Figure 2-5. Note that, as the number of SKUs in the category increases, profitability rises, reaches a maximum, and finally decreases. The dashed line indicates the number of SKUs that produces optimal profitability (around 35 SKUs in this example). However, short-term profitability is not the only business goal of most retailers. Other business objectives, such as increasing customer equity and market share, should also be considered when deciding on the optimal product assortment.

But what do we mean when we talk about costs? Because of the complex nature of the retail industry, there are many contributors to a retailer's costs. For example, costs can originate from transportation, distribution, warehousing, labor, in-store ordering and stocking, inventory analysis, administrative overhead, etc. However, in the context of assortment optimization, there are only two relevant costs: *avoidable* costs and *opportunity* costs.

Avoidable costs are, as the name suggests, costs that can be avoided by changing the assortment. Opportunity costs represent the income that is foregone by changing the assortment. For example, suppose that we know with certainty that an item's unit cost is

$1.00. If we delete the item from the assortment, we have avoided a per-unit cost of $1.00. In this case, the avoidable cost is $1.00. But suppose that the item generates a per-unit *income* of $0.75. When we delete the item from our assortment, we are foregoing $0.75 in income. This is the opportunity cost of deleting the item from the assortment. If we consider the item in isolation, we have incurred a per-unit cost of $0.75 by not carrying the item (the foregone income). But suppose that we replace the item with another item that generates an income of $1.25 (with the same sales velocity). This assortment change generates a net income increase of $1.25 − $0.75 = 0.50.

If we replace the deleted item with another item, we must also worry about how the new item affects the sales of the remaining items in the assortment in comparison to the old item. For example, if the new item cannibalizes more sales from existing items than the old item, the old item's opportunity cost is comparatively less than it would be otherwise. Moreover, suppose the old item was a traffic generator that stimulated the sales of other items (whether within the category or not). In this case, switching to the new item may result in a negative contribution to net income because of the high opportunity costs of deleting the old item.

Other issues that we must consider are an item's "segment value," and "exclusivity." In other words, even if an item is not highly profitable by itself, it may attract customers that are deemed valuable because of their overall purchase patterns. Therefore, it may be worthwhile to keep the unprofitable item in the assortment in order to build loyalty or "equity" among the segment of valuable customers. An item's exclusivity refers to the percentage of all customers that are loyal to that item. If an item has a large following, it may be worthwhile including it in an assortment in order to maintain customer loyalty. Many of these considerations are crucial to effective assortment optimization and can be addressed by analyzing transactional data.

## 2.6 Prediction

Once models are built to represent patterns and trends within data, these models can be used to successfully predict the outcomes of future events. While historical data cannot foretell the future, patterns do tend to repeat themselves, so that if a representative model of a data set can be built, predictions can be made from it.

The process of prediction is straightforward. With a set of inputs, a prediction is made on a certain outcome. While the validation process uses prediction, it is really comparing known results to predictions made to calculate an accuracy level. With true prediction, the outcome to be predicted will not be known.

In the example at the beginning of this chapter of a customer retention model created through classification, we can use this model to predict between the two outcomes: *Cust_Type* Loyal and *Cust_Type* Lost.

There is other information that such a prediction process may make, as discussed below.

### 2.6.1   Challenger Outcomes

Not only do you want to know what outcome will be predicted, it may be interesting to calculate challenger predictions. For example, in the case above, the customer was predicted to be *Cust_Type* Loyal. There will also usually be some type of weighting associated with this score. There is another possible outcome, *Cust_Type* Lost, and it will have a score. In the case where there are more than two outcomes, the challenger outcome, or next best prediction, is also very interesting.

### 2.6.2   Margin of Victory

Margin of victory is the difference between the best prediction score versus the challenger outcome. If a prediction is calculated by a score or weight of some sort, then the difference in the prediction scores can also be calculated. For example, in this case, *Cust_Type* Loyal was predicted as the outcome with a score of 732, and the challenger *Cust_Type* Lost was predicted with a score of 534, which is a margin of victory of 27%. The larger the percentage, the more likely it is the winning prediction is true.

Prediction accuracy can be improved by only making predictions on the rows of data where the margin of victory is greater than a set percentage. You will not make predictions for every row, but the rows you do make predictions on may have a better margin of victory. This will allow for more accurate predictions on fewer rows of information.

### 2.6.3   Conducting a Cost Benefit Analysis

Analyzing predictions against known results provides the ability to help you assess the business value of a predictive model. Consider the example where you want to send a direct mailer to those people most likely to close accounts. If you send a random mailer to 10% of the population you are likely to reach 10% of the people who are going to close accounts; however, if you use a predictive model, you can send 10% of your population a mailer and reach a much greater percentage of those likely to close their accounts, thereby increasing your effectiveness, which in turn should result in cost savings or profit.

*How do you use the cost and benefit trade-offs of using your model to identify the percentage of individuals to target through a direct mailer?*

Marketers routinely use a "lift" chart to show the effectiveness of using prediction to direct whom to mail to. From a lift chart, a cost benefit analysis can then be done.

For example, the graphical image in Figure 2-7 is known as a lift chart.

This lift curve represents the predictive "lift" the data-mining model provides on customers that are likely to close accounts. If you mailed randomly to 80% of your customers you would, on average, reach 80% of the people who close accounts. That is what the diagonal line in Figure 2-7 represents.

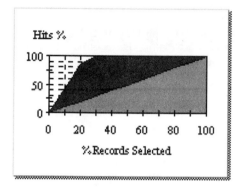

**Figure 2-7**   The lift chart.

The goal of a lift curve is to see if you can reach more people who are likely to close accounts, while only mailing to a limited subset, thereby increasing efficiency. This model says you can reach 80% of your customers likely to close an account and only mail to 20% of your customer base. That is what the area above the diagonal line in Figure 2-7 depicts. The higher the curve, the better the "lift." The lift is dependent on how good a predictive model you have.

Now, let's say you want to do cost analysis. To send this offer, which includes a promotional gift, it costs you $10 for each customer you mail to. You also know that for every customer you prevent from leaving, you will gain $90 in revenue this quarter. You would specify the following values in the Cost area:

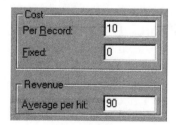

**Figure 2-8**   Cost analysis.

In Figure 2-9, you see the cost/profit trade-offs:

| Interval | | | Cumulative | | | Analysis | | | Cumulative | | |
|---|---|---|---|---|---|---|---|---|---|---|---|
| Score | Hits | % | Hits | % | % of total | Cost | Revenue | Profit | Cost | Revenue | Profit |
| 270.00 | 43 | 98.4 | 43 | 98.4 | 42.2 | 440.00 | 3870.00 | 3430.00 | 440.00 | 3870.00 | 3430.00 |
| 70.00 | 43 | 98.4 | 86 | 98.4 | 84.3 | 440.00 | 3870.00 | 3430.00 | 880.00 | 7740.00 | 6860.00 |
| -110.00 | 16 | 36.6 | 102 | 77.8 | 100.0 | 440.00 | 1440.00 | 1000.00 | 1320.00 | 9180.00 | 7860.00 |
| -180.00 | 0 | 0.0 | 102 | 58.4 | 100.0 | 440.00 | 0.00 | -440.00 | 1760.00 | 9180.00 | 7420.00 |
| -230.00 | 0 | 0.0 | 102 | 46.7 | 100.0 | 440.00 | 0.00 | -440.00 | 2200.00 | 9180.00 | 6980.00 |
| -280.00 | 0 | 0.0 | 102 | 38.9 | 100.0 | 440.00 | 0.00 | -440.00 | 2640.00 | 9180.00 | 6540.00 |
| -320.00 | 0 | 0.0 | 102 | 33.3 | 100.0 | 440.00 | 0.00 | -440.00 | 3080.00 | 9180.00 | 6100.00 |
| -360.00 | 0 | 0.0 | 102 | 29.2 | 100.0 | 440.00 | 0.00 | -440.00 | 3520.00 | 9180.00 | 5660.00 |
| -410.00 | 0 | 0.0 | 102 | 25.9 | 100.0 | 440.00 | 0.00 | -440.00 | 3960.00 | 9180.00 | 5220.00 |

**Figure 2-9** Cost/profit analysis.

The cumulative profit values are in the rightmost column. Locate the largest value: $7,860 as shown on the righthand side of Figure 2-9 in row 3. That is the maximum amount of profit that you can make. It also shows that you should mail to 30% of you customer base to realize this profit, since every row number represents 10% of the population and the maximum profit appeared in row three. Now, notice that a prediction score of –110 appears in the first column of row 3. You would have to contact every customer likely to churn whose prediction score is –110 and greater to potentially realize $7,860 in profit. Also notice tha the *Cumulative % of Total* field says 100% in row 3. This means you would approach 100% of the customers likely to churn, or 102 customers in this case, after mailing to 30% of the base. It would be foolish to mail to the remaining 70% if you can identify all those likely to churn in the top.

You would have to decide whether the additional potential profit warranted the additional cost. Were you to approach only 85% of those likely to churn, your cost would be significantly less, $880, but your profit would also be less, $6,860.

## 2.7 Estimation

Models that are built with classification predict discrete categories. For instance, a model calculating someone's credit risk might predict them as "high," "medium," or "low." Estimation works with outcomes that have continuous values (for example, real numbers between 1 and a million). For instance, a model calculating the stock price for Sun Microsystems™ next week might output 74.53. Another example is a model that predicts what the average global temperature will be at a particular time. In the context of estimation, statisticians call handling of discrete value outcomes as classification and the handling of continuous value outcomes as "regression."

### 2.7.1  Examples of Estimation

KnowledgeMiner from Script Software is widely used in "estimation" problems, which are useful in manufacturing, financial, and academic areas. For example, manufacturers want to predict the likely probability of failure of a chemical process and compare this with the actual results. KnowledgeMiner is in use by NASA, Boeing, MIT, Columbia, Notre Dame, the University of Hamburg, Mobil Oil, Pfizer Inc., Dean & Company and many other corporations, universities, and research institutions. They have sample data sets and examples that range from the prediction of global temperature, to stock market trends, medical diagnosis, and failure of materials (like the Challenger Space Shuttle O-Ring).

In Chapter 8, this book discusses NETPROPHET by Neural Applications that is a commercial product for stock forecasting, that provides estimation for stocks.

## 2.8  Summary

This chapter discussed different ways in which data mining can be used. Approaches like classification, clustering, visualization, and association are all lumped under the term data mining and yet they do very different things. Data mining owes much to the field of artificial intelligence, and therefore, it is understandable that there are many different approaches, because artificial intelligence encompasses such a wide range of techniques and styles.

Chapter 3 discusses a more detailed example of the methodology of performing a data-mining study. It uses a classification approach, but the discussion is valuable to all approaches because the data-mining process has common threads, like properly preparing data before data mining. There is much to be discussed in the area of data preparation and data quality. Data mining is not, of course, very useful if the quality of your data is bad.

# The Data-Mining Process

$\mathbf{T}$his chapter explains the data-mining process in much greater detail by using an example and stepping through the stages of data mining. While it discusses data mining using an example from the health care industry, the intent is to highlight the process and not discuss issues of that particular industry. Chapter 8 discusses different industry applications of data mining.

The chapter is organized as follows:

## 3.1  Discussion of Data-Mining Methodology

When viewed as a methodology, data mining becomes much easier to understand. Most data-mining vendors define a methodology for building models, evaluating them, refining them, and using them for prediction. Here is a brief summarization of the data-mining methodology we use in this book. This methodology defines five main steps:

1. Data manipulation
2. Defining a study
3. Reading the data and building a model
4. Understanding the model
5. Prediction

In this chapter each of these steps in the data-mining process is described. Note that data mining is a circular process. One study sparks ideas that will lead to refining it as well as the creation of new studies which, in turn, may lead to more new studies.

Although not discussed in this chapter, one of the most popular methodologies is the SEMMA methodology used by SAS Institute.

### 3.1.1  The SEMMA Methodology from SAS Institute

The following data-mining methodology described by SAS Institute outlines the process they employ with their data mining tool, Enterprise Miner (see Figure 3-1). They use the SEMMA (Sample, Explore, Modify, Model, and Assess) methodology to help structure the process.

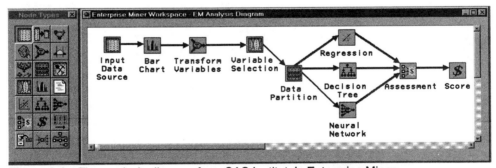

**Figure 3-1**    The analysis diagram from SAS Institute's Enterprise Miner.

Within Enterprise Miner is an analysis diagram, as shown in Figure 3-1, which maps to the SEMMA methodology. *Sampling* involves creating one or more data tables — samples that are large enough to contain the significant information, yet small enough to process. *Exploring* the data entails searching for anticipated relationships, unanticipated trends, and anomalies in order to gain understanding and ideas. The data is then *modified* by creating, selecting, and transforming the variables to focus the model selection process.

*Modeling* is using analytical tools (regression, decision tree, and neural networks, for example) to find patterns in the data that reliably predict a desired outcome. During *assessment*, the usefulness and reliability of the findings from the data-mining process are evaluated.

SAS Institute defines data mining as the process of selecting, exploring, modifying, and modeling large amounts of data to uncover previously unknown patterns in data for a business advantage. The data-mining process is applicable across a variety of industries and provides methodologies for such diverse business problems as fraud detection, customer retention and attrition, database marketing, market segmentation, risk analysis, affinity analysis, customer satisfaction, bankruptcy prediction, and portfolio analysis.

Enterprise Miner software is an integrated product that provides an end-to-end business solution for data mining. A graphical user interface (GUI) provides a user-friendly front-end to the SEMMA data-mining process:

- Sample the data by creating one or more data tables. The samples should be large enough to contain the significant information, yet small enough to process.

- Explore the data by searching for anticipated relationships, unanticipated trends, and anomalies in order to gain understanding and ideas.

- Modify the data by creating, selecting, and transforming the variables to focus the model-selection process.

- Model the data by using the analytical tools to search for a combination of the data that reliably predicts a desired outcome.

- Assess the data by evaluating the usefulness and reliability of the findings from the data-mining process.

You may or may not include all of these steps in your analysis, and it may be necessary to repeat one or more of the steps several times before you are satisfied with the results. After you have completed the assess phase of the SEMMA process, you apply the scoring formula from one or more champion models to new data that may or may not contain the target. Scoring new data that is not available at the time of model training is the end result of most data mining problems.

The SEMMA data-mining process is driven by a process-flow diagram, which you can modify and save. The GUI is designed in such a way that the business technologist who has little statistical expertise can easily navigate through this data-mining methodology, while the quantitative expert can go "behind the scenes" to fine-tune the analytical process.

## 3.2  The Example

The example used in this chapter is selected from the healthcare industry. Data from the field of healthcare make for interesting data mining studies because of the volume and variety of information available. Table 3-1 displays information on patients undergoing surgery or treatment for severe back pain. There is information about the patient, the doctor, the hospital, the insurance, and the type of medication used. From these data, a series of studies can be defined and run.

**Table 3-1**   Data on Patient Recovery from Severe Back Pain

| Column Name | Values | Explanation |
| --- | --- | --- |
| PATIENT ID | Unique | Unique patient identifier |
| HOSPITAL BRANCH | Valley, Central, Western, Coast | The hospital branch patient used |
| RECOVERY TIME | 0–2 weeks, 2–3 weeks, 3–6 weeks, 6+ weeks | How long it took for patient to be up and walking without significant pain |
| HOSPITAL_STAY | Outpatient, Overnight, 2 days, 3+ days | How long patient stayed in hospital |
| AGE | Numeric, in years | Age of patient |
| SMOKER | Yes, No | Whether the patient is a smoker |
| SMOKER_TYPE | Never, Occasional, Frequent, Daily | Smoker type, by frequency |
| MARITAL_STATUS | Single, Married, Divorced, Widowed | Marital status of patient |
| OCCUPATION | Civil servant, Manual worker, Unemployed, Retired, Professional, Business owner | Occupation of patient |
| INSURANCE | Self-insured, Medicare, Company policy | Type of insurance policy |
| PAIN RELIEVER USED | Mild, Codeine equivalent, Severe narcotic | Type of pain reliever prescribed for patient |

*(continued)*

**Table 3-1**   Data on Patient Recovery from Severe Back Pain

| Column Name | Values | Explanation |
|---|---|---|
| DOCTOR_YRS | Numeric | Number of years doctor has been in practice |
| DOCTOR_#_OPERATIONS_ PERFORMED | High, Very high, Medium, Low, Very low | Number of operations performed by a doctor |
| #BEDS_IN_HOSP | Numeric, Integer value | Number of beds in hospital |
| HIGH_BLOOD_PRESSURE | Yes, No | Whether patient has high blood pressure |
| ALLERGIES | Yes, No | Whether patient has allergies |
| ARTHRITIS | Yes, No | Whether patient has arthritis |
| PREVIOUS SURGERIES | Numeric, Integer | Number of surgeries patient has previously undergone |
| BACK_PROBLEMS | Yes, No | If patient has a history of back problems |
| QUARTER | Winter, Spring, Summer, Fall | The season that patient was admitted |
| FOLLOW_UP_EXAM | Critical, Poor, Fair, Good, Excellent | Condition of patient during follow- up exam |
| OBJ_PAIN | Low, Med, High | Doctors' objective findings on pain |
| OBJ_SWELLING | Yes, No | Doctors' objective findings on whether patient has swelling |
| OBJ_STIFFNESS | Yes, No | Doctors' objective findings on whether patient has stiffness |
| PATIENT_AREACODE | Area codes in the U.S. | Area code for patient's home phone. |
| HEIGHT | Numeric, in inches | Height of patient |
| WEIGHT | Numeric, in pounds | Weight of patient |
| WEIGHT_LAST_YEAR | Numeric, in pounds | Weight of patient last year |

Given the data shown in Table 3-1, specific examples of the kinds of issues you are likely to face in preparing data-mining studies appear immediately. The first issue is how to get at your data. This seems straightforward, but actually can be quite a formidable task if your data is stored in many places. This issue involves data preparation, and it begins the data-mining process.

## 3.3  Data Preparation

Data preparation involves finding the answers to several questions, including: How do you create a table like Table 3-1? How do you mine data that are not in the right form? How do you handle data that are not entirely clean? This section will discuss these questions, and look at solutions that are currently being used in the industry.

Some people would like to view data mining as a magical process that somehow takes raw data and distills them into a diamond that will save your business millions of dollars.

The reality is that data mining should always be considered as a *process,* and that data preparation is at the heart of this process. For example, if you want to find out who will respond to a direct marketing campaign, you need data about customers who have previously responded to mailers. If you have their name and address, you should realize that this type of data is unique to a customer and therefore not the best data to be mined.

Information like city and state provides descriptive information, but demographic information is more valuable: items like a customer's age, general income level, types of interests, and household type. This information can be purchased from many companies, but to mine it, the data must be merged.

There are several things to consider about data preparation in a data-mining study.

**Data Cleaning.**   Data is not always "clean." For example, a column containing a list of soft drinks may have the values "Pepsi," "Pepsi Cola," and "Cola." The values refer to the same drink, but are not known to the computer as the same. This is a consistency problem.

Another cleaning issue is stale data. Mailing lists have to be continually updated because people move and their addresses change. An old address that is no longer correct is often referred to as stale.

Another data-cleaning issue is typographical errors. Words are frequently misspelled or typed incorrectly.

**Missing Values.**   Data often contain missing values. Some data-mining approaches require rows of data to be complete in order to mine the data. Also, if too many values are missing in a data set, it becomes hard to gather any useful information from this data set or to make predictions from it.

**Data Derivation.**  Often the most interesting data may require derivation from existing columns. For example, if I have a column called *maximum$_94* and *maximum$_95* to describe the dollars spent in 1994 and 1995, an interesting derivation is *$_difference*, which is the change in the amount of money spent between 1994 and 1995.

**Merging Data.**  The most commonplace situation with data for business systems is for the data to be stored on a mainframe or in a relational database on a UNIX server or Windows NT workstation. Data in these systems are stored in the form of tables. For example, Figure 3-2 shows an entity-level diagram of sales transactions for a retailer.

In order to mine these tables, it is often useful to manipulate the data into a two-dimensional table. Merging data in a relational system can be achieved in a number of ways, including merging these tables through a view, an SQL statement, or an export of the data into a flat file. Views are created by a database administrator to make a series of tables look like one table. Query tools can merge tables by building a query that joins the tables into a resultant table.

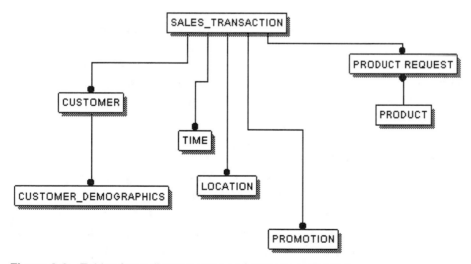

**Figure 3-2**  Tables for mailer response and customer information.

### 3.3.1  Getting at Your Data

The data for the patients suffering severe back pain look understandable enough when laid out in the form of a table, but data about doctors, about insurance, about patient information, and about hospitals may be stored in different databases. Even if the data are in one relational database, they are likely to be stored in multiple tables.

Below are some alternative ways to access data for data mining. Appendix A lists vendors who offer solutions that make data access easier, such as data-warehouse vendors, data-conversion vendors, and query-tool vendors.

### Accessing Data Warehouses

Data mining is often discussed as an after-market for *data warehouses* and *data marts*. This is not because data mining requires a data warehouse or data mart. Data mining is discussed as an after-market of data warehousing and data marts because taking the time to build such decision-support systems forces companies to undergo the task of bringing all their disparate data together.

An interesting trend in data mining is the integration of data warehousing databases directly with data-mining tools. Many tools today require intermediary steps to be performed before data in these tables can be mined.

### Accessing Data through Relational Transaction-Based Databases or PC-Based Databases

Even if data are not stored in a data warehouse, you can access data from a relational, transaction-based database or PC-based database directly by using connectivity. Many vendors today offer integration with ODBC, a connectivity standard to most databases of this kind (or the new OLE DB standard). There can be a problem with accessing multiple tables at once, but this can be solved by relational databases by creating what is known as a *view* on the database side, which is a way to make multiple tables appear as one.

### Accessing Data through Data-Conversion Utilities

If a data warehouse is not in place or if it is in a format that a data-mining tool does not understand, there are other alternatives to getting data. For example, there are several *data-conversion utilities* that allow you to merge data sets and/or change formats.

A common problem you may face is that your data are stored in a different format than what the tool supports. Mainframe data are often stored in a fixed format, which is not easily transformed into comma- or tab-delimited data. Often tools will require tab-delimited or comma-delimited files in lieu of a database connection.

There are a few PC-based data-formatting tools, such as Data Junction™ or DBMS Copy™, out on the market today that will take data of virtually any format and put it into another. The data-warehousing vendors also have a series of vendors who will synthesize data on a much larger scale, for example, Prism®.

## Accessing Data Using Query Tools

Another alternative to creating a data source suitable for mining is using a query tool to join tables from existing databases and then creating files from them. Vendors like Business Objects®, Brio Technology®, and Cognos Corporation® even offer levels of integration with data-mining tools to facilitate this issue.

Standard query tools will solve the problem of collating data from several relational tables.

## Accessing Data from Flat Files

The last alternative for getting a table ready for data mining is using a two-dimensional text-based or flat file. Almost all data-mining tools today mine flat files. The main advantage is that text-based files are very fast to read. The obvious drawback is that they either have to be extracted from an existing database/data warehouse, or they have to be input manually. Once they are created, they are difficult to manipulate.

Smaller text-based files can be loaded into spreadsheets like Microsoft Excel, where they can be manipulated, but there are limitations to this; for example, how many columns and rows are allowed.

An example of a healthcare data set loaded from a flat file into Excel is shown in Figure 3-3.

| | 1 | 2 | 3 | 4 | 5 | 6 | 7 |
|---|---|---|---|---|---|---|---|
| 1 | PATIENTID | HOSPITAL | RECOVERY_TIME | LENGTH_HOSP_STAY | AGE | HEIGHT | DOCTOR_YRS |
| 2 | 670 | CENTRAL | 0-2Weeks | 2days | 18-25 | 71 | 2TO5 |
| 3 | 645 | CENTRAL | 0-2Weeks | 2days | 18-25 | 67 | 2TO5 |
| 4 | 13 | CENTRAL | 0-2Weeks | 2days | 18-25 | 68 | 1TO2 |
| 5 | 18 | WESTERN | 0-2Weeks | 2days | 18-25 | 67 | 2TO5 |
| 6 | 1 | CENTRAL | 0-2Weeks | overnight | 18-25 | 60 | 1TO2 |
| 7 | 662 | WESTERN | 0-2Weeks | overnight | 18-25 | 69 | 2TO5 |
| 8 | 83 | WESTERN | 0-2Weeks | overnight | 18-25 | 73 | 5TO10 |
| 9 | 97 | WESTERN | 0-2Weeks | overnight | 18-25 | 70 | 2TO5 |
| 10 | 70 | VALLEY | 0-2Weeks | overnight | 18-25 | 66 | 5TO10 |
| 11 | 79 | CENTRAL | 0-2Weeks | overnight | 18-25 | 62 | 5TO10 |
| 12 | 72 | WESTERN | 0-2Weeks | overnight | 18-25 | 60 | 5TO10 |
| 13 | 58 | WESTERN | 0-2Weeks | overnight | 18-25 | 61 | 10+ |
| 14 | 8 | COAST | 0-2Weeks | overnight | 18-25 | 65 | 2TO5 |
| 15 | 597 | COAST | 0-2Weeks | 2days | 18-25 | 66 | 2TO5 |
| 16 | 646 | CENTRAL | 0-2Weeks | overnight | 18-25 | 61 | 10+ |
| 17 | 643 | VALLEY | 0-2Weeks | outpatient | 18-25 | 65 | 2TO5 |
| 18 | 676 | CENTRAL | 0-2Weeks | outpatient | 18-25 | 74 | 1st-YEAR |
| 19 | 695 | CENTRAL | 0-2Weeks | outpatient | 18-25 | 75 | 5TO10 |
| 20 | 4 | CENTRAL | 0-2Weeks | 2days | 18-25 | 63 | 5TO10 |
| 21 | 22 | COAST | 0-2Weeks | overnight | 18-25 | 70 | 1TO2 |

**Figure 3-3**   An example of a text-based file for data mining.

### 3.3.2    Data-Qualification Issues

A common issue people face when approaching data mining is that of qualification. For example, consider the following fields of data: *Customer_ID, First_Name, Last_Name, Address, Phone_No, Area_Code, City, State,* and *Zip_Code.* You would not mine a field like *Customer_ID* because it is a unique field and there are no patterns to be found in unique fields. Similarly, there are usually no patterns to find in *First_Name, Last_Name, Address,* or *Phone_No* because they are most often unique.

*Area_Code, City, State*, and *Zip_Code* might be interesting fields for studies, but *City, Area_Code* and *Zip_Code* have another issue: There can be thousands of city names or zip code numbers, and hundreds of area codes. Even if you mine these data fields, are the results going to be understandable to the end user? Potentially, yes, but, on the other hand, for small data sets, these types of fields may be too unique to offer any interesting trends.

For classification studies, a data set must also have data fields that can be used as the output of a study. For instance, the churn rate example in Chapter 1 had a field, *Cust_Type*, that contained the values Lost or Loyal.

Fields that are inherently qualified for the output of a data-mining classification study are derived from experience. For example, over time, a bank will have information on certain customers who have balanced accounts and certain customers who have over-draft accounts. From this information, you have derived fields *good customers* and *bad customers*.

In the healthcare example in Table 3-1, there are several fields that could be used as the output of a study, including *Length_of_stay, Recovery_time,* and *Allergies*.

### 3.3.3    Data-Quality Issues

Data are rarely 100% "clean." The quality of data on which decisions are made in the corporate world is often suspect. Data mining is at best as good as the data it is repre-senting.

Let us look at how data-quality issues might affect the sample data set in this chapter.

#### Redundant Data

Look at the data distribution shown in Figure 3-4 for a sample file derived from our healthcare example.

**Figure 3-4**  An example of unclean data.

In Figure 3-4, the area circled and denoted with the letter A shows that there are 34 rows of data for the patient with patient ID 937. This particular study was supposed to show only one patient record for each patient, because it was a week's worth of data and the patient would not have undergone surgery in this period more than once. The fact that 34 rows show up means that we have redundant data in this study, and it must be cleaned.

### Incorrect or Inconsistent Data

Look at Figure 3-5, which shows another page of the data distribution from the same study shown in Figure 3-4.

The circles marked B and C clearly show incorrect data. The year 1995 should definitely not show up in a column named *HOSPITAL_BRANCH* and there are inconsistencies in the value that should read "0-2Weeks."

| Field Name | Usage | Type | Values | Unique values | Occur. | Category | Min | Max |
|---|---|---|---|---|---|---|---|---|
| PATIENTID | Input | Discrete | 990 | | 1024 | | | |
| HOSPITAL_BRANCH | Input | Discrete | 6 | | 1024 | | | |
| | | | | CENTRAL | 347 | | | |
| | | | | WESTERN | 349 | | | |
| | | | | VALLEY | 214 | | | |
| | | | | COAST | 112 | | | |
| | | | | Central | 1 | B | | |
| | | | | 1995 | 1 | | | |
| RECOVERY_TIME | Output | Discrete | 6 | | 1024 | | | |
| | | | | 0-2Weeks | 196 | | | |
| | | | | 0-2WEAeks | 1 | C | | |
| | | | | 0-2WEeks | 1 | | | |
| | | | | 2-3Weeks | 298 | | | |
| | | | | 3-6Weeks | 286 | | | |
| | | | | 6+Weeks | 242 | | | |
| AGE | Input | Discrete | 5 | | 1024 | | | |
| | | | | 18-25 | 198 | | | |
| | | | | 25-35 | 314 | D | | |
| | | | | 35-45 | 221 | | | |
| | | | | 45-65 | 211 | | | |
| | | | | 65-up | 80 | | | |
| SMOKER_TYPE | Input | Discrete | 4 | | 1024 | | | |
| | | | | DAILY | 211 | | | |
| | | | | FREQUENT | 334 | E | | |
| | | | | NO | 221 | | | |
| | | | | OCCASIONAL | 258 | | | |

**Figure 3-5**   Several data-quality issues.

### Typos

The circles marked B and C are not only inconsistent, but also show misspellings. Note that circle B also shows the central region has been represented by both *CENTRAL* and *Central*, which is a capitalization problem.

### Stale Data

The data denoted by circle D may be stale. If this data set was from 1994, someone who was 24 will be 26 now. In other words, the data changed from then to now. Addresses are great examples of where stale data exists. People change addresses frequently in our society, so addresses more than a year old become suspect. A customer profile is two years old and the customer has moved, but this is not reflected in the address listed.

Another important factor in data staleness is that the "state of the world" changes. For example, customer behavior and trends change over time.

### Variance in Defining Terms

Looking at the values marked by circle E brings up an interesting question: What makes a person an occasional smoker versus a frequent smoker? If two hospitals vary in their definition, your data may be skewed. For example, the Central Region hospital may define frequent smokers as those who smoke more than two packs a day, while the Valley hospital may say frequent smokers are those who smoke more than three cigarettes an hour.

### 3.3.4  Binning

The field *Age*, denoted by circle D in Figure 3-5, shows that people had been grouped into categories by age: 10–25, 25–35, 35–45, 45–55, 55–up. In this example, the field was already binned before you mined it; however, the field could have been a numeric field with each number a discrete value. When you have fields that are a range of numbers, it is often best to bin them, or rather, define them in categories, not unlike what was done for you with the field *Age*.

Most data-mining tools will offer ways to bin data for you. There are many different approaches to binning data, and the way you bin the data can affect your overall result. In Chapter 1, a data-distribution chart was shown where the categories were binned in an arbitrary way. Figure 3-6 shows the distribution chart again.

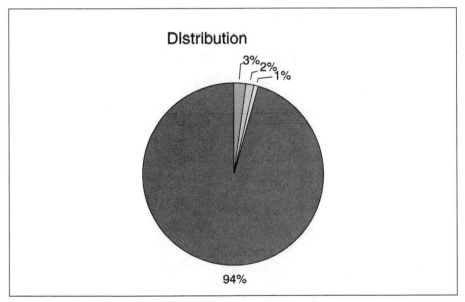

**Figure 3-6**  An example where most data falls into one bin.

In this case, numeric values were binned into four distinct categories, but 94% of all data elements fit into just one category.

The question is often asked: How many bins should you have? The answer to this is not straightforward. It is necessary to look at a data distribution to figure out how many unique groupings of numbers are in your data set. Some statisticians believe that data should not be binned at all; however, doing this can greatly increase the complexity and computing time of your model.

### 3.3.5    Data Derivation

There are two fields in the healthcare data set for a patient: *Weight* and *Weight_Last_Year*. The two fields are interesting for use in data mining, but it might also be interesting to have a field that shows the difference in a patient's weight from this year to last year. A field like this can be derived by taking the difference between the two columns, *Weight* and *Weight_Last_Year*.

Data fields can be derived in several different ways. You can use SQL in a relational database to do it, query tools will allow you to do it, and this example data set is small enough that you could do it using an Excel spreadsheet and some mathematical functions.

In this study, there is another field, *Patient_AreaCode*, which is not the best way to represent the data for a data set of 1,000 patients. Let us say that you want to know what state a patient lives in, but the data set does not provide this information; the information can be derived from the area code. In this example, the author used SQL to derive a field showing the patient's state from the area code. The patient's state may be shown by using SQL's query capability to update a field *Patient_State* with the value West for all the following area codes:

| | |
|---|---|
| Colorado: | 303, 719, 970 |
| Washington: | 206, 360, 509 |
| Oregon: | 503, 541 |
| California: | 213, 310, 408, 415, 510, 619, 707, 805, 818, 909, 916 |
| Idaho: | 208 |
| Utah: | 801 |
| Nevada: | 702 |
| Arizona: | 520, 602 |
| Montana: | 406 |
| Wyoming: | 307 |
| New Mexico: | 505 |

## 3.4  Defining a Study

Defining a study is the second step in the data-mining process. You needn't have finished preparing data to perform a data-mining study, because data mining is a process and is likely to be honed and redone. Over time, the data you use, how you bin it, and how well it is cleaned will change and hopefully improve the overall model.

Assuming you have prepared a data set for mining, you then need to define the scope of that study. This involves several things, including understanding the limits of a study, choosing good studies to perform, determining the right elements to study, and understanding sampling.

### 3.4.1   Understanding Limits

In defining a study, you will be faced with many questions: Where do you start? What data should you examine? How much data should you use? Just how far will data mining go for me? Data mining has often been sold as a miracle process, and people often struggle between the reality of the benefits and the promises of the sales organizations. Here are a few of the questions concerning the limits of data mining, along with the answers.

*No goal should be necessary in defining a study. Shouldn't data mining find relevant patterns for me without specifying what to look at?*

While there is some truth to this statement, the choices you make in preparing data and defining how those data are presented will always reveal some goals or objectives. Even in unsupervised or clustering studies where no dependent variable is necessary, the choices in data dictate what you look at. It is not necessary to define specific goals, but, for example, if your data concern surgeries on patients suffering from severe back pain, then your studies are likely to revolve around learning more details about these surgeries.

*How will data mining work if I have bad data?*

Data mining will not ignore bad data, but then, you have to start somewhere. A goal of data mining should always be to improve processes. By understanding a data set, it is to be hoped that you will better understand how to improve its reliability.

*If I have a model built, why should I continue to use a data mining tool?*

Data mining is a process, and it will usually raise questions when you see the results. Are there other ways to examine the data? Maybe you will perform the same study on a subset of your data. For example, you may study only surgeries performed in the central region rather than the whole.

*If I perform a study and find out no new, useful information, then why should I mine data?*

Data mining will not always reveal something new. If you have analyzed your data for several years and are intimately familiar with it, chances are that data mining will not provide a golden nugget.

There are two good reasons to use data mining when data are already understood. The first is that data mining often validates what you already assume to be true. It is reassuring to have information back up your hunches. The second is that data mining can quickly spot trends. You can build the same model using new information every month and compare results. If one month's data indicates something that your previous models have not been telling you, then you may have a change in patterns and need to investigate further.

### 3.4.2   Choosing a Good Study

When you're not sure of the proper place to start, it is often useful to imagine presenting your overall purpose to someone else. For good studies, you should find it easy to explain how the outcome of a study will potentially provide a solution or work towards solving a need that you have.

Examples of good studies (goals):

- My purpose is to profile what type of patients have allergies or not so that we can improve the process of treating patients with or without allergies in the future.
- My purpose is to understand what type of patients undergoing surgery for severe back pain recover in 0–2 weeks, 2–3 weeks, 3–6 weeks, and 6+ weeks, so that I can potentially help reduce a lengthy recovery process, and understand areas that may hinder recovery.
- My purpose is to determine which patients are most likely to use mild pain relievers, codeine-equivalent drugs, or severe narcotics in order to reduce the overall level of addiction to a certain drug.

### 3.4.3   Types of Studies

The following are a few suggestions of areas to consider for studies. Examples are provided for each type of study using the healthcare data set from Table 3-1.

Studies can be used both to understand why certain conditions are occurring, as well as to predict sets of criteria that will cause an outcome.

#### Profiling Customer Habits

**Example.**   Based on existing data of people who smoke or do not, what are the characteristics of patients who are smokers versus non-smokers?

### Profiling Customer Demographics

**Example.**   Based on information about patients' occupations, what are the differences in their patient histories?

**Example.**   Based on information on the type of insurance people use, what are the differences in their patient histories?

### Time-Dependence Studies

**Example.**   Based on the season that a surgery was performed (winter, fall, summer, spring), what are the differences in patient success and recovery rates?

### Retention Management

We could add a field to our data indicating whether patients, within a year's time, have continued to use this hospital system, had no further need of health services, or moved to another hospital system after their back surgery. If we added an indicator of loyal patients versus patients who have no more need of services, or those no longer using the system, we can start to understand the set of characteristics that cause a person to stay, have no need for services, or leave.

This set of data would do a retention study only for patients who had surgery for severe back pain.

### Risk Forecast

**Example.**   Based on patient-recovery information, what types of patients will have the most risk of taking a long time to recover?

With surgeries, there is always a risk of fatalities, however small, which this data set does not cover. A more critical study is to understand what characteristics make someone likely or less likely to survive surgery.

### Profitability Analysis

**Example.**   Another column to this data set could be added to indicate the profitability of a surgery. Based on categories of net profit (e.g., high profit, low profit, low loss, high loss), what sorts of surgeries yield the highest amount of profit or loss to the organization?

Profitability studies, especially in healthcare, are the first to generate protests of the ethics of data mining. Any organization has to understand its costs to understand how to remain profitable, but there are always ethical implications for such information.

### Data-Trends Analysis

**Example.**   Based on pre-built models that show trends in length of hospital stay, customer recovery rates, or any other monitoring metric, flag data that differ from what is considered normal.

Trend analysis is often performed by running a study with a data set containing past history and then running the same study using a data set with only this month's data. The differences in the results will show trends over the specified periods of time.

### Employee Studies

**Example.**   Based on the number of surgeries performed by a doctor, what set of characteristics of patients are there for doctors who perform more surgeries versus those who do not?

### Regional Studies

**Example.**   Based on where a surgery was performed (valley, central, western, or coast hospitals), what are the differences in patient histories?

### Classification, Clustering, and Visualization Studies

All the examples so far have been worded so that you can perform a classification study. As an exercise, you can reread them and determine which column should be used as a dependent variable for each type of study; however, clustering and visualization studies can also be performed for each type of study.

For example, for the study profiling smokers versus non-smokers, a clustering study could be performed to potentially identify groups or segments of a patient population who are more likely to be smokers versus non-smokers.

The data on smokers and non-smokers can also be graphed against any number of other variables to visualize the importance of certain elements and characteristics of the two groups.

The number of possible studies is endless. This exercise was meant to spark thought on what you can do. In Chapters 7 through 8, specific examples will be given for several different industries.

### 3.4.4    What Elements to Analyze?

Whether you perform a clustering study, look at data visually, or perform a classification study, the process of choosing elements to analyze are the same. If you are data mining for the first time, then you might choose to include any number of columns and let the data-mining process tell you what elements are important. The second pass may involve narrowing down the list of elements to the most important ones.

In performing a classification study, it is often important to recognize what types of data, or *dimensions*, you have and what other types you may want in the future.

There is a column, *Allergies*, in Table 3-1 from our sample healthcare data set. If we choose this as the dependent variable, then we are performing a study to classify the difference between those patients who have allergies and those who do not.

**Goal.**   I want to understand the profile of who is likely to have allergies and who is not.

**Subject of the Study.**   Looking at the data set in Table 3-1, there are different types of information that can be used for a study. These types of information are what the decision support industry commonly refers to as *dimensions*. It is always a good idea to identify what dimensions you may have in the data set you are studying. Here are the dimensions found in the healthcare demo:

- *Patient's physical information*
  Fields that tell us about a patient's physical information are: Age, Height, Weight, Weight_Last_Year
- *Patient's medical information*
  Fields that tell us about a patient's medical information include Recovery Time, Hospital Stay, Pain Reliever Used, High_Blood_Pressure, Allergies, Arthritis, Previous Surgeries, Back Problems, 2nd_Day_Exam, Obj_Pain, Obj_Swelling, and Obj_Stiffness
- *Patient's demographic information*
  Fields that tell us about a patient's demographic information include Smoker, Insurance, and Occupation
- *Doctor information*
  Fields that tell us about the doctor include Doctor_Yrs and Doctor_#_OP_Performed
- *Hospital information*
  Fields that tell us about a hospital include Hospital Branch and #Beds_in_Hosp
- *Time information*
  The field about time of surgery is Quarter

In all, there are six dimensions identified here: patient's physical, patient's medical, patient's demographic, doctor information, hospital information, and time information.

The first question to ask for a study on profiling people with allergies and those without is:

***What dimensions are useful to profiling people with allergies and those without?***

Clearly, any dimension describing the patient is useful. Is doctor information or hospital information useful? There is not as clear a link unless your purpose is to understand if certain hospitals or doctors tend to treat more people with allergies or vice versa. The time dimension is useful in determining a seasonal relation to allergies.

The second question to ask is:

*How descriptive are the fields in the identified dimensions?*

The patient's medical dimension has many elements, but the patient's demographic and time dimensions are sparse. If you are looking at what type of information to add, then the patient demographic and time dimensions would be a good place to start. Examples of patient's demographic information might include marital status, gender, income level, household type, type of exercise, or religion. The time dimension might include day of year, hour of day, or day of week.

A third question to ask is:

*What types of dimension might one add to this study?*

In this case, one could add a dimension about the drug a patient used, including describing side effects and efficacy rates. Another dimension might be a regional dimension describing the types of trees, animals, and environmental conditions that affect a person's allergies. If you think about it, there are several other dimensions that could be useful to a study like this.

Don't limit yourself when you are starting the data mining process. Data mining should help filter out fields that don't provide any information. More importantly, identify the dimensions of data you have and where you might add information in the future.

### 3.4.5   Issues of Sampling

Almost all data miners ask this question at one time or another:

*How can I mine only a subset of my data and get good results if I have millions of rows of information?*

Data mining does not always require your entire data set to model appropriately. The follow-up question is, how much is enough? While no exact amount can realistically be given, a fair statement would be to start out small and build up. If you are building models that accurately represent your data, increasing your data sets should not alter the results that you are finding; however, it can increase the robustness of the results.

Another thing to know is that a model can be created from a small sampling and then validated on the whole data set. If a sample data set is valid, then it is able to predict outcomes for other data samples and the results of known outcomes for other data sets can be compared.

## 3.5  Reading the Data and Building a Model

For the next three sections, a classification study has been chosen to show the process of building a model. Below is the goal:

**Goal.** *My purpose is to understand what type of patients undergoing surgery for severe back pain recover in 0–2 weeks, 2–3 weeks, 3–6 weeks, and 6+ weeks, so that I can help reduce lengthy recovery processes and understand areas that may hinder recovery.*

Once this study has been defined and the input data specified to evaluate recovery time, it is left to the data-mining tool to read a data set and build a model from it.

Chapter 1 discussed the various types of models briefly. It is not the purpose of this book to go into the details of how each type of model works. Many of the works that are pointed to in Appendix A will help with that.

For this example, a modeling tool will build a model that indicates the factors that make a person more likely to recover in 0–2 weeks, 2–3 weeks, 3–6 weeks, or 6+ weeks. It's most important for a business professional to be comfortable with the accuracy, understandability, and performance of the model.

### 3.5.1  On Accuracy

The fact that it is possible to find important relationships that help determine why someone takes more than six weeks to recover is one thing; proving that this relationship is a certain percentage accurate within a margin of error is another. Data mining has not completely replaced statistics toward this end. Data mining is a process for extracting meaningful information from data; statistics is an entire field of study that includes extracting meaningful information from data.

Data mining will produce models that can be proven to have a certain degree of accuracy over time, but when accuracy is regulated by the government and must be proven, a combination of approaches is necessary. For example, HNC's Falcon is a great product for determining credit fraud, but it is not widely used to grant or deny credit because government regulations demand that the user justify what is done down to the mathematical equations.

### 3.5.2  On Understandability

Being able to understand a model can be a personal comfort issue. Some people are more comfortable with one approach over another; however, understandability is not a yes/no check-off item. There are several aspects to a model that should be understandable.

*First, does the model let you understand what inputs affect an outcome?*

Earlier, I mentioned that neural-net approaches are often black-box approaches that can be used for prediction, but it is hard to understand why predictions are made. For new-generation products, this does not have to be true, but it can be an issue. Decision trees do have a good method for understanding how data segments best cluster together to affect an outcome.

*Second, does a model let you understand why it fails or succeeds in predictions?*

Some models will produce reports that tell you why a model succeeds in predicting (when compared against known outcomes) and where it may be falling short.

*Third, does a model let you predict an outcome for complex data sets?*

Decision trees have been criticized for their inability to predict outcomes of complex data sets. Again, new products may overcome past criticisms, but a model should allow you to predict outcomes on very large data sets.

*Fourth, does a model validate its results?*

All models should be able to tell you how accurate they are in predicting data, and where they can compare the predictions against known results.

### 3.5.3    On Performance

The performance of a model can be divided into two areas: how fast can you build a model and how fast can you predict from it. Historically, neural nets have again been criticized for the time they take to build a model. HNC provides special hardware to speed up the process. Once a model has been built, prediction is very fast. Bayesian Belief modeling can be very fast for model building and prediction. For model building, it has linear performance as a data set grows past millions of rows (it does not take three times as long to read twice as much data); however, there usually is some trade-off between performance and accuracy of any model.

## 3.6  Understanding Your Model

Understanding a model has many different dimensions to it. This section describes the types of reports and what information you might expect from a data set describing recovery time of patients.

### 3.6.1 Model Summarization

Regardless of the model you use, the reports tell you what information has a relationship to the specified outcomes. Saying the input data has an impact on a particular outcome does not necessarily mean a causal relationship. There could be a relationship between driving speed on freeways and darkness: for example, people drive 10 miles per hour faster at night (on average). This does not mean that darkness causes people to drive faster. Rather, traffic congestion during the day causes them to drive slower.

The following are examples of definite relationships a model might find for our data set:

- *Recovery: 0–2Weeks*
  Roughly 7.5% of all patients who recovered in this time had the occupation of professional. If someone had the occupation professional, they always recovered in 0–2 weeks.
  Roughly 73% of all patients who recovered in this time period were self-insured. If someone was self-insured, there was a very strong chance they recovered in 0–2 weeks.
- *Recovery: 2–3Weeks*
  Roughly 34% of all patients who recovered in this time period did not smoke. If they did not smoke, there was a very strong chance that they recovered in 2–3 weeks.
- *Recovery: 3–6Weeks*
  Roughly 41% of all patients who recovered in this time period were daily smokers. If the patient was a daily smoker, then there was a good chance they recovered in 3–6 weeks.
- *Recovery: 6+Weeks*
  Roughly 18% of people who are retired and are over 65 years of age recovered in over six weeks. If someone is retired and over 65 years of age, there was a good chance that they took six weeks to recover.
  Roughly 13% of people who recovered in over six weeks had a history of back problems. If someone has a history of back problems, there is a strong chance they took six weeks or more to recover.

The findings that were presented by the model provided several pieces of information. First, the frequencies of occurrence were calculated: How often did something happen? Second, the weight or probability that an input affected an outcome was measured in some way. Finally, something called a *conjunction* was shown. In this case the conjunction was: If someone was retired and they were over 65, then they were likely to recover in six weeks.

### 3.6.2   Data Distribution

One field in the example data set is *Weight*, which is a numeric value representing a patient's weight in pounds. The data for the column *Weight* can be binned into five categories as follows:

| Category 1 | 83–111 pounds |
|---|---|
| Category 2 | 111–139 pounds |
| Category 3 | 139–168 pounds |
| Category 4 | 168–196 pounds |
| Category 5 | 196–224 pounds |

In order to show a data distribution, the number of values in each category is totalled. Category 1 has 75 values within its range; Category 2 has 300 values; Categories 3, 4, and 5 have 320, 211, and 115 values, respectively. The data distribution for this column looks like Figure 3-7.

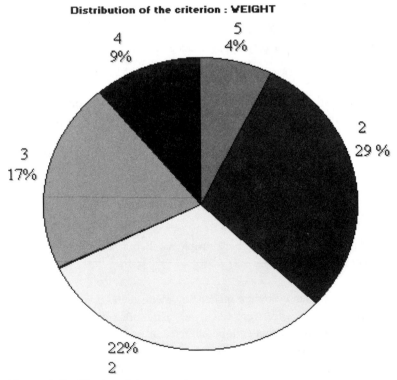

**Figure 3-7**  Binning data properly.

The data are not evenly distributed among categories, and this creates an obvious question:

***How do you bin these data to optimize your results?***

There are several ways to answer this question. Decision trees, using a CHAID algorithm, are especially good at finding these types of results. Another way is to sort the values and see what the weight values look like. Figure 3-8 is an Excel chart of sorted weight values.

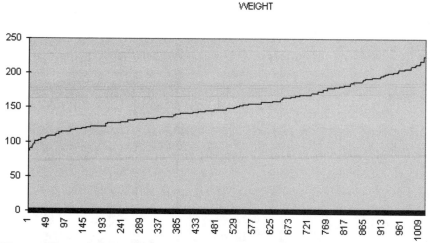

WEIGHT

**Figure 3-8** A chart showing patient weights for 1,009 patients.

The chart shows that the data are fairly evenly distributed among weight values, and interesting groupings are not readily identifiable. Figure 3-9 shows a much more unusual distribution of patient weights.

### 3.6.3 Validation

The validation report is a way to evaluate how good your model is at predicting patterns in the data set. In one example, a model came up with these results for our sample data set:

- The model predicted patients recovering in 0–2 weeks with 84% accuracy.
- The model predicted patients recovering in 2–3 weeks with 69% accuracy.
- The model predicted patients recovering in 3–6 weeks with 62% accuracy.

• The model predicted patients recovering in more than six weeks with 85% accuracy.
• Overall, the model predicted outcomes with a 73% accuracy.

A couple of questions that you might have about the validation process are:

### *Is the model evaluated on the same data set that it was created with?*

You may have better results evaluating a model against data that was used to build it than if you evaluate a model on a *holdout sample.* A holdout sample is a set of data not used to build a model that is used to evaluate the model's accuracy. A holdout sample is a better litmus test to validate a model's robustness.

### *Is the model better at predicting certain outcomes than others?*

In the case of a direct-mail campaign, the marketer cares more about how well the model predicts the person likely to respond, not the person who will not respond.

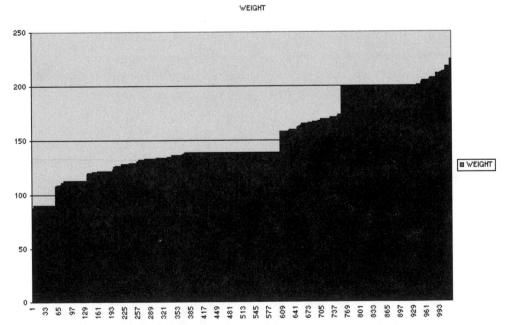

**Figure 3-9**  Another example of unusually distributed patients weights.

*How can I improve my model's predictive accuracy?*

There are several ways to improve upon a model once it is created. There is, however, a danger of "over-fitting" the model, so that it is highly predictive for a training set, but is less efficient when predicting from data not used in building the model. Here are a few suggestions to improve the model:

- After identifying types of input data that have a strong influence on certain outcomes, try to gather more detailed information similar to these data points.
- Data used in creating a model is always in jeopardy of being "unclean." Data cleaning will always improve a model.
- Change the way numeric values are binned. Binning ranges can have a strong impact on model efficiency
- Use evaluation information, if available, that explains when a model fails or succeeds to predict successfully. For example, the model that was evaluated reported that it failed to predict correctly for recoveries that took more than six weeks when the number of operating rooms in the hospital were from one to 10. This condition occurred roughly 6% of the time the recovery time was six weeks.
- A data set can be divided into subsets and mined individually. Sometimes mining a series of subsets will yield stronger results than mining the whole.
- If you know the conditions that should always lead to a certain outcome, filter out these data and mine the rest. For example, if input A leads to output B 95% of the time, then assume all rows of data with input A are linked to output B and mine the rest.

## 3.7 Prediction

The process of prediction is straightforward. With a set of inputs, a prediction is made on a certain outcome. While the validation process uses prediction, it is really comparing known results to predictions made to calculate an accuracy level. With true prediction, the outcome to be predicted will not be known.

In our example of modeling recovery time, one row of data looks like the following:

| | |
|---|---|
| HOSPITAL_BRANCH | Western |
| LENGTH_HOSP_STAY | 0-2Days |
| AGE | 18-25 |
| HEIGHT | Unknown |
| WEIGHT | Unknown |
| SMOKER | Yes |
| SMOKER_TYPE | Occasional |
| MARITAL_STATUS | Married |

| | |
|---|---|
| OCCUPATION | Civil Servant |
| INSURANCE | Self-Insured |
| PAIN_RELIEVER_USED | Mild-Pain-Reliever |
| DOCTOR_YRS | 2-5 |
| D_#_OPERS | Med |
| #BEDS | 951-1149 |
| #OPER_RMS | 10-20 |
| HIGH_BLOOD_PRESURE | N |
| ALLERGIES | N |
| ARTHRITIS | N |
| PREVIOUS_SURGERY | 3 |
| HIST_BACK_PROBS | N |
| BLOOD_PRESURE | High |
| QUARTER | Summer |
| 2ND_DAY_EXAM | Excellent |
| OBJ_PAIN | LOW |
| OBJ_SWELLING | Y |
| OBJ_STIFFNESS | N |
| HISTORY_NEUROSIS | N |

The recovery time of this particular patient will be predicted. Using one technique, the patient is predicted to recover in 0–2 weeks.

There is other information that such a prediction process may make, as discussed below.

### 3.7.1   Challenger Outcomes

Not only do you want to know what outcome will be predicted, it may be interesting to calculate challenger predictions. For example, in the case above, the patient was predicted to recover in 0-2 weeks. There are three other possible outcomes. What will be the next likely prediction? In this case, 6+ weeks was predicted as the next likely outcome, or *challenger* outcome.

### 3.7.2   Margin of Victory

One very interesting point of data is the difference in the best prediction versus challenger outcome. If a prediction is calculated by a score or weight of some sort, then the difference in the prediction scores can also be calculated. For example, in this case, 0–2 weeks was predicted as the outcome with a score of 831 and the challenger outcome was predicted with a score of 640, which is a margin of victory of 23%. The larger the percentage, the more likely the prediction is to be true.

You can make predictions on only the rows of data where the margin of victory is greater than some percentage. You will not make predictions for every row, but the rows you do make predictions on may have a better margin of victory.

### 3.7.3 Understanding Why a Prediction Is Made

You may want to know why a prediction was made. For the example above, the top three reasons this prediction was made were: the patient was self-insured, the doctor found in objective findings a low occurrence of pain, and the patient was considered in excellent shape in the second day exam.

## 3.8 Summary

This chapter has covered the data-mining process in much more detail. A sample data set was used to discuss issues and step through the data mining process of preparing a data set, defining a study, building a model, understanding the model, and performing prediction. The chapter explores the types of information you expect when mining. This chapter is deliberately general. The subsequent chapters will explore the process in more detail. The next chapter looks at the various algorithms used in data mining. Chapter 5 discusses vendors in the data-mining industry. Chapters 6 and 7 will step through the data-mining process again, using different tools to familiarize you with how different products approach data mining. To examine types of studies for different industries, Chapters 8 and 9 will look more at the specifics.

# Data-Mining Algorithms

**T**oday's leading data-mining tools offer a wide variety of algorithms to choose from. The most simple reason for this is that some technologies perform better for different types of tasks. This chapter looks at some of the most popular data-mining algorithms used today, including neural networks, decision trees, and genetic algorithms, among others. The technologies are discussed as well as some of the strengths and weaknesses of the approaches. This chapter also elaborates on the discussions in Chapter 2 on market-basket analysis and assortment optimization.

This chapter is organized as follows:

## 4.1 Introduction

At the heart of data mining is the process of building a *model* to represent a data set. The process of building a model to represent a data set is common to all data-mining products; what is not common to all data-mining products is the manner in which a model is built. Many different algorithms are used to perform data mining.

To confuse this situation, there are hundreds of derivative approaches under the generic guise of names like neural networks, decision trees, genetic algorithms, and belief networks. For example, one vendor offers a neural network product set that offers more than 25 different neural-network approaches. This section will discuss different modeling techniques. Several books are recommended for continued reading in this area, as this is not the main focus of this book.

Modeling is the process of creating a model to represent a data set. A model will not usually represent a data set with 100% accuracy. You can create a model that is 100% accurate with some approaches using one training set, but if you are using such a model for prediction, then you may have *overfit*, or *overtrained*, the model by making it too specific. Overfitting leads to poor generalization when encountering data that the model has never "seen" before. For example, a model predicting whether someone will respond to an ad campaign is built with a sample data where all people with blue eyes responded to the ad campaign. The model generalizes that all people with blue eyes will respond. If you evaluate the model accuracy using the same sample data, this generalization will remain true, but when using this model against other data, this generalization will likely be proven false.

It is then left to the modeler to determine which set of algorithms are best for which set of applications. For future cases, your model may be less accurate because, over time, general trends are more important than specific cases.

## 4.2 Decision Trees

Creating a tree-like structure to describe a data set has been used for quite some time in computer science, but it has not been a preferred process of knowledge discovery. The book *Classification and Regression Trees,* written in 1984 by L. Breiman, J. Friedman, R. Olshen, and C. Stone, was an important work in gaining credibility and acceptance for decision trees in the statistics community. The decision-tree approach discussed in this work is commonly referred to as the CART algorithm.

J.R. Quinlan added popular new algorithms in a paper, "Induction of Decision Trees," published in the *Machine Learning Journal* in 1986, which introduced the ID3 algorithm. In 1993, Quinlan also published the book *Programs for Machine Learning*, introducing the extremely popular decision-tree algorithm C4.5; the book includes source code for programmers.

In addition to ID3, C4.5, and CART, classification-tree analysis has many different algorithms. A commonly used algorithm is CHAID (Chi-Square Automatic Interaction Detection) for categorical outputs.

Figure 4-1 shows a decision tree.

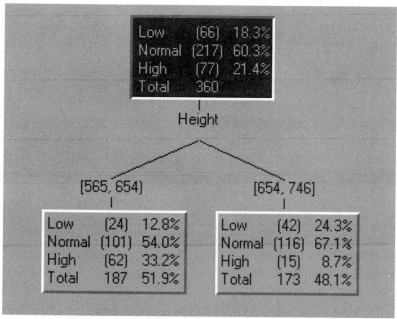

**Figure 4-1**   Viewing a decision-tree model.

The greatest benefit to decision-tree approaches is their understandability; however, to successfully model data using the decision-tree approach, several splits may be necessary. The tree subdivides the data according to height. It may be necessary to subdivide further on the basis of age and weight to learn, for example, that short, heavier people above a certain age have a greater incidence of high blood pressure.

### 4.2.1   How Decision Trees Work

Below is a simplified, stepwise discussion of building a decision tree. It should be noted that there are many approaches to decision trees used today. One is a statistical approach, and CART is the best example of this approach. It uses statistical prediction in which there are exactly two branches from each nonterminal node. Another approach is where the number of branches off a nonterminal node is equal to the number of categories.

Examples of this approach are the CLS, ID3, and C4.5 algorithms. Yet another approach varies the number of nodes on a nonterminal node from two to the number of categories. This approach is exemplified by the AID, CHAID, and TREEDISC algorithms. Many vendors use a combination of these approaches. For example, Angoss KnowledgeSEEKER uses a combination of algorithms.

While all decision-tree algorithms undergo a similar type of process, they employ different mathematical algorithms to determine how to group and rank the importance of different variables. For example, Quinlan, in *C4.5 Programs for Machine Learning,* discusses a gain-ratio algorithm that "expresses the proportion of information generated by the split that is useful, i.e., that appears helpful for classification."

**Step 1.** Variables are chosen from a data source. From the variables presented in the data source, a dependent variable is chosen by the user. In the example in Figure 4-1, hypertension is chosen as the dependent variable, with outcomes low, normal, and high. An input variable for this study is height. This variable is shown in Figure 4-1, but there may be many such input variables.

**Step 2.** Each variable affecting an outcome is examined. An iterative process of grouping values together is performed on the values contained within each of these variables. For example, in Figure 4-1, the optimal groupings of values for height are examined. Through an interactive process of grouping and merging the numeric values for the variable height, the values are shown as divided into two categories: (565–654) and (654–746). The conclusion that these are the two groupings for the variable height is done by statistical tests like Chi-Square that attempt to maximize variations between the groups and minimize variations within the groups. The determination that two groups, not three or four, is the right number of groups is also dependent on the type of functional tests used for grouping the data.

**Step 3.** Once the groupings have been calculated for each variable, a variable is deemed the most predictive for the dependent variable, and is used to create the leaf nodes of the tree. In our example, the variable height is selected as the leaf node of the tree because height was determined to be more predictive of hypertension than other variables. Frequency information is usually supplied to show the number of occurrences, by groups for the values of a dependent variable. In Figure 4-1, it is shown that shorter individuals are more likely to have higher blood pressure (32.2% of the people in the shorter height range had high blood pressure versus 8.7% of the taller individuals).

### 4.2.2   Strengths and Weaknesses of Decision Trees

Most people understand decision trees intuitively. This is the technology's greatest strength. As shown in Chapter 6, which demonstrates a decision-tree product, picking up and learning a decision-tree tool takes relatively little time. The negative side of decision trees is the fact that they get harder to manage as the complexity of the data increases. This is because of the increasing number of branches in the tree. There is also an issue with the handling of missing data, because without a data element being present, how do you traverse a tree node dependent on that datum? (This issue has been dealt with in most production decision-tree products, but it still is cumbersome at best.)

## 4.3 Genetic Algorithms

Genetic algorithms are a method of combinatorial optimization based on processes in biological evolution. The basic idea is that over time, evolution has selected the "fittest species." Applying this idea to data mining usually involves optimizing a model of the data using genetic methods to obtain "fittest" models. There is much active research in the area of genetic algorithms today, and, of all the modeling techniques, this appears to be the least understood. The roots of genetic algorithms start with Charles Darwin's work, the *Origin of Species*, in 1859. In 1957, G.E.P. Box wrote *Evolutionary operation: a method of increasing industrial productivity,* which was influential in linking genetic algorithms with business problems. Other influential works include a work by A.S. Fraser, *Simulation of genetic systems by automatic digital computers*; another very influential work in this area was H.J. Bremermann's *Optimization through evolution and recombination*, 1962. Genetic algorithms have often been used in conjunction with neural networks to model data.

### 4.3.1 How Genetic Algorithms Work

Genetic algorithms are good at clustering data together. For example, you want to divide, or cluster, a data set into three groups. A process for doing this is discussed below.

**Step 1.** For a genetic algorithm, you can start with a random grouping of data. Think of each of three clusters to be created as an organism. The genetic algorithm will have what is called a *fitness function* that determines if a data set is a match for one of the three "organisms" or clusters. This fitness function could be anything that identifies some data sets as "better fits" than others. As data sets are read, they can be evaluated by the fitness function to see how well they relate to the other data elements in a cluster. In our example, a fitness function could be a function to determine the level of similarity between data sets within a group.

**Step 2.** Genetic algorithms have *operators* that allow for copying and altering of the descriptions of groups of data. These operators mimic the function found in nature where life reproduces, mates, and mutates. If a row of data in a data set is found to be a good fit by the fitness function, then it survives and is copied into a cluster. If a row of data is not a good fit, it can be crossed over to another set, or, in other words, it can be mated with other clusters to create a better fit. A cluster will alter itself to create optimized fits as new data sets are read.

### 4.3.2    Strengths and Weaknesses

Genetic algorithms solved complex problems that other technologies have a difficult time with; that having been said, however, genetic algorithms are the least understood of the approaches as well as the most "open." For example, fitness functions can vary widely. The main requirement is that a fitness function must have certain properties that allow for convergence to minimal error, yet that leaves a lot of room for varying implementations.

Genetic algorithms have often been used in conjunction with neural networks to provide a higher level of model understanding. While neural networks (described in Section 4.4) have often been said to be "black boxes," genetic algorithms in conjunction with neural networks can record groups of input variables that impact an outcome directly into a database, providing more detailed documentation of each neural network model. After experimenting with various models, a final model can be built by reading one of the earlier model's variable sets.

## 4.4  Neural Networks

The concept of an "artificial neuron" that mimics the process of a neuron in the human brain was captured in 1943 in a paper by McCulloch and Pitts discussing a Threshold Logic Unit (TLU). In 1959, Frank Rosenblatt introduced the concept of a Perceptron. Neural nets fell into disfavor following publication of a book, *Perceptrons*, by Minsky & Papert in 1969, which showed that perceptrons could not solve a simple decision problem known as the XOR problem. Neural networks came into favor again when people realized that perceptrons with nonlinear thresholding units connected in multiple layers had considerably more power than a single perceptron and could in fact solve the XOR problem (and all other non-linearly separable classification problems). In 1982, John Hopfield published a paper showing how neural networks could be used for computational purposes. In 1984, Teuvo Kohonen introduced a new algorithm he called an *organizing feature map*, which allowed for a process of using neural networks for unsupervised learning. This opened a new branch of neural network research where no "correct" answer is required to learn or train a network. In 1986 Rumelhart, Hinton, and Williams wrote a seminal paper on the error back-propagation method, which opened up a flurry of activity in the late 1980s and 1990s and made neural networks what they are today (*Nature*, Vol. 323, page 533, 1986).

Neural networks are used extensively in the business world as predictive models. In particular, the financial services industry widely uses neural networks to model fraud in credit cards and monetary transactions.

### 4.4.1 How It Works

Neural networks attempt to mimic a neuron in a human brain, with each link described as a processing element (PE). Neural networks learn from experience and are useful in detecting unknown relationships between a set of input data and an outcome. Like other approaches, neural networks detect patterns in data, generalize relationships found in the data, and predict outcomes. Neural networks have been especially noted for their ability to predict complex processes.

A processing element, or PE, processes data by summarizing and transforming it using a series of mathematical functions. One PE is limited in ability, but when connected to form a system, the neurons or PEs create an intelligent model. PEs are interconnected in any number of ways and they can be retrained over several, hundreds, or thousands of iterations to more closely fit the data they are trying to model.

Processing elements, or PEs, are linked to inputs and outputs. The process of training the network involves modifying the strength, or *weight*, of the connections from the inputs to the output. Increases or decreases in the strength of a connection is based on its importance for producing the proper outcome. A connection's strength depends on a *weight* it receives during a trial-and-error process. This process uses a mathematical method for adjusting the weights, and is called a *learning rule*.

Training repeatedly, or iteratively, exposes a neural network to examples of historical data. PEs summarize and transform data, and the connections between PEs receive different weights. That is, a network tries various formulas for predicting the output variable for each example.

Training continues until a neural network produces outcome values that match the known outcome values within a specified accuracy level, or until it satisfies some other stopping criterion.

Figure 4-2 demonstrates a neural network. Each of the processing units takes many inputs and generates an output that is a nonlinear function of the weighted sum of the inputs. The weights assigned to each of the inputs are obtained during a training process (often back-propagation) in which outputs generated by the net are compared with target outputs. The answers you want the network to produce are compared with generated outputs, and the deviation between them is used as feedback to adjust the weights.

The process of readjusting weights is important to increasing a model's accuracy. Notice there are also four "hidden nodes," or middle layer nodes, in Figure 4-2. These four hidden nodes are associated with the weighting process. The number of hidden nodes can be adjusted, and, in fact, there can be multiple levels of hidden nodes, just to confuse matters. The number of inputs, hidden nodes, outputs, and the weighting algorithms for the connections between nodes determine the complexity of a neural network. In general there is a trade-off between the complexity of a neural network, its accuracy, and the time it takes to create the neural network model. Because the configuration of hidden nodes and weights is so critical to neural networks, there are many approaches for finding the right number of hidden nodes and readjusting weights.

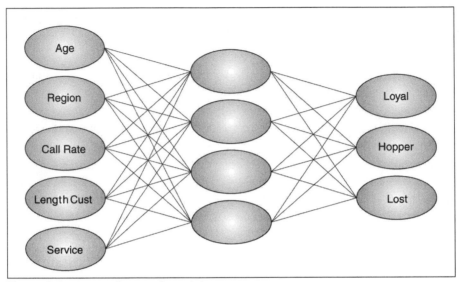

**Figure 4-2**   A neural-network model.

This is at best an introductory view of neural networks, but it does give a starting point from which to understand how they work.

### 4.4.2   Different Types of Models to Build — Unsupervised Learning

This example made use of what is referred to as a *feed-forward* network, which is commonly used with *supervised learning* studies. Feed-forward networks are very popular due to their relative simplicity and stability. *Back-propagation* is a training rule used with feed-forward networks.

It is possible to perform *unsupervised learning* with neural networks as well. The process is very similar, but of course no output is specified during training. In contrast to supervised learning, an unsupervised network is not given the desired response, but organizes the data in a way it sees fit. Such self-organizing networks divide input examples into clusters depending on similarity, each cluster representing an unlabeled category. *Kohonen learning* is a well-known method in self-organizing neural networks.

If you are interested in learning more about the neural-network algorithm, there are several books available, and, for the developers out there, you can even get source code. One book on neural networks that provides source code is *Neural Network and Fuzzy*

*Logic Applications in C++* by Stephen T. Welstead. Another good source is *Elements of Artificial Neural Networks* by Mehrotra *et al.*

### 4.4.3 Strengths and Weaknesses of a Model

The greatest strength of neural networks is their ability to accurately predict outcomes of complex problems. Neural networks are a preferred technique in performing estimation, or continuous numeric outputs, which are popular in financial markets and manufacturing. The book, *Neural Networks in the Capital Markets*, by Apsotolos-Paul Refenes, demonstrates just how pervasive they are in financial institutions. Neural networks are used in many applications today. IBM, SAS, SPSS, HNC, Angoss, RightPoint, Thinking Machines, and NeoVista are a few of the vendors with neural network products. HNC's Falcon, a neural-network product, is used in detecting fraud in the financial market to the point where a sizable portion of all the credit cards in America have been analyzed by HNC. On searching the Web, several hundred sites can be found discussing neural networks; you may find as many variations of them as well. In accuracy tests against other approaches, neural networks are always able to score very high.

There are some downfalls to neural networks. First, they have been criticized as being useful for prediction, but not always in understanding a model. It is true that early implementations of neural networks were criticized as "black box" prediction engines; however, with the new tools on the market today, this particular criticism is debatable.

Secondly, neural networks are also susceptible to *over-training*. If a network with a large capacity for learning is trained using too few data examples to support that capacity, the network first sets about learning the general trends of the data. This is desirable, but then the network continues to learn very specific features of the training data, which is usually undesirable. Such networks are said to have memorized their training data, and lack the ability to generalize. Commercial-grade neural networks today have effectively eliminated overtraining through bootstrapping holdout (test) samples, and by monitoring test versus training errors.

Over-training can be measured by periodically checking the results of your test data set. Early stages of a training session yield lower error measurements on both the training and the test data. This continues unless the network capacity is larger than need be, or unless there are too few data sets in the training file. If at some point during learning, your test data begin to produce worse results, even though the training data continue to produce improved results, over-training is occurring.

Another issue with neural networks is training speed. Neural networks require many passes to build. This means that creating the most accurate models can be very time consuming. It is only fair to mention that all regression techniques require time to converge; and, while back propagation is slow, training neural networks can be sped up dramatically with methods like conjugate gradient.

## 4.5  Bayesian Belief Networks

Bayesian Belief Networks, although gaining in popularity, are not as commonly used in the data-mining community as decision trees and neural networks, yet recent research in this area suggests that this may change. Microsoft has invested much research in this area, and even has a Windows-based "Belief Network Tool" that can be downloaded from the Web. RightPoint, demonstrated in this book, uses some algorithms that are loosely based on Bayesian Belief Networks. BBN have also been referred to as causal networks, probabilistic networks, influence diagrams, and knowledge maps.

In 1763, Reverend Thomas Bayes (1744–1809) came up with a theorem that states how opinions made before any experimentation should be modified after evidence is collected on the outcomes being examined (known as the Bayes Theorem of Probability). For example, if you were reaching into your refrigerator for a can of cola, your opinion that there are an equal number of cans of cola and cans of ginger ale might drastically change after you pulled out seven cans of ginger ale.

When variable events are linked together in the form of a network, they can help predict the outcomes of events that are dependent on other events.

### 4.5.1  How They Work

Take a simple example of one variable affecting an outcome. Let's say we want to predict if a call made on a cell phone will go through as shown in Figure 4-3.

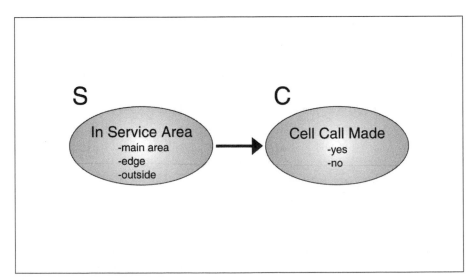

**Figure 4-3**   A simple Bayesian Network.

Figure 4-3 shows the dependence of a cell call on whether the customer was in the service area. Let's say, in this example, that the probabilities, P(S), of being in the service area, S, are:

P (S = main area) = .825
P (S = edge) = .105
P (S = outside) = .070

These probabilities affect whether a cell call was made, and we denote P(C|S) as the probability that the call was made, given that the caller was in service area S when he placed the call. Let's say that for these we have:

P (C = yes|S = main area) = 1.0
P (C = no|S = main area) = 0.0
P (C = yes|S = edge) = 0.76
P (C = no|S = edge) = 0.24
P (C = yes|S = outside) = 0.0
P (C = no|S = outside) = 1.0

This Bayesian Network model is very simplistic, and indicates that where you are in relation to your service area will impact whether or not you can make a successful call.

Let's take a look at a more complex Bayesian Network where we add the following factors:

- is phone operational (o)
- is the Send button pushed (p)
- is the phone display indicating everything OK (d)

The diagram for this is shown in Figure 4-4. The Bayesian Network shown in Figure 4-4 has several interesting aspects. For one thing, notice that there is no link from "operational" to "in service area." This is because whether or not a cell call completes, the fact that you are in or out of a service area won't have any bearing on whether your cell phone is operational. Some of the notation is interesting as well. For example:

- P(p|o) is the probability that you will push the send button, given that the phone is operational. If the phone is not operational, then it really doesn't matter if you push the button.
- P(c|s,p) is the probability you will make a cell call, given that you are in the service area and you pushed the button.

- Notice that although P(d), or the probability that the display reads OK, is not a direct dependency of the cell call being made, the fact that the display reads OK will affect the probability of the phone being operational and the phone being in the service area.

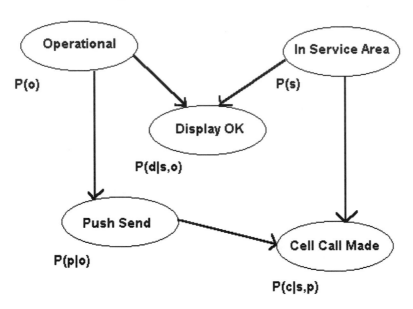

**Figure 4-4**   A Bayesian Network.

### 4.5.2   Strengths and Weaknesses of Bayesian Belief Networks

The greatest strength of a Bayesian Belief Network is that it can be easily understood and can predict outcomes well. This means that it marries the benefits of decision trees and neural networks. One problem with this technology is that, in true probabilistic networks, outcomes that occur with very little frequency will have much lower probabilities associated with them, which leads to skewing toward the most frequently occurring outcomes. This is a problem in situations where you are trying to predict, for example, whether a certain claim is fraudulent: since less than 1% of all claims are fraudulent, you can have a 99% accurate model just by predicting all claims to be good. There are ways to work around this type of problem, and Bayesian networks hold much promise.

## 4.6 Statistics

Statistics have long been used to create a model of data sets. The process of linear regression is a process using probability, data analysis, and statistical inference. Blaise Pascal and Pierre De Fermat introduced probability in a series of letters aimed at solving a gambling problem. Regression analysis was introduced around the turn of the century by geneticist Francis Galton, who discovered what is called *regression towards the mean*. He used probability and statistics to show that the height of children regressed toward a mean (taller fathers had shorter sons; shorter fathers had taller sons). The term "regression" is no longer used in the context of "regression toward the mean" as in Galton's law (this is just historical coinage). Regression stands for any conditional expectation. In the context of data modeling, it's usually the conditional expectation of a dependent variable given independent variables.

Some mathematicians may argue that all models used in data mining are really statistical methods. The field of statistics includes the realms of probability and statistical inference, which are routinely used to create models that represent data sets.

### 4.6.1 On Discriminant Analysis

Discriminant analysis is the study of finding a set of coefficients or weights that describe a Linear Classification Function (LCF), which maximally separates groups of variables.

Discriminant analysis is popular for vendors attempting to find common groupings of variables. For example, this technique is useful when performing customer segmentation for marketing purposes. A threshold is used to classify an object into groups. If LCF is greater than or equal to the threshold, it is in one group; if LCF is less than the threshold, then it is in another group.

The weights are called *discriminant coefficients*. The data-mining process of clustering attempts a similar process.

### 4.6.2 On Regression Modeling

A *regression equation* is one that estimates a dependent variable using a set of independent variables and a set of constants. Classification studies discussed in this book could be constructed with traditional statistic regression techniques.

Linear regression models attempt many of the same things that data-mining tools do; e.g., making predictions of a customer's response for direct-mail campaigns.

Regression techniques can be used to perform prediction when techniques of conditional probability are introduced. The regression model used for predictive response is sometimes called the linear probability model (LPM). One type of regression model is the *logit model*, which is a model where all independent variables are categorical. A *logistic regression model* is similar to the logit model, but has continuous variables as well.

There are many types of regression models. For situations where no linear functions easily fit with data, there are nonlinear regressions and nonlinear multiple regression models. Coefficients of multiple and partial correlation can be defined using a variety of statistical methods.

### 4.6.3    Strengths and Weaknesses

The strengths of statistical approaches are that not only are these approaches accurate, they are well understood and widely used. Statistical approaches are viewed by many to be the "truest" form of data mining, and in fact, many data-mining techniques make use of statistical techniques that have been around for many years. CHAID, a popular decision-tree approach, uses the Chi Square metric. Association algorithms use the statistical metrics of support and confidence, and clustering techniques use statistical metrics like the K-means algorithm. Bayesian Networks use the Bayes Theorem of Probability, a statistical formula that has been with us since 1763.

The biggest criticism of statistics has been the perceived difficulty of using it effectively. While data mining is a process for extracting meaningful information from data, statistics is an entire field of study that includes extracting meaningful information from data. There has often been a "wall" between statisticians and other business professionals who wish to make use of predictive models. Many business professionals are confused by the terminology used in statistics. Moreover, industry analysts have historically distinguished between statistics and "data mining." Data mining was said to be different from statistics: it was easier for business professionals to get their arm around data mining. IBM, SPSS, and SAS have come a long way in breaking down this perception by including standard statistics models right next to neural networks, decision trees, and other techniques associated with data mining.

## 4.7  Advanced Algorithms for Association

Chapter 2 discussed association and the two most common metrics for performing association: confidence and support. Both the merits and shortcomings of these approaches were shown. This section discusses more advanced association algorithms. Along with Section 4.8, on assortment optimization, it introduces algorithms and techniques not as commonplace as neural networks or decision trees. There has been little industry agreement in the area of association and assortment optimization on what algorithms are the "standards." The discussions in this section and in Section 4.8 were provided courtesy of Dr. Miguel Castro of Dovetail Solutions.

### 4.7.1   A Better Way of Discovery Associations

Associations of the form "If customers buy A they also tend to buy B, x% of the time" are most meaningful when x (the percent of co-occurrence) is different from what would be expected by random chance. In our Coke and Pepsi example in the last chapter, both Coke and Pepsi occurred separately in 50% of all the market baskets, and we expected that they should occur together in 25% of all baskets by random chance alone. The expected (random) percent of co-occurrence was 25%, but the actual percent of co-occurrence was 0.01%. The difference between the expected and the actual co-occurrences was so large that we identified the association between Coke and Pepsi as representing valuable and action-able information. This is the general idea behind the *Dependence Framework*, as opposed to the Support-Confidence Framework.

The Dependence Framework looks at associations where the items in a transaction database are statistically dependent. In other words, it considers only items whose percent of co-occurrence is significantly different from random chance. Here's how it works. We know from statistics that two events are independent if the probability of their co-occur-rence is the same as the product of the probabilities of the individual events. To bring it back to our Coke and Pepsi example, the probability of both Coke and Pepsi occurring in the same basket is expected to be the same as the product of the probabilities of either one occurring individually: (Probability of Coke + Pepsi together) = (Probability of Coke alone) × (Probability of Pepsi alone). If this is true, the co-occurrence of Coke and Pepsi is said to be random or "independent." On the other hand, if the actual co-occurrence of Coke and Pepsi in the same basket is observed to be very different from the expected co-occurrence, we say that Coke and Pepsi are "statistically dependent."

In our Coke and Pepsi example, the example random co-occurrence was:

$$\text{Expected(Coke + Pepsi together)} = 25\%$$

and, the actual observed co-occurrence was:

$$\text{Actual(Coke + Pepsi together)} = 0.01\%$$

In this case, the difference between the expected and actual co-occurrences is so large that we can safely assume that Coke and Pepsi are not independent, but that they are in fact very much dependent on one another. In other words, the presence of Coke signifi-cantly affects the presence of Pepsi in the same basket (and vice-versa). On the other hand, suppose that in the bread-and-milk example we had the expected random co-occurrence as:

$$\text{Expected(Bread + Milk together)} = 12\%$$

and the actual observed co-occurrence as:

$$\text{Actual(Bread + Milk together)} = 12\%$$

In this case, bread and milk are independent, since the actual observed co-occurrence is equal to the expected (random) co-occurrence. Therefore, the presence of bread in a basket tells us nothing about the presence of milk, and vice-versa. (The 12% comes from multiplying 30% by 40%, assuming that milk and bread occur in 30% and 40% of all transactions, respectively.)

Most cases are not this clear-cut, however. For example, if the actual observed co-occurrence of bread and milk together had been 12.1%, would we have concluded that they are dependent because this is different from the expected co-occurrence of 12%? The answer is that we need to determine how *statistically significant* the differences between actual and expected co-occurrences are. In order to do this, we use the well-known Chi-Squared statistical test.

We start out by determining the frequency of occurrence of each item individually. For example, we may find that milk occurs in 30% of all baskets, and that bread occurs in 40% of all baskets. Subsequently, we compute the expected co-occurrence. Under the assumption that the items are independent, this expected co-occurrence is just the product of the individual frequencies of occurrence. For example, in the case of milk and bread, the expected co-occurrence is $30\% \times 40\% = 12\%$. Finally, we compute the Chi-Squared statistic as follows:

$$X^2 = \frac{[ExpectedCoOccurrence - ActualCoOccurrence]^2}{ExpectedCoOccurrence}$$

Note that the Chi-Squared statistic measures deviation from the expected random co-occurrence. It is equal to zero if the deviation from random co-occurrence is zero (this is the "null hypothesis," which states that the items are independent), and it is greater than zero if the items are dependent (the "alternative hypothesis," which states that the items are dependent). This statistic has a Chi-Squared distribution, and we can compare it against Chi-Squared tables. We can thus obtain a $p$ value that will tell us if the null hypothesis of independence is true. Good p values are small values, for example, if $p = 5\%$, we say that we reject the null hypothesis of independence at the 5% level. Equivalently, we can say that the items are dependent with 95% confidence.

### 4.7.2  Beyond Statistical Dependence

Once we know that two (or more) items are dependent, how do we use this information? Recall that statistical dependence between two or more items means that the presence of one of the products in a basket gives us information about the presence of the other items. This is already powerful information, since it can suggest actionables like store layout, cross-marketing, and the like. However, we can do better by understanding how strongly dependent the products are.

One way of quantifying dependence is by looking at the *impact*, which is the ratio of the actual or observed co-occurrence divided by the expected co-occurrence:

$$Impact = \frac{ActualCoOccurrence}{ExpectedCoOccurrence}$$

The impact is equal to about one if the products are independent, and it is different from one if the products are dependent. For example, in the Coke and Pepsi case, we have:

$$Impact(Coke + Pepsi) = 0.01/25 = 0.0004$$

which is very different from one, indicating that the products are very dependent. In the bread and milk example, we have:

$$Impact(Bread + Milk) = 12.1/12 = 1.008$$

which is very close to one, indicating that the products are independent.

A more intuitive quantity is the *Lift* of item A on item B, defined as the difference between the expected and the actual co-occurrences of A and B divided by the frequency of A:

$$Lift(AonB) = \frac{[ActualCoOccurrence - ExpectedCoOccurrence]}{FrequencyofOccurrenceofA}$$

Notice that the Lift is a number between −1 and 1. The lift is close to zero if the items are independent, it is positive if the items are positively dependent (they "attract" each other), and it is negative if the items are negatively dependent (they "repel" each other). To illustrate, the lift in the Coke and Pepsi example is:

$$Lift(Coke\ on\ Pepsi) = (0.001 - 0.25)/\ 0.50 = -0.498$$

This negative lift implies that the two products "repel" each other. In other words, Coke and Pepsi tend not to be in the same baskets together. Knowing that these two products "repel" each other can already suggest actionable recommendations such as pricing, promotions, etc. Better, more targeted actionable marketing decisions can be made, however, if we dissect non-zero lifts further.

### 4.7.3   Understanding Associations

In order to take more precise marketing actions, we should find out why products occur together more (or less) frequently than by random chance. For example, there could be at least two underlying reasons why products "repel" each other. One is that they are substitutes, meaning that they compete in the same market segment. Another is that they serve different market segments, and thus do not compete. Likewise, two products may "attract" each other either because they are complements, or because a third product complements both. These distinct reasons can lead to very different marketing strategies.

We can use transactional data to measure the degree of substitutability or complementarity between two products by looking at cross-purchase skews with third products. The cross-purchase skew methodology that we describe below was developed by Dovetail Solutions, a San Francisco-based consulting company. Their version of this method in the context of market basket analysis is called Product Triangulation™. (Conjoint Value is a trademarks of Dovetail Solutions.)

For example, suppose that orange juice and soda "repel" each other, leading one to suspect that they may be substitutes. But suppose that they exhibit different cross-purchase profiles (in other words, different co-occurrence percentages) when compared against whole-wheat bread and potato chips. This "triangulation" might reveal customer segments within which the two products are not substitutes and thus do not compete. For example it might be that "healthy" foods, such as whole-wheat bread, tend to be purchased more often with orange juice than with soda, revealing preferences of different buyer segments.

On the other hand, consider the Coke and Pepsi case. Here we may find little or no cross-purchase skews when "triangulating" with different third products. This may reveal that Coke and Pepsi are substitutes that compete in the same markets. If we have customer-specific transactional data, however, we may be able to discover cross-purchase skews when the "third product" is a demographic such as age. For example, it may be revealed that younger customers tend to buy Pepsi more often than Coke. This would indicate that the products address different markets. However, if the most significant skew occurs when "triangulating" with respect to promotion or pricing, we would conclude that the products are in fact substitutes.

As another example, we may be able to explain why baby food and calcium supplements 'repel' each other by triangulating these items with demographics. We may find, for example, that calcium supplements are bought more often by women over 50, while baby food is bought more often by women between 20 and 30. Thus, like Coke and Pepsi, these items "repel" each other, but unlike Coke and Pepsi, they "repel" because they are consumed by different market segments, not because they compete in the same segment.

Item "roll-ups" or taxonomies can also be very useful from a marketing perspective. Item "roll-ups" refer to analyzing associations involving entire categories or classes or products. As an example, suppose that an entire category is substantially less price-elastic than the individual items in the category. This means that changing overall category prices does not change the category sales much, while changing individual brand prices causes brand switching.

Suppose further, that the category is not a traffic generator that stimulates sales in other categories, and that specific brand promotions stimulate stock-up effects (i.e., household inventory build-up of the category's products). This suggests that the price of the whole category should be raised, while brand-specific promotions should be avoided.

### 4.7.4 Actionable and Effective MB Analysis

In summary, market-basket analysis can be very effective in generating actionable information that leads to strategic marketing decisions. The examples above are simple because they were handpicked for illustration. However, much subtler and surprising patterns emerge when market basket analysis is carefully applied to real-world data. Successful market basket analysis requires that we follow a few guidelines.

First, we must be careful when considering associations of the type: *"If customers buy product A they also tend to buy product B, x% of the time."* While looking at these types of associations is common practice when carrying out market basket analysis, this tends to generate many useless associations that occur by random chance. We should limit our search to only those associations that are different from what would happen by random chance, because these associations have the best likelihood of leading to actionable marketing decisions (refer to the bread and milk example above). One of the most effective ways of detecting statistically significant non-random associations (or dependencies) is by using the Chi-Squared test in the context of the dependence framework of market basket analysis.

Second, we must not blindly discard associations that have "low support" (in other words, low frequency of co-occurrence in the database). Again, this is a common practice that can lead to throwing away the baby with the bath water. While low support might be a manifestation of low statistical significance, it can also be the result of items that "repel" each other with a very high statistical significance. These associations can be valuable (see the previous Coke and Pepsi example). Our focus should be on high statistical significance, and not necessarily on high support.

Third, once we have found groups of items that exhibit statistically significant non-random associations, we must further analyze these groups of items to determine what causes their non-random associations. For example, if we know that two products "repel" each other, we need to know why they "repel": Are they substitutes, or do they address totally different market segments? To see how essential this information is from a marketing strategy perspective, suppose we are trying to determine how to price the two products relative to each other. If they are substitutes, we must worry about one product "cannibalizing" the sales of the other, while if the products serve two different market segments, the price of one product will be relatively independent of the other's price. As we mentioned, a powerful technique used to measure the degree of substitutability or complementarity is the Product Triangulation™ method. This technique is especially useful when we do not have enough customer-specific transactional data, or when we wish to complement our understanding of market-segment purchasing patterns with general trends in the overall transaction database.

The concepts of substitutability and complementarity are also useful in assortment optimization, as we explain in the next section.

## 4.8  Algorithms for Assortment Optimization

In Chapter 2 we discussed sales volume versus variety and how variety curves should be used to help us look at the trade-offs of adding or removing items from an assortment.

We must improve the method of using variety curves to estimate changes in category sales because it is not very precise. It assumes that only the number of items in the assortment matters, and not which item is being added or removed. In fact, this is usually not the case, because different items sell at different rates and have different substitutability.

Transactional data can be used to supplement the variety curve method to overcome these deficiencies. The idea is to better estimate the transferable demand by considering each item individually. If items "repel" (refer to the Market Basket Analysis section), we still need to find out whether they are substitutable or whether they address different market segments. If we have customer-specific transactional data, we can gauge how substitutable an item is by looking at how many times consumers switch from the item in question to other items. Pricing data can also give information regarding substitutability. For example, if an item is purchased consistently by the same consumers despite promotions of other items, this item is less substitutable than it would be otherwise. Useful information can also be gathered when the item in question is absent from the store shelves, for example, when the item is out of stock. In summary, the more substitutable an item is, the more demand it will transfer to (or will be transferred from) similar items in its category when that item is deleted (or added).

When a new or unfamiliar item is added to the assortment, we obviously cannot rely on in-house transactional data. In this case, we may want to match the new item as closely as possible to one or more items in the current assortment based on how similar the new item's attributes are to attributes of items in the current assortment. In this way, we can make inferences about the item's substitutability and transferable demand. We may also rely on information from the variety curve, or perform trials of the item in question to better gauge the item's long-run demand.

Once we have estimated the transferable demand of a given item, we must determine how the demand will be transferred to or from the other items in the assortment. This can be achieved by extracting "switching data" from customer-specific transactional data. A viable alternative (or supplement) to in-house transactional data is panel data supplied by outside vendors. The idea is to track the purchases of individual consumers over time and count how many times consumers switch from one item to another (within the category of interest).

As an example, suppose we have four items labeled A, B, C, and D, in a given category. We start by tracking the purchase sequence of these four items for each consumer or household over time (see Figure 4-5). We then count how many times each consumer has switched from item A to item B, from item A to item C, etc. for all combinations of pairs of items. Next, we add up all the instances of switching over all the consumers and summarize this information in a matrix of "Switching Counts" (Figure 4-6). Finally, we divide each entry in the Switching Counts matrix by the row totals to produce a matrix containing the (conditional) probability of switching (Figure 4-7) from one item to another. For example, the entry in the second row, third column represents the probability of switching from B to C (= 0.333 in our example). This is also known as the "Switching Rates" matrix or the Markov matrix.

## Purchase Histories

| | |
|---|---|
| Customer 1 | ABBBBBCBBBB |
| Customer 2 | CCBCBBAAAAACADDDAA |
| Customer 3 | AAAADADDDACDDDDBBBB |
| Customer 4 | ABDDCBDDDADBBDDDD |
| Customer 5 | AAACCCCBAAACCCCCCBCCD |
| Customer 6 | BBBCBAABABBBAA |
| . | . |
| . | . |
| . | . |

**Figure 4-5**  Customer purchase histories. The purchases of four items (A, B, C, and D) are tracked over time for each consumer in the database. This information is used to track how many times brand switching occurs. For example, Customer 6 has switched twice from A to B, three times from B to A, once from B to C, and once from C to B.

## Item Bought in Subsequent Purchase

| Item Bought in Previous Purchase | A | B | C | D |
|---|---|---|---|---|
| A | - | 4 | 4 | 3 |
| B | 5 | - | 4 | 3 |
| C | 1 | 6 | - | 2 |
| D | 4 | 2 | 1 | - |

**Figure 4-6**  Switching counts. This table tracks how many times switching has occurred from one product (or brand) to another, using the information in Figure 4-5. For example, switching from B to A has occurred five times over all six customers tracked in Figure 4-5.

## Item Bought in Subsequent Purchase

| Item Bought in Previous Purchase | A | B | C | D |
|---|---|---|---|---|
| A | - | 0.364 | 0.364 | 0.273 |
| B | 0.417 | - | 0.333 | 0.250 |
| C | 0.111 | 0.667 | - | 0.222 |
| D | 0.571 | 0.286 | 0.143 | - |

**Figure 4-7**  Switching Rates Matrix (or Markov Matrix). Each entry in this table contains the probability of switching from one product to another. For example, the probability of switching from B to A is 0.417, while the probability of switching from A to B is 0.364. These numbers were obtained by dividing each entry in Figure 4-6 by the sum of the corresponding row entries.

The Switching Rates matrix allows us to distribute the transferable demand among the remaining items in the assortment. Suppose, for example, that we delete item D from the assortment. Suppose also that we have already determined that D's transferable demand is $100 (recall the above discussion on estimating transferable demand). How much of this demand is transferred to A, B, and C? We can determine this by multiplying the $100 by the corresponding conditional probability entry in the Switching Rates matrix. In our example, $57.10 is transferred to A, $28.60 to B, and $14.30 to C. Likewise, if we've just *added* item D, its transferable demand of $100 will come from cannibalization of the sales of A, B, and C. Again, this is determined by multiplying $100 by the corresponding entries in the Switching Rates matrix. In this way, we arrive at how the sales volume of each of the items changes as we change the assortment.

But knowing how adding or deleting items affects sales is only half the story. We must also consider how changing the assortment affects costs, store traffic generation, and the like, before we can determine what resulting mix of products best meets the retailer's business goals.

### 4.8.1  Cost: As Easy as ABC?

Above, we looked at optimizing sales volumes by changing a category assortment. In Chapter 2, we also discussed how costs are affected. In this section, we expand on the discussion of costs.

Because costs are such a significant component of the assortment optimization process, it is very important to estimate item costs accurately. For this reason, a cottage industry has sprung up in recent years proposing the use of activity-based costing (ABC) methodologies for assortment optimization. The aim of ABC methodology is to allocate fixed costs to individual items. As an example, consider the cost of keeping dairy products refrigerated. This is a fixed cost in that it has to be incurred as long as the retailer sells dairy products, and it is largely independent of what specific items or brands are inside the refrigerator. How do we allocate the cost of refrigeration among the different items? One way is by how much physical volume different items occupy inside the refrigerator. Another is by how fast items sell. Yet another is by the items' prices. In general there are many ways of allocating overhead or fixed costs, and it is not always clear which way is the best.

ABC uses the costs of "activities" as drivers of item costs. For example, stocking an item requires labor, which in turn is costly. If we analyze the process of stocking an item, we will see that it involves many steps, including storage, retrieval, and placement on the shelves. Each of these "activities" consumes labor hours. Therefore, we can split labor costs among the different items according to how many "activities" the different items consume. Likewise, we can allocate the cost of storage and retrieval to a specific item by measuring how many cubic feet a case of this item occupies, how many cases fit in a crane pallet, how many trips an employee needs to take from the stockroom to the shelves, and other "time-and-motion" types of measurements. There is virtually no limit to how detailed our analysis of costs may get. However, a very detailed "time-and-motion" ABC analysis may be very costly, and, more importantly, it is also often *misleading* in the context of assortment optimization.

For example, suppose we perform an assortment optimization analysis using detailed ABC considerations, and decide to replace item X with item Y. We may find that this decision was arrived at because of a combined warehouse and labor-cost reduction of $75 per store per week when replacing X with Y. However, close inspection may reveal that the cost savings came from a reduction of 3½ pallet moves, 2 trips from the stockroom to the shelves, and 57 cubic feet of warehouse space. The problem with these reductions in "activities" is that they may well not represent avoidable costs. If we save 20 minutes of labor per week and 57 cubic feet of warehouse space, this is unlikely to lead to cost savings from employee layoffs or reduced warehouse rent, since we would continue to employ the same number of employees and pay the same amount of rent.

There are two situations where this type of detailed ABC analysis can be helpful in performing assortment optimization. The first such situation arises if we can efficiently redeploy the resources consumed by activities. In our example above, this would entail a careful assessment of alternative activities for employees to efficiently spend the extra 20 minutes per week, and an assessment of how much would be saved by alternative uses of the extra warehouse space. These assessments would likely be expensive to generate and too imprecise to be of much use. The second situation arises if the change in assortment is so large that the retailer may avoid costs by making drastic changes like laying off employees, moving all inventory to a smaller warehouse, eliminating trips from the distribution center to the warehouse, etc. Since assortment optimization usually entails adding or deleting relatively few items from an assortment, it is unlikely that these additions/deletions will be large enough to merit such drastic changes. Therefore, lengthy, expensive, and detailed "time-and-motion" types of ABC are usually unnecessary and could be misleading when applied to assortment optimization.

### 4.8.2  Relevant Costs

As we mentioned before, avoidable costs and opportunity costs are very important when performing assortment optimization. Fortunately, most of these costs can be obtained directly from transactional data. One notable exception is unit wholesale cost (an avoidable cost), which must be supplied in addition to transactional data. Other types of costs come from "displacement" and "purchase stimulus." Both of these are opportunity costs, which we will briefly discuss below.

Shelf space is a scarce commodity in the retail sector, and "displacement costs" refer to how much shelf space is consumed by an item in a category. More specifically, we look at how many display surfaces or "facings" are taken up by an item and where on the shelf the item is located. The idea here is that the more "facings" an item occupies, the more alternate items it displaces, and the higher its opportunity cost. Moreover, shelf space that is closer to shoulder level is more valuable than shelf space that is closer to ankle level. This is because, all else being equal, shoulder-level shelf space tends to generate higher sales velocities than ankle-level shelf space. The closer an item is to the shoulder-level shelves, the higher its opportunity cost. Therefore, both display surface and shelf location represent opportunity costs that affect assortment optimization.

"Purchase stimulus" relates to an item stimulating the purchase of another. For example, suppose chips and dip "attract" each other, which means that they occur in transactions more often than expected by random chance (see the Market Basket Analysis section). We may ask whether chips are causing the purchase of dip, whether it's the other way around, or whether it goes both ways. Pricing information can be used to *quantify* the direction of purchase stimulus. For example, if raising the price of dip has little effect on the sales of chips while vice-versa has a large impact on the sales of dip, one may conclude that chips are driving the sales of dip.

In general, when a product (A) stimulates the purchase of another product (B), it adds value to the second product. We call this "stimulus value" or Conjoint Value™ Product (Conjoint Value is a trademarks of Dovetail Solutions) that A adds to B. Therefore the value of A should not be determined in isolation, as we must consider the value that A adds to other products. For example, changing the price of A would not only affect the sales of A, but would also impact the sales of all the products having high Conjoint Values coming from A. In the context of Assortment Optimization, we must consider the ripple effects that A will have on the sales of other products both inside and outside A's category, before deciding whether to remove A from our assortment. In other words, Conjoint Value represents an opportunity cost that must be accounted for when optimizing an assortment.

Conjoint Values can be used to identify "traffic generators." That is, products that add significant Conjoint Value to many other products. For example, milk may have a low or even negative profit margin when considered in isolation. But much of its value derives from the many other products whose sales are stimulated by the purchase of milk. This could lead to a recommendation of identifying and heavily promoting traffic generators in an effort to increase store traffic and sales of products having high Conjoint Value deriving from milk.

Conjoint Value can help us decide how to bundle products. An example is bundling a high-margin but rare item with a lower-margin but higher-volume item that contributes a high Conjoint Value to the high-margin item.

### 4.8.3 Business Goals: Bringing It All Together

We have seen that transactional data can be used to determine how sales volume and costs change when we modify an assortment. From this, we can immediately calculate how profitability changes when we modify the assortment. If our goal is to increase profitability, we can think of the assortment optimization problem as finding that assortment which maximizes profitability. We first start by producing new candidate assortments through additions or deletions of items from the old assortment. For each candidate assortment, we compute the profitability and pick the assortment having the highest profitability.

However, short-term profitability is usually not the only goal of a retailer. For example, sales volume can be a goal in itself when a retailer aims to increase or defend market share. Customer "equity" is also a desirable business goal, when a retailer endeavors to cultivate the loyalty of valuable customers. As mentioned earlier, the effect of assortment changes on customer "equity" can be found by measuring the "segment values" and "exclusivity" of the items that are added or deleted from the current assortment. These quantities can, in turn, be obtained from transactional data.

Strictly speaking, maximizing each of these three goals simultaneously is not possible. For example, we cannot maximize both *profits* and sales volume *simultaneously*. The optimal approach is to consider the best compromise among all three goals reflecting our business objectives. This compromise consists of a weighted average of P̲rofitability, S̲ales Volume, and Customer E̲quity, called PSE:

$$PSE = (\text{Profitability Weight} \times \text{Profitability}) + (\text{Sales Weight} \times \text{Sales})$$
$$+ (\text{Equity Weight} \times \text{Equity})$$

The weights are numbers between zero and one, and they must add up to one. They are chosen to reflect our business objectives, depending on how much importance we attach to each of the individual goals. For example, a PSE like this:

$$PSE = (0.60 \times \text{Profitability}) + (0.30 \times \text{Sales}) + (0.10 \times \text{Equity})$$

attaches the most importance (60%) to short-term profitability, secondary importance (30%) to sales volume, and least importance (10%) to customer equity.

PSE is known as a multi-goal objective function, and the process of maximizing PSE is known as *goal programming*. Assortment optimization, therefore, consists of finding the assortment that maximizes PSE. We start out by choosing those weights in the objective function (PSE) that best reflect our business goals. Subsequently, we produce new candidate assortments through additions or deletions of items from the old assortment. For each candidate assortment, we compute PSE and pick the assortment with the highest PSE.

## 4.9  Summary

In this chapter, we looked at some of the algorithms used in data mining. The intent was to provide an overview of different technologies used today. There have been many papers written and much research done on these algorithms, and while this chapter can only hope to be an introduction, it should get you familiar with the terminology and issues relating to these technologies.

# CHAPTER 5

# The Data-Mining Marketplace

This chapter provides insight into the data-mining market today. Not only are many of the leading commercial data-mining vendors discussed, but this chapter also lists useful Web sites where you can learn more about them, as well as where to purchase information for data mining and, for those programmers out there, where to find public domain source code.

This chapter is organized as follows:

- Section 5.1    Introduction (Trends)
- Section 5.2    Data-Mining Vendors
- Section 5.3    Visualization
- Section 5.4    Useful Web Sites/Commercially Available Code
- Section 5.5    Data Sources for Mining
- Section 5.6    Summary

## 5.1 Introduction (Trends)

Central to data mining's increased popularity is the advancement in computational power. Decreases in hardware costs have made data mining available to a much wider audience. Not long ago, a mainframe was required to process what PCs can do today. (The PC on which this book was written has also mined more than 20 million rows of data.)

Beyond the rise in computational power, there also have been several trends in the industry that ensure a broader use of data mining. A few of the most noticeable trends that directly affect the interest level in data mining appear below. All products are trademarks or registered trademarks of their respective companies.

### 5.1.1    Data Warehousing is Becoming Commonplace

Data warehousing has become much more widely accepted today than it was few years ago. While data mining does not require the presence of a data warehouse, data mining is often viewed as an after-market product of data warehousing because people who have made the effort to create a data warehouse have the richest data available to mine. It stands to reason that the broader acceptance of data warehousing will lead to increased interest in data mining.

### 5.1.2    Data Mining on the Internet

Many vendors are applying data-mining techniques to e-business to improve on how Internet sites relate to their customers. Earlier in this book, we noted that Yahoo! not only uses data mining, but bought a data-mining company, HyperParallel. IBM has released a Web-centric data-mining solution called SurfAid Analytics. SurfAid tracks traditional Web statistics and then analyzes them to determine how customers are interacting with a site. Using IBM's data-mining techniques, SurfAid allows cyber-marketers to easily determine how users are interacting with their site. Hilton Hotels was one of the earliest adopters of this new software.

Levi Strauss makes use of data mining with Blue Martini Software Inc.'s electronic-merchandising system. The system will manage Levi's product data catalogs, which hold 7,000 stock-keeping units each with 50 to 100 pieces of information, universal product code numbers and pricing information. "This will allow us to really watch what's selling quickly and to get more sophisticated in targeting consumers," says Bob Knowles, director of U.S. electronic-commerce at San Francisco-based Levi Strauss.

Net Perceptions is a vendor that provides dynamic data-mining technologies to more than a hundred Web commerce sites examining what customers are most likely to buy.

RightPoint software has a dynamic data-mining engine used by telecommunication and banking firms to help retain, cross-sell, and increase the value of their existing customer base.

### 5.1.3    EIS Tool Vendors Integrating Data Mining

EIS and query vendors are also involved in integrating data mining with traditional query and decision-support tools. Query and EIS tools in the past have required end users to formulate questions in order to get interesting answers, an assumptive-based process.

Integrating data mining with query and EIS tools will enable a discovery-based process, whereby an end user can be told the most interesting things to look at and then can formulate questions based on the new information.

Business Objects, in cooperation with ISoft SA, announced a data-mining integration in 1996. Business Object's data-mining solution, BusinessMiner, provides a data-mining solution that's aimed at mainstream business users.

Cognos Software has announced the availability of its Scenario data-mining tool, which integrates their query and OLAP tools with data mining.

### 5.1.4 Information More Accessible

Data mining requires information, and information is more available than ever before, as are the larger disk drives to hold the data.

Customer, household, and industry demographic information has become widely and cheaply available. Not only can you purchase a CD-ROM with millions of home and business users, but you can purchase complete geographic information from the U.S. Census Bureau. Further in this chapter, many data providers are mentioned.

While it often evokes issues of privacy, and will make many uncomfortable, it is astonishing to note how much information providers can learn about us from our credit information. For example, if you have ever purchased cat food, dog food, baby food, or squash, there are assumptions that can be made, especially if you continue a pattern.

### 5.1.5 Data-Mining Vendors Focusing More on Vertical Markets

Data mining involves an implicit understanding of the data with which you are working; therefore it is not surprising that vendors are focusing on vertical markets.

For example, HNC resells a product line named Falcon that focuses on credit fraud analysis in banking and insurance. Not only has this product been successful in this market, a significant percentage of all credit-card transactions are analyzed by the software to determine potential fraud.

RightPoint Software (formerly DataMind) transformed itself from a data-mining company to a real-time marketing company that helps companies deliver intelligent content to customers. Data mining is now a component of their software package.

NeuralWare, a data-mining software vendor highlighted in the first edition of this book, was purchased by Aspen Technology, Inc. Aspen Technologies focuses on enabling process manufacturers to improve their profitability by designing, operating, and managing their enterprise with the help of business intelligence and data mining.

Thinking Machines, a leading data-mining vendor, was purchased by Oracle Corporation, with the intention of including the data-mining technology Oracle's vertical applications.

## 5.2  Data-Mining Vendors

Following is a list of major data-mining vendors in the market today. This list is by no means complete, but is meant to represent the more dominant players. All products are trademarks or registered trademarks of their respective companies.

**Angoss Software Corporation (KnowledgeSEEKER, KnowledgeSTUDIO)**
34 St. Patrick Street, Suite 200
Toronto, Ontario
Canada, M5T 1V1
(416) 593-1122
Web: http://www.angoss.com

**Product.**  KnowledgeSEEKER, KnowledgeSTUDIO

**Position.**  KnowledgeSTUDIO is the next-generation data-mining tool provided by Angoss, delivering a wide variety of data-mining techniques. Initially, five decision tree algorithms, three neural net algorithms, and one "unsupervised" algorithm are being used, and more are being added. KnowledgeSTUDIO can be integrated with your applications and business processes because it is completely programmable. Through the use of Active X and Java technologies, data mining can be embedded into in-house or vertical market applications.

KnowledgeSEEKER, shown in Chapter 6, performs data mining using decision tree techniques, employing two well-known algorithms: CHAID and CART. The program graphically shows decision trees, automatically forming decision trees on all significant relationships and also allowing the user to "force" a graphical tree on any relationship not already built. The program is understandable for end users and ODBC compliant to access relational back ends. Cognos, a software developer of decision support tools, has signed a relationship with Angoss to provide Angoss's technology with their product set. Angoss also has numerous other partnerships announced.

**Attar Software USA (XpertRule Miner)**
Two Deerfoot Trail on Partridge Hill
Harvard, MA 01451
(978) 456-3946
Web: http://www.attar.com

**Product.**  XpertRule Miner, XpertRule KBS

**Position.** Attar is a British data-mining company with a set of products for data mining. XpertRule KBS is a development package with in-built resource optimization for building knowledge-based systems. XpertRule Miner is a client-server software package for data mining. The client-server processes are accomplished through ODBC connectivity to back-end databases.

### Business Objects (BusinessMiner)

2870 Zanker Road
San Jose, CA 95134
(408) 953-6000
Web: http://www.businessobjects.com

**Product.** BusinessMiner

**Position.** BusinessMiner is an integrated client-sided data-mining solution with Business Object's query, reporting, and OLAP solutions. The product is developed with the Alice technology from ISoft SA, which is a decision-tree approach to data mining. Business Objects has an impressive list of clients using BusinessMiner including Bank of America, British Airways, Chevron, Fannie Mae, LA Cellular, Pacific Bell, Seagram, and Victoria's Secret.

### Cognos Incorporated (Scenario)

3755 Riverside Drive
P.O. Box 9707, Station T
Ottawa, ON Canada K1G 4K9
(613) 738-1440
Web: http://www.cognos.com

**Product.** Scenario

**Position.** Cognos, a leader in providing query and OLAP tools, is shipping Scenario, a data-mining solution for integration with their tools, Powerplay and Impromptu. This client-side data-mining solution is based on decision tree CHAID (Chi-Squared Automatic Interaction Detection) technology. Cognos also announced its intent to include neural network modeling based on their purchase of Right Information Systems.

**Dovetail Solutions ("Value, Activity, and Loyalty Technique,"**
**Product Triangulation, Conjoint Value)**
2261 Market Street, #457
San Francisco, CA 94114
(510) 583-0831
Web: http://www.dovetailsol.com

**Product.**   "Value, Activity, and Loyalty Technique," Product Triangulation, Conjoint
Value

**Position.**   Dovetail Solutions is a software development and information technology
consulting firm. They specialize in business strategy and information technology, particularly in data warehousing, data mining, modeling, and forecasting for the retail and
catalog industries. Dovetail provides end-to-end customized solutions to solve the specific business needs of their clients. These include deployment and integration of off-
the-shelf software as well as their own proprietary technologies, and building customized high-end computer hardware to suit the customer's business needs.

The "products" listed are actually trademarked techniques that Dovetail has
developed for their customers. Conjoint Value and Product Triangulation techniques
are discussed in more detail in Chapter 4, under Market Basket Analysis and Assortment Optimization. The Value, Activity, and Loyalty Technique is discussed in
Chapter 8.


**HNC Software Inc. (wide range of data-mining solutions based on industry)**
5930 Cornerstone Court West
San Diego, California 92121-3728
(619) 546-8877
Web: http://www.hnc.com

**Product.**   Capstone, Falcon, ProfitMax,
VeriComp, ECM, SPYDER, Retek Active Retail Intelligence,
Retek Behavior Profiling, ATACS 5

**Position.**   HNC Software offers a suite of software applications based on neural
network predictive models as well as a number of other advanced technologies.
HNC divides its solutions by six business units: HNC Financial, HNC Insurance,
HNC Telecommunications, HNC Retek Retail, HNC Aptex Internet, and HNC
Advanced Technologies.

In the area of finance, HNC offers Falcon, a set of software products that are
used to detect credit and debit-card fraud. It also offers Capstone Decision Manager
which performs functions like credit decisioning. ProfitMax is also used to help analyze customer profitability.

In insurance, HNC offers VeriComp Claims, which looks at fraud in the claims industry; SPYDER, which looks at claim fraud in Medicare and Medicaid; and eCM Director, which analyzes what claims to inspect in more detail.

In retail, HNC Retek's division has data-mining solutions for Active Retail Intelligence and Behavior Profiling. Their Aptex Internet solution also has a solution for text mining, which, for one thing, determines how to respond to incoming customer inquiries via e-mail, Web form, chat room or call centers. The product intelligently interprets incoming inquiries in order to deliver the right responses.

In telecommunications, HNC has applications for fraud (ATACS 5), and for analyzing customer behavior (ProfitMax).

**IBM Corporation (Intelligent Miner for Data, Intelligent Miner for Text)**
Old Orchard Road
Armonk, NY 10504
(914) 765-1900
Web: http://www.ibm.com

**Product.**   Intelligent Miner for Data, Intelligent Miner for Text

**Position.**   IBM sells a suite of software data-mining tools under the name Intelligent Miner to provide a high-end data-mining solution. Intelligent Miner for Data offers a wide variety of different algorithms to solve separate problems like clustering, visualization, classification, and link analysis. The tool has a Java based GUI and includes a statistics package, parallel data mining, a published API for application development, and access to relational databases like DB2. This tool runs on a host of different platforms.

IBM's Intelligent Miner for Text helps interpret information from text sources, such as online news services, e-mail, and the Web. The tool extracts patterns and trends from text and then provides methods to organize and search the information.

**Information Discovery, Inc. (The Data Mining Suite,**
**The Knowledge Access Suite)**
703B Pier Avenue, Suite 169
Hermosa Beach, CA 90254
(310) 937-3600
Web: http://www.datamining.com

**Product.**   The Data Mining Suite, The Knowledge Access Suite, and industry-specific modules for retail, banking and finance, direct marketing, Web-log and access, and manufacturing.

**Position.** The Data Mining Suite is an advanced data-mining tool that works directly on large SQL repositories with no need for sampling or extract files. It accesses large volumes of multi-table relational data on the server, and incrementally discovers powerful patterns.

The Knowledge Access Suite is sold as an automatic analysis package that discovers patterns, generates rules and performs prediction on the constructed models. This product provides business users with access to knowledge that has been "pre-distilled" from data and is stored in a pattern-base. Business users need not perform data analysis, but simply query explainable knowledge on the intranet that has been automatically pre-mined. The product supports most relational database systems.

Information Discovery has also targeted several vertical industries, offering industry-specific modules for retail, banking and finance, direct marketing, Web-log and access, and manufacturing.

### ISoft (AC2, Alice d'ISoft)

Chemin de Moulon

F-91190 Gif sur Yvette

33-1 69 35 3737

Web: http://www.alice-soft.com

**Product.**  AC2, Alice d'ISoft

**Position.**  ISoft is a French company that has implemented decision-tree-based data-mining software. Alice d'Isoft is a PC-based data mining solution with a graphical front end. ISoft has formed a partnership with Business Objects, where Business Objects will be adding their software as an add-in module that integrates directly with their tools.

AC2 is available as a development environment, with a C++ library and OLE support. Both products support SQL access to relational databases through ODBC.

### NeoVista Solutions, Inc. (Retail Decision Suite, SmartCRM, Decision Series)

10710 N. Tantau Ave.

Cupertino, CA 95014

(408) 777-2929

Web: http://www.neovista.com

**Product.**  Retail Decision Suite, SmartCRM, Decision Series

**Position.** NeoVista markets a suite of products, the Decision Series, that focuses on data mining. The suite of products is a server-side product offering. The product offers modules for prediction and descriptive analysis. For predictive analysis they have Decision Net, Decision Cubist, Decision Tree, and Decision Bayes. Each of these modules provides predictive modeling, but they use different algorithms: neural networks, regression, decision trees, and Bayesian algorithms. For descriptive analysis, they have Decision Cluster, Decision Kmeans, and Decision AR. Decision Cluster is a clustering solution with advanced clustering algorithms for supervised and unsupervised learning. Decision Kmeans uses a statistical clustering technique for understanding hierarchical clusters. Decision AR is solution generating association rules, used to model how likely events occur together or sequentially over time, i.e., 73% of the time events X and Y occur together, and in half of those cases, event Z occurs within a week.

NeoVista has industry vertical packages for retail solutions, financial solutions, insurance solutions, and customer-relationship management. The Retail Decision Suite is particularly strong in handling companies in retail that distribute large numbers of products.

NeoVista, which has remade itself after formerly being known as Maspar, is tackling the enterprise-level data-mining market. They have referenced that they aggressively market at WallMart and the Army Air Force Exchange. They were one of the first vendors to enter a relationship with Informix to construct a Data Blade for Informix's Universal Server.

## Neural Applications Corporation (NetProphet, Aegis)
2600 Crosspark Rd.
Coralville, IA 52241
(319) 626-5000
Web: http://www.neural.com

**Product.** NetProphet, Aegis Development System

**Position.** Net Prophet is a stock browser for the Internet. It is a Java enabled application that monitors stock and mutual funds at home. There are intelligent stock-filtering tools and neural network ratings for most stocks traded.

Aegis is a development environment for intelligent process-control applications. Industrial process control applications require process optimization. Aegis makes use of neural networks, fuzzy logic, and genetic algorithms.

Neural Applications entered an exclusive partnership with Net Perception. Neural Applications provides data-mining technology to Net Perceptions which enhances Net Perceptions technology to intelligently cross-sell products on the Web.

### Oracle Corporation (Darwin)

500 Oracle Parkway

Redwood Shores, CA 94056

(650) 506-7000

Web: http://www.oracle.com and http://www.think.com

**Product.**  Darwin

**Position.**  Oracle acquired Thinking Machines Corp, the provider of the data-mining software Darwin, on June 7, 1999. Oracle wants their new data mining capability to be an integral part of their customer relationship management (CRM) suite and their e-business strategy.

Oracle emphasizes the parallel scalable approach to data mining. Their tool also employs a multi-algorithmic approach and can generate C, C++, and Java business models. In particular, Darwin has attracted much interest within the banking/ financial, telecommunications, and database marketing, as well as in government.

Darwin is a suite of data-mining products that exploits parallel computing to deliver in hours results that require days or weeks using traditional methods. Darwin offers decision-tree algorithms, neural networks, linear regression, logistic regression, memory-based reasoning, Bayesian learning, and clustering with a variety of techniques including k-means and self-organizing maps.

### RightPoint Software (DataCruncher)

2121 S. El Camino Real

Suite 1200

San Mateo, CA 94403

(415) 287-2000

Web: http://www.rightpoint.com

**Product.**  DataCruncher

**Position.**  RightPoint Software, headquartered in San Mateo, California, is a privately held company that produces enterprise applications for delivering real-time, one-to-one marketing campaigns via interactive customer touch points. This technology includes a data-mining tool with "assistants" to help create predictive models used in marketing for common problems like churn, cross-selling, product bundling, customer segmentation, direct mail, and up-selling. The product also has a dynamic learning engine that automatically creates predictive models that learn how likely the next customers are to respond, based on current customer responses on the Web or through the call center.

Using the RightPoint Real-Time Marketing Suite, companies are empowered to leverage each customer interaction to maximize customer satisfaction, loyalty, and revenue generation potential. Formerly known as DataMind Corporation, RightPoint Software has relationships with companies like Oracle, Fair, Isaac and Company Inc., and Edify Corporation.

### Silicon Graphics Computer Systems (MineSet)

2011 N. Shoreline Blvd.

Mountain View, CA 94043

(415) 960-1980

Web: http://www.sgi.com

**Product.**  Silicon MineSet

**Position.**  MineSet provides a suite of data-mining tools for visual exploration of data and data-mining results. Decision-tree algorithms, probabilities, and association algorithms are also incorporated. The tools utilize animated 3-D landscapes.

The MineSet version supports many visual data-mining tools including the Association Rule Visualizer, Map Visualizer, Scatter Visualizer, Tree Visualizer, Stat Visualizer, Data Mover, and Record Viewer.

The Map Visualizer supports the analysis of spatially related data and information. By applying data onto height and color of pre-built or user-generated map elements, users have the ability to quickly identify trends, patterns, relationships, and anomalies in data.

Many times, data sets are just too complex for representation in two or even three dimensions. The MineSet Scatter Visualizer is ideal for analyzing the behavior of data in many dimensions all at once.

The Tree Visualizer provides the capability to visualize trees and hierarchical data structures. Using a three-dimensional fly-through navigational paradigm, users can move through data to discover trends, patterns, and anomalies.

The Association Rule Visualizer graphically displays results from the Association Rule Generator. By analyzing rules discovered using the Association Rule Generator, users gain greater insight into the nature of a particular data set.

### SPSS Inc. (SPSS Clementine)

232 S. Wacker Drive, 11th Floor.

Chicago, IL 60606

(800) 543-2185

Web: http://www.spss.com

**Product.**  SPSS Clementine

**Position.**   SPSS purchased Integral Solutions LTD, the maker of the data-mining tool, Clementine. Data Warehousing Tools Bulletin awarded Clementine the "Best Data-Mining Product of 1998." Clementine is based on a visual programming interface and is an application development environment as well as a data-mining tool. Any model developed can be represented with C source code. Clementine boasts an impressive number of users, including Reuters, Unilever, Halfords Department Store, and Winterthur Insurance.

SPSS is a leader in the statistical software arena, competing head-to-head with SAS Institute. SPSS is incorporating its own initiatives in offering data-mining solutions. SPSS has SPSS and SYSTAT statistical packages that perform such things as linear regressions.

SPSS CHAID is a decision-tree-based data-mining software tool for analysts that develops predictive models and produces easy-to-read tree diagrams. Market and customer segmentation is one key area where this product has been used. This SPSS CHAID product can also be run as an add-on module to the SPSS Base for the Windows package.


### SAS Institute Inc. (SAS Enterprise Miner)

SAS Campus Dr.

Cary, NC 27513-2414

(919) 677-8000

Web: http://www.sas.com/

**Product.**   Enterprise Miner

**Position.**   SAS Institute's Enterprise Miner had not been released when the first version of this book was published, but is already a leading tool in the data-mining market. SAS Institute has bridged the gap between traditional statistics packages and data-mining tools. A case study of using Enterprise Miner at US WEST is discussed in Chapter 1. SAS Institute has won many awards for their tool including Datamation Magazine's Data Warehousing Product of the Year. Currently their software is used by over 33,000 business, government, and university sites in more than 115 countries.

Enterprise Miner is used in areas like customer relationship management (customer acquisition and retention, cross-selling, and market basket analysis), fraud detection, and credit scoring.

### Trajecta (dbProphet)

611 S. Congress, Suite 420

Austin, Texas 78704-1736

(800) 250-2242

Web: http://www.trajecta.com

**Product.** dbProphet

**Position.** dbProphet is a neural-network-based data-mining tool. The tool incorporates advanced neural network algorithms as well as data visualization and variable manipulation tools. dbProphet also has a runtime model that can be accessed by a C programming interface.

### Unica Technologies, Inc. (Model 1)

55 Old Bedford Rd.

Lincoln, MA 01773

(781) 259-5900

Web: http://www.unica-usa.com

**Product.** Model 1

**Position.** Unica was founded in 1992 by an MIT alumnus to focus on providing data-mining solutions. The tool has four components: Response Modeler, Cross Seller, Customer Valuator, and Customer Segmentor/ Profiler. Unica formed a marketing relationship with Group 1 Software, a well-known marketing software company, to distribute its MODEL 1 series of data-mining products.

### Wizsoft Inc. (WizRule, WizWhy)

3 Beit Hillel Street

Tel Aviv, Israel 67017

(972) -3-5631948

Web: http://www.wizsoft.com

**Product.** WizRule, WizWhy

**Position.** WizSoft markets its software to thousands of customers in varied businesses and institutions all over the world, providing data-mining tools for a number of industries. WizRule is a data-auditing application based on data-mining technology. WizRule discovers the rules that govern a given data, and points at the deviations from the discovered set of the rules as cases to be audited.

WizWhy is a data-mining application that discovers the rules governing the data and predicts, based on these rules, the outcome of new or future cases. There is a demo that can be downloaded from their Web site for Microsoft Windows users.

## 5.3  Visualization

The essence of data mining is the process of creating a model. A model is a representation of complex data that makes complex data more understandable. Because pictures often represent data better than reports or numbers, data visualization is clearly another way to data mine.

### 5.3.1  Examples of Data Visualization

Figure 5-1 exemplifies how a picture can help make raw data more understandable. The figure, courtesy of MapInfo, shows product sales overlaid on top of a map.

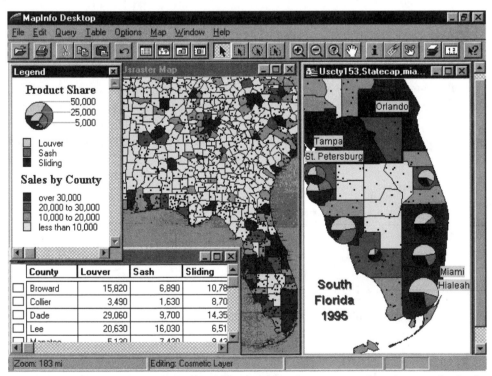

**Figure 5-1**   This figure, courtesy of MapInfo, graphically shows product share and sales by county.

The map has an area zoomed in on southern Florida and shows pie charts of product sales in specific counties. This picture provides a concise way to understand how product sales vary depending on the state, county, and city at which you are looking. Colors are also used to denote the number of sales by county to help indicate where the most product sales are happening.

There are several graphical information systems, or GIS products, on the market today, and they are very useful in showing graphical representations of data. Microsoft has a mapping feature integrated directly into Microsoft Excel, based on an arrangement with MapInfo.

Data visualization tools go beyond simply two-dimensional mapping of data, and fortunately, with the advancements in personal computing, many of the visualization techniques that were only available on high-power servers are moving into the end-user market space.

Silicon Graphics is a leader in data-visualization techniques. Silicon Graphics' data-mining package, MineSet, has several visualization components to it. For example, it too has a map visualizer, but it allows for three-dimensional visualization as well as a method for showing changes over time, while mapping data such as product sales over a geographic region.

Figure 5-2 shows a representation of the Map Visualizer. This tool displays quantitative and relational characteristics of your spatially oriented data. Data items are associated with graphical "bar chart" objects in the visual landscape. However, the objects have recognizable spatial shapes and positions, such as those found in geographical maps. The landscape can consist of a collection of these spatially related objects, each with individual heights and colors. You can dynamically navigate through this landscape by panning, rotating, zooming, drilling down to see increased granularity of geographic details, drilling up to aggregate data into more coarse-grained graphical objects, and using animation to see how the data changes across one or two independent dimensions.

Silicon Graphics also has a Tree Visualizer as shown in Figure 5-3. The Tree Visualizer is a graphical interface that displays data as a three-dimensional "landscape." It presents your data as clustered, hierarchical blocks (nodes) and bars through which you can dynamically navigate, viewing part or all of the data set.

The Tree Visualizer displays quantitative and relational characteristics of your data by showing them as hierarchically connected nodes. Each node contains bars whose height and color correspond to aggregations of data values. The lines connecting the nodes show the relationship of one set of data to its subsets. Values in subgroups can be summed and displayed automatically in the next higher level. The base under the bars can provide information about the aggregate value of all the bars.

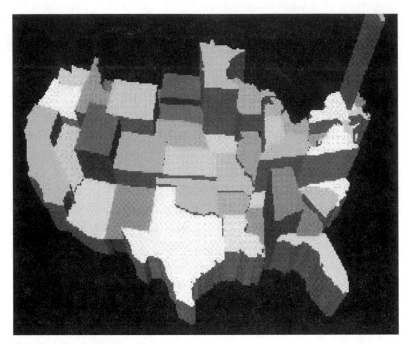

**Figure 5-2**   Map Visualizer.

**Figure 5-3**   Tree Visualizer.

The Tree Visualizer takes data at the lowest level of the hierarchy as input. Data is then aggregated up through the visualization automatically, as defined by the user. Full support is also provided for visual filtering, querying, and marking.

The Tree Visualizer is also used for the display of the decision trees resulting from the Decision Tree Inducer. The Tree Visualizer shows decision and leaf classification nodes. Information about classification distribution and classification purity is shown at each node. The Tree Visualizer allows for further understanding and analysis of the decision trees.

### 5.3.2  Vendor List

Below is a list of vendors who provide data-visualization tools. All products are trademarks or registered trademarks of their respective companies.

**Advanced Visual Systems (AVS/Express)**
300 Fifth Ave.
Waltham, MA 02115
(617) 890-4300
Web: http://www.avs.com

**Product.**  AVS/Express

**Position.**  Advanced Visual Systems provides three- dimensional visualization and imaging techniques for complex data, and offers both end-user and developer versions of products. Their graphical components include visualization blocks, image processing, and database connectivity.

**Alta Analytics, Inc. (NetMap)**
929 Eastwind Drive, Suite 203
Westerville, Ohio 43081
(800) 638-6277
Web: http://www.ALTAanalytics.com

**Product.**  NetMap

**Position.**  NetMap is a mapping tool designed for more sophisticated data visualization. It has features that allow for clustering, link analysis, and integration with the visualization components. This allows for graphical knowledge discovery to identify trends and patterns. The product has been used in uncovering corporate fraud as well as in analyzing corporate securities. Some customers include the Australian Securities Commission, the U.S. Government, and the United Kingdom's Special Fraud Office in London. Five of the top 15 property and casualty insurance carriers use NetMap for claims.

**Belmont Research, Inc. (CrossGraphs)**
84 Sherman St.
Cambridge, MA 02140
(617) 868-6878
Web: http://www.belmont.com

**Product.**   CrossGraphs

**Position.**   CrossGraphs is a unique data-visualization tool that divides data into subsets and displays complex data in arrays of graphs, one graph per subset, on one or many pages without programming. Graph arrays let you easily spot trends, identify anomalies, and see relationships among different variables or subsets of your data in a single display. For example, sales and marketing managers gain business knowledge by using CrossGraphs to view sales performance data in many graphs — by competition, product, attribute, region, sales channel, market segment, time period, or a combination of these dimensions. The product can be run interactively or in batch and has links to Oracle and ODBC databases, and ASCII, dBase, and SAS data files. Belmont Research has done much work in the healthcare industry, and several of their graphs are shown in Chapter 9.

**Environmental Systems Research Institute, Inc. (MapObjects, ARC/INFO, Arc GIS, Spatial Database Engine)**
380 New York St.
Redlands, CA 92373
(909) 793-2853
Web: http://www.esri.com

**Product.**   MapObjects, ARC/INFO, ARC GIS, Spatial Database Engine

**Position.**   ESRI supports a suite of GIS software products that allow for viewing maps, geocoding, and performing more sophisticated data visualization. ARC and ARC/INFO come with a macro language to support embedding this technology into other applications. Their Spatial Database Engine allows for support of spatial information into databases like Oracle, DB2, Informix, and Sybase.

**MapInfo Corp (MapInfo, SpatialWare)**
1 Global View
Troy, NY 12180
(518) 285-6000
Web: http://www.mapinfo.com

**Product.**   MapInfo Desktop, MapInfo Professional, MapMaker, SpatialWare, MapX

**Position.**   MapInfo provides a suite of products for data visualization and mapping. They support geocoding as well as data overlay onto maps to help visualize data trends. MapInfo works with many partners and its products have a programming interface. Its mapping technology is integrated as a module within Microsoft Excel, and it has also introduced a SpatialWare technology that allows users of relational databases like Oracle and Informix to examine and store complex data for spatial analysis within their database.

**Silicon Graphics Computer Systems (MineSet)**
2011 N. Shoreline Blvd.
Mountain View, CA 94043
(415) 960-1980
Web: http://www.sgi.com

**Product.**   MineSet

**Position.**   SGI has been discussed in this section. The Map Visualizer, Tree Visualizer, Scatter Visualizer, and Evidence Visualizer all provide enhanced data visualization.

## 5.4   Useful Web Sites/Commercially Available Code

The data-mining community offers several Web sites with a great deal of information about data mining vendors, data, and even source code. Below is a start at listing some of the more interesting sites. You will inevitably find many more sites. Using these Web sites, you may find:

- More information about data mining.
- Data sites with which to experiment.
- Data sources and vendors who provide this data.
- Code for some data-mining algorithms.

### 5.4.1    Data-Mining Web Sites

Of the data-mining Web sites that were listed in the first book, very few managed to stay around. Therefore, the "list" of data-mining Web sites is actually very short: one site (and the URL for this site changed). The following site is a "must see" if you want more information on data mining.

**Knowledge Discovery Mine**

Web: http://www.kdnuggets.com

**Description.**   This site has put together an impressive, comprehensive data-mining resource. The home page of this site provides many valuable pointers, including:

- Other Web sites on data mining.
- S*I*FTWARE (a list of many public domain tools available for data mining).
- Companies that provide data-mining tools.
- *Knowledge Discovery Nuggets* — a newsletter.
- Upcoming meetings for the data-mining community.
- Reference materials.
- Pointers to available Web sites.

### 5.4.2    Finding Data Sets

**StatLib (sample data sets)**

Web: http://lib.stat.cmu.edu/datasets

**Description.**   StatLib contains a collection of data sets that have been contributed by many statisticians, authors, and academicians for use by all. They include everything from performance and salary ranges of major league baseball players to Dow-Jones industrial averages from 1900 to 1993. You are free to use any data set and to contribute your own. If you use any algorithm or data set from StatLib, they ask that you acknowledge StatLib and the original contributor.

**U.S. Census Bureau**

Web: http://www.census.gov

**Description.**   The United States Census Bureau is undergoing a massive effort to make census information available on the Web. If you are interested in geographic information for the United States, the United States Census Bureau has a TIGER/Line® product it distributes (at a cost) with extensive geographic information.

**Edgar**

Web: http://www.edgar-online.com

**Description.** Reports filed to the SEC by publically held companies. These reports are available to you if you visit this Web site.

### 5.4.3 Source Code

**SGI Source (MLC++)**

Web: http://www.sgi.com/Technology/mlc/source.html

**Description.** MLC++ (A Machine Learning Library) is C++ source code that provides general machine-learning algorithms. This source code was developed for Silicon Graphics by Ronny Kohavi. Silicon Graphics is making source code available as public domain (compiled on SGI's IRIX 5.3 using their C++ compilers) in order to promote the development of new and better data-mining algorithms. Many of the better-known algorithms and graphing styles are available.

**Source Code for C4.5 Decision-Tree Algorithm**

Web: ftp://ftp.cs.su.oz.au/pub/ml/

**Description.** J.R. Quinlan makes the decision-tree algorithm C4.5 available, with source, in his book, *C4.5 — Programs for Machine Learning*, Morgan Kaufmann, 1993. Patches, papers, and more information are available on the Web site mentioned above.

**Source Code for OC1, a Decision Tree Algorithm**

Web: http://www.cs.jhu.edu/~salzberg/

Web (code): ftp://ftp.cs.jhu.edu/pub/oc1/

**Description.** OC1 (Oblique Classifier 1) is a decision tree induction system available with C source code and a paper that Sreerama K. Murthy, Simon Kasif, Steven Salzberg, and Richard Beigel wrote on the algorithm for AAAI in 1993. OC1 is freely available via anonymous FTP from the Department of Computer Science at Johns Hopkins University at *ftp.cs.jhu.edu*. Go to the directory *pub/oc1*.

## 5.5  Data Sources for Mining

The availability and detail of information about what people buy, where they live, how much they earn, and what types of hobbies they have is astonishing. You may be troubled by the privacy issues this raises, but the fact remains that this type of information not only exists, it is easy to get.

Adding purchased information to augment customer lists is one of the most effective ways for corporations to understand their customers. It also makes data mining an interesting endeavor. Many, if not all, data providers are involved in data mining activities of their own.

Below is a list of vendors who sell information. This is certainly not a complete list, but it is representative of the larger data providers in consumer and business-related information. All products are trademarks or registered trademarks of their respective companies. A very brief description of each one's services is provided.

**ACNielsen**
177 Broad Street.
Stamford, CT 06901
(203) 961-3000
Web: http://www.acnielsen.com

**Description.**  ACNielsen is a market leader in providing information for consumer packaged goods manufacturers and retailers. ACNielsen monitors 47,000 households in the United States and Canada electronically to understand consumer-purchase behavior.

**Acxiom Corporation**
301 Industrial Blvd
Conway, AR 72032
(800) 922-9466
Web: http://www.acxiom.com

**Description.**  Acxiom is a leading provider of comprehensive information on consumers and businesses, for decision-support activities in marketing, merchandising, and risk management. Founded in 1969 as Demographics, Acxiom, by one account, has over four terabytes of data and 500,000 magnetic tapes.

**CACI Marketing Systems**
1100 Glebe Road
Arlington, Virginia 22201
(703) 841-7800
Web: http://www.caci.com

**Description.** This vendor provides demographic and consumer-spending data, focusing on customer-relationship management. Several government agencies work directly with CACI.

**CorpTech**
12 Alfred Street, Suite 200
Woburn, MA 01801
(800) 454-3647
Web: http://www.corptech.com

**Description.** CorpTech provides information about technology companies and industry markets, offering more than 45,000 company profiles and national, regional, and state-level industry reports.

**Claritas**
1525 Wilson Blvd., Suite 1000
Arlington, VA 22209
(703) 812-2700
Web: http://www.claritas.com

**Description.** Claritas offers customers demographic information, including a suite of products referred to as PRIZM®. Claritas supplies detailed lifestyle segmentation and PRIZM +4 micro-neighborhood segmentation.

**Equifax, Inc.**
1600 Peachtree St. N.W.
Atlanta, GA 30302
(404) 885-8000
Web: http://www.equifax.com

**Description.** Equifax has been a leading provider of comprehensive customer and business demographic information since 1899. Equifax has expanded well beyond the role of credit bureau to provide a diverse range of information.

## Harte-Hanks Data Technologies
PO Box 269
San Antonio, TX 78291
(210) 829-9000
Web: http://www.harte-hanks.com

**Description.** Harte-Hanks is a market leader in providing direct marketing, including consumer and business-to-business market research. Harte-Hanks Data Technologies is part of Harte-Hanks Communications, based in San Antonio, Texas.


## Healthdemographics
4901 Morena Blvd., Suite 701
San Diego, CA 92117
(800) 590-4545
Web: http://www.healthdemographics.com

**Description.** Healthdemographics is a market leader in providing health-demographic information for government agencies, providers, and payors. They specialize in helping sort through the complex data requirements of managed-care organizations, hospitals, and pharmaceuticals.


## Polk & Company
1621 18th St.
Denver, CO 80202
(303) 292-5000
Web: http://www.polk.com

**Description.** Polk, with more than 125 years in business, is a leading information provider to corporations. They have extensive data on motor vehicles, customer demographics, and purchasing behavior, as well as many other areas.


## TRW Communications
1900 Richmond Rd.
Cleveland, OH 44124
(216) 291-7000
Web: http://www.trw.com

**Description.** A leading provider of consumer credit, business credit, direct marketing, and real-estate information, TRW has expanded beyond its role of credit bureau into a provider of many different types of data services.

## 5.6  Summary

This chapter discussed industry trends in the data-mining industry. It also mentioned several of the leading data-mining vendors that are around today, and introduced visualization tools, Web sites for data miners, and several of the sellers of customer and industry demographics. With this information, you can readily familiarize yourself with what is open to you in the data-mining arena.

Many vendors who are involved in data preparation and in the decision-support arena are invariably connected with data mining. For more information, refer to Appendix A.

The next several chapters examine a few of the data-mining tools in much more depth, and will give you a better idea of how these tools solve industry problems.

# PART 2

# A Rapid Tutorial

Chapters 6 and 7 introduce two leading data-mining software products. The CD-ROM included with this book contains demo versions of Angoss KnowledgeSEEKER and RightPoint DataCruncher. Appendix B steps you through the installation process you'll need to complete in order to follow along with the demonstrations in these chapters.

# A Look at Angoss: KnowledgeSEEKER

This chapter looks at a popular application that uses a decision-tree approach to data mining: KnowledgeSEEKER.

The chapter is organized as follows:

- Section 6.1   Introduction
- Section 6.2   Data Preparation
- Section 6.3   Defining a Study
- Section 6.4   Building the Model
- Section 6.5   Understanding the Model
- Section 6.6   Prediction
- Section 6.7   Summary

## 6.1  Introduction

The purpose of this chapter is to familiarize you with a decision-tree approach to data mining. While the process is demonstrated with KnowledgeSEEKER from Angoss Software Corporation, you will find similarities in all decision-tree approaches. The user interface for KnowledgeSEEKER is easy to understand.

### 6.1.1    KnowledgeSTUDIO

While the demonstrations in this chapter discuss Angoss Software Corporation's decision-tree tool, KnowledgeSEEKER, Angoss has expanded its product offering beyond just this type of tool. They also offer a new data-mining product suite, KnowledgeSTUDIO. Unlike KnowledgeSEEKER, KnowledgeSTUDIO delivers a wide variety of data-mining techniques. Initially, five decision-tree algorithms, three neural-net algorithms, and one "unsupervised" learning/clustering algorithm are offered, with more algorithms to be added in new releases. Because KnowledgeSTUDIO was implemented as a framework, third-party companies are able to add their own algorithms as well.

KnowledgeSTUDIO has a user interface that looks and feels like Office '97 and has an advanced user interface. KnowledgeSTUDIO tightly integrates with data warehouses and data marts, and has a dedicated high-performance data server.

KnowledgeSTUDIO can also be integrated with your applications and business processes through a programmable interface, through the use of Active X and Java technologies.

KnowledgeSTUDIO imports data from all major statistical products. Not only does it read and write SAS data files, it also generates SAS code. This allows your existing statisticians and modelers to quickly and easily adapt and integrate.

Angoss has been working with a number of application vendors to create vertical applications using their technologies. Like other vendors in the industry, they are moving towards a solution-oriented product offering.

### 6.1.2    KnowledgeSEEKER and Decision Trees

KnowledgeSEEKER is a decision-tree-based analysis program. This program is a comprehensive program for classification-tree analysis. KnowledgeSEEKER makes use of two well-known decision-tree algorithms: CHAID and CART. CHAID, or Chi-Square Automatic Interaction Detection, is used to study categorical data, like states in a country or gender. CART (Classification and Regression Trees) works with continuous dependent variables, such as monthly expenses (0–1000 dollars, 1001–2000 dollars, and 2000 and above dollars). There are several commercially available decision-tree algorithms (see Chapter 3). Angoss has put much work into making the process user-friendly.

There are many decision-tree approaches and algorithms. Dr. Gordon B. Kass introduced the CHAID method in 1976 in his doctoral dissertation. CART was popularized in 1984. A popular decision-tree algorithm, complete with source code, may be purchased from Morgan Kaufman Publishers: *C4.5 Programming for Machine Learning* by J. Ross Quinlan.

### 6.1.3    How Decision Trees Are Being Used

Many vendors are offering decision-tree approaches. AC2, from Isoft, is a popular decision-tree algorithm. Isoft has formed a relationship with Business Objects, in which

Business Objects sells a data-mining module that makes use of Isoft's decision-tree approach. SPSS markets a product based on the algorithm, called SI-CHAID. Many other vendors use combinations of algorithms to best fit approaches. A decision-tree algorithm is also used in many data-mining packages that combine a variety of approaches, including IBM's Intelligent Miner, SAS Enterprise Miner, SPSS, Thinking Machine's Darwin, and Silicon Graphic's MineSet.

Angoss recently announced a deal with Andyne, a maker of end-user querying and decision support programs, to jointly market with KnowledgeSEEKER. Angoss has aggressively looked at many other partnerships to move this technology into the mainstream. For example, Customer Insight Company (CIC), a provider of database marketing tools, signed on to be a value-added reseller for KnowledgeSEEKER.

Decision-tree approaches are good for handling classification problems. Classification is the process of using historical data to build a model for the purpose of understanding and prediction. Chapter 2 discussed this in more detail.

Angoss widely advertises its product to solve a wide variety of problems and points to many industry examples. The IRS is using KnowledgeSEEKER to predict the likelihood of tax fraud, using important factors associated with tax claims. *Reader's Digest Canada* incorporates Angoss to use market-segment analysis as well as predicting cost. The *Washington Post* uses KnowledgeSEEKER for direct marketing. Angoss is being used by the Oxford Transplant Center in London to analyze the mortality rates of kidney transplants recipients, based on historical patient information. KnowledgeSEEKER is used by Hewlett-Packard to analyze rules for production control systems. The Canadian Imperial Bank of Commerce uses the software to look at risk management.

## 6.2 Data Preparation

The demonstration in this chapter studies the important dietary factors that can lead to low, normal, and high blood pressure. KnowledgeSEEKER helps you understand the aspects of individual dietary behavior that can lead to hypertension. This type of study is interesting to many in the medical profession, including medical researchers, health-care insurers, or pharmaceutical researchers seeking cures for hypertension.

This chapter uses a sample data set based on a study of high blood pressure from a community health survey; Angoss includes this data set with its demonstration. Table 6-1 shows the values in the data set.

When the demonstration software included in the back of this book is loaded onto a PC and started, this data set automatically comes up prepared and ready to go. There are, however, steps that had to be taken to prepare this data set for mining. For example, several of the fields contain integer values to which labels were applied. *Hypertension* is a field that has the values 1, 2, and 3. These fields are labeled to be low, normal, and high.

*TypeOfMilk* is another field that has labels added. The field has values 1–5 which are labeled to mean whole milk, 2%, skim, powder, or no milk at all.

**Table 6-1**    Data on a Hypertension Study

| Column Name | Values | Explanation |
|---|---|---|
| TypeOfMilk | Integer: 1–5 | Type of milk person drinks. Integer values labeled to denote whether milk is whole milk, 2%, skim, powder, or no milk at all. |
| DeepFriedLastWeek | Integer: 0–7 | Number of times person had deep-fried food last week. |
| BeefLastWeek | Integer: 0–7 | Number of times person had beef last week. |
| PorkLastWeek | Integer: 0–7 | Number of times person had pork last week. |
| PoultryLastWeek | Integer: 0–7 | Number of times person had poultry last week. |
| FishLastWeek | Integer: 0, 1, 2 | Number of times person had fish last week. |
| LambLastWeek | Integer: 0–7 | Number of times person had lamb last week. |
| OtherMeatLastWeek | Integer: 0, 1, 2, 3, 7 | Number of times person had other meat last week. |
| CheeseLastWeek | Integer: 0–7 | Number of times person had cheese last week. |
| EggsLastWeek | Integer: 0–7, 9 | Number of times person had eggs last week. |
| Meat2MealsLstWk | Integer: 0–7, 9 | Number of times person had meat in two meals last week. |
| SaltInFood | Integer: 1–5, 9 | Does a person use salt? Numbers are labeled to denote a lot, moderate, very little, or none. |
| SaltConsumption | Integer: 1–5, 9 | What is the person's level of salt consumption? Numbers are labeled to denote very low, low, moderate, high, or very high. |
| ButterFood | Integer: 1–3 | Does a person butter their food? Numbers are labeled to denote frequently, sometimes, and never. |
| SportsActivity | Integer: 1–5, 9 | Does a person exercise? Numbers are labeled to denote daily, weekly, occasionally, rarely, and never. |

*(continued)*

**Table 6-1**  Data on a Hypertension Study

| Column Name | Values | Explanation |
| --- | --- | --- |
| SleepTime | Integer: in hours: 0–24 | The number of hours a person sleeps, on average. |
| Smoking | Integer: 1–4 | Does a person smoke? Numbers are labeled to denote regular, occasional, former, never, and ??? <br><br> (??? for unknown). |
| DrinkPattern | Integer: 1–5 | Does a person drink? Numbers are labeled to denote regular, occasional, former, and never. |
| DrinksEveryDay | Integer: 1, 2, 9 | Does a person drink every day? Numbers are labeled to denote yes or no. |
| Age | Integer: 1–3 | Age of person. Numbers are labeled to denote 32–50, 51–62, and 63–72. |
| YearsEducation | Integer: 1–5 | How many years' education has a person had? |
| Income | Integer: 3–21 | What is person's income? |
| Gender | Integer 1, 2 | What is gender of person? Numbers are labeled to denote male and female. |
| Weight | Integer: in kilograms | What is the person's weight in kilograms? |
| Height | Integer: in centimeters | What is the height of customer in centimemers? |
| Hypertension | Integer: 1, 2, 3 | What is the person's level of hypertension? Numbers are labeled to denote low, normal, and high. |

In order to label these values, a user would pull down the edit menu from Knowledge-SEEKER and choose *Map Data*. You would then choose a column, like *TypeOfMilk*, and choose the *Map* push-button. The map editor for *TypeOfMilk* looks like Figure 6-1.

In Figure 6-1, integer values have been mapped to text strings with much more meaning.

Derived columns should be considered with this data set. For example, the column *Age* has the values 1, 2, and 3, which are labeled 32–50, 51–62, and 63–72. Normally, a column named *Age* does not come with the values 1, 2, and 3, but with the actual age of a person. In this data set, *Age* was encoded into three ranges. The column was derived before data mining began and the choice of the age ranges 32–50, 51–62, and 63–72 were made.

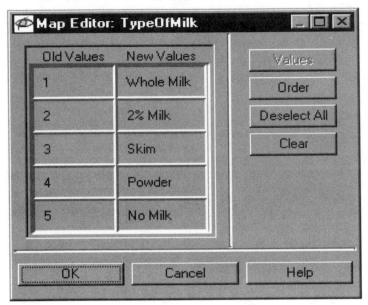

**Figure 6-1**   Defining data fields.

The demonstration in this chapter has already provided the data preparation for you, but you should be aware of the steps that occurred to actually mine a data set. For many data sets, no mapping is needed.

## 6.3   Defining the Study

In this section, we will step through the process of defining a study that examines hypertension.

### 6.3.1   Defining the Goal

In order to start using KnowledgeSEEKER, it is useful to define the goal of your study. The demonstration in this chapter profiles what dietary factors have the most influence on different levels of blood pressure. This goal can be stated clearly as:

*Profile the dietary factors that most influence low, normal, and high blood pressue.*

### 6.3.2 Starting Up

The following steps run through an example of using the KnowledgeSEEKER product. If you would like to follow along, load the demonstration by following the instructions in Appendix B.

The first step is to open the application. Open KnowledgeSEEKER. Pull down the File menu and select **Open.** You will see the screen shown in Figure 6-2.

**Figure 6-2** Selecting the blood-pressure data set, *bpress.*

By highlighting *bpress* and selecting **OK,** the data set on blood pressure, described in the last section, is automatically loaded for you.

### 6.3.3 Setting the Dependent Variable

The column *Hypertension* has been automatically set as the dependent variable. Later on, this variable will be changed.

Upon opening KnowledgeSEEKER, you will see the screen shown in Figure 6-3.

The box highlighted in black is known as the root node. Notice that the root node for the dependent variable classifies high blood pressure into three categories: low, normal, and high. We are profiling which people are more likely to have low, normal, and high blood pressure. What you are being told here is:

- 18% of the people, or 66 people in the study, have low blood pressure.
- 60% of the people, or 217 people in the study, have normal blood pressure.
- 21% of the people, or 77 people in the study, have high blood pressure.

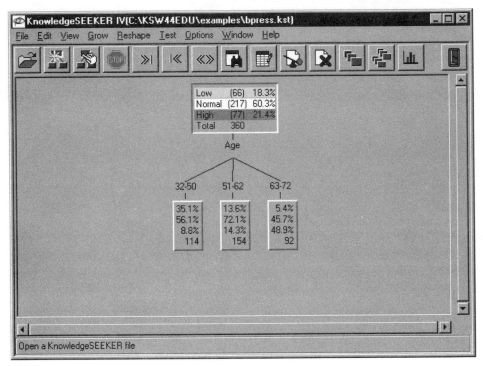

**Figure 6-3**  Starting up.

## 6.4 Building the Model

KnowledgeSEEKER has built the next level of the tree model. The tree can also be generated automatically to multiple levels, as will be shown later in the chapter.

The next level of the tree in Figure 6-3 is shown dividing patients by age. Age is just one variable that affects the outcome high blood pressure, but in this case, age appears to be the most significant factor that affects whether someone has high blood pressure.

You will now see age groups as follows:

- Age 32–50
- Age 51–62
- Age 63–72

The leaf nodes of this tree can be created using a column other than age. Specifying another column is know as a *split*. In this example, there are 12 splits automatically found. They are listed in the next section. Other splits can be created by your specification.

## 6.5 Understanding the Model

We can continue to grow this model, but first it is useful to explore the first leaf nodes and to clarify the concept of a split, which was just introduced. We have found age to be the most important criterion for characterizing the categories of blood pressure, but it is reasonable to assume that this is not the only factor that affects it.

### 6.5.1 Looking at Different Splits

This application shows the importance of variables other than age on blood pressure. KnowledgeSEEKER evaluates all variables for their effectiveness in describing low, normal, and high blood pressure, and constructs a ranked list of the most descriptive variables. To see another variable used to construct leaf nodes directly below the root node, you will go to another *split*. You can look at the other data elements that affect high blood pressure easily.

To see other splits, press the following button:

If you press this button, or alternatively choose **Reshape** and choose **Next Split**, you will see the next split. In this example, there are twelve different splits detected automatically. In order of importance, they are:

- *Age*
  Generalization:  Age was divided into three groups: (32–50), (51–62), and (63–72). From this split you can make a generalization that the older you are, the higher the likelihood you will have high blood pressure. You will see that 35.1% of people age 32–50 have low blood pressure, 13.6% of people age 51–62 have low blood pressure, and only 5.4% of people age 63–72 have low blood pressure.

- *Height*
  Generalization: Height was divided into two groups: (565–666) and (666–746). It appears that taller people have lower blood pressure! Certainly something you would not expect. You can see in Figure 6-4, 30.4% of those 565–666 have high blood pressure while only 8.2% of people 666 to 746 have high blood pressure.

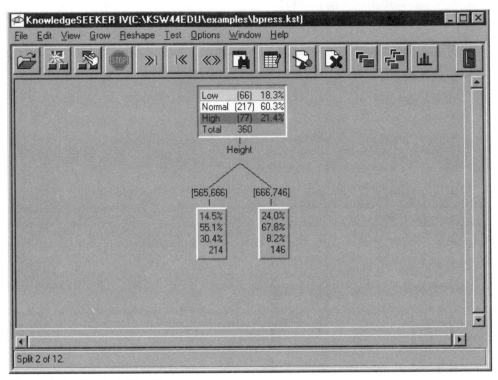

**Figure 6-4**  The height split.

- *Gender Male and Female*
  Generalization: The data suggests that women are more likely to have high blood pressure. Only 14.1% of men had high blood pressure in this study versus 30% of females. Of course, follow-up studies would be valuable to determine whether or not the study didn't just pick a lot of women with high blood pressure.

- *SportsActivity*
  Generalization: The tool grouped *SportsActivity* into two groups: (Daily, Weekly, Occasionally, Rarely) and (Never). Those people who had some form of sports activity were much more unlikely to have high blood pressure. Only 12.8% of active people had high blood pressure versus 30.2% of inactive people.

- *DrinkPattern*
  Generalization: The tool grouped *DrinkPattern* into two groups: (Regular, Occasionally, Former) and (Never). Those people who had some form of drinking activity were much more unlikely to have high blood pressure. Only 16.9% of drinkers had high blood pressure versus 34.4% of non-drinkers.

- *Income*

  Generalization: *Income* has been grouped into five groups: (3, 4, 5, 6, 7), (8, 9, 10), (11), (12, 13, 14, 15), and (16–98). The numbers indicate a percentage; for example, the people in group 3–7 have the lowest income levels, with 3 representing the lowest income, whereas the people in the 16–98 group have the highest incomes, with 98 representing the highest income. The lowest blood pressure was in group 11 and 16–98 with 2.6% and 5.4% having high blood pressure, respectively. The highest blood pressure was in group 3–7 with 39.5% blood pressure.

- *PorkLastWeek*

  Generalization: *PorkLastWeek* has been grouped into two groups: (0–4) and (5–7). You can see 63.6% of people in group 5–7 had low blood pressure versus only 16.9% of people in group 0–4.

- *SaltInFood*

  Generalization: *SaltInFood* has been grouped into two groups: (A Lot, Moderate) and (Very Little, None). You can see that 32.4% of people in the first group had high blood pressure versus only 16.7% of people in the second group.

- *Smoking*

  Generalization: *Smoking* has been grouped into two groups: (Regular) and (Occasional, Former, Never, ???). First notice that categories were grouped. We have regular smokers and all others (??? denotes unknown data). Not surprisingly, regular smokers appear to have higher blood pressure.

- *TypeOfMilk*

  Generalization: *TypeOfMilk* has been grouped into three groups: (Whole Milk, Powder, and No Milk), (2% Milk), and (Skim). People who regularly drink skim milk are the least likely to have high blood pressure. Only 10.5% of the people who drink skim milk have high blood pressure versus 17.7 for 2% milk and 30.9% for those who drink whole milk, powder, or no milk at all.

- *YearsEducation*

  Generalization: *YearsEducation* was divided into two groups, (1, 2, 3, 4) and (5). Those whose *YearsEducation* was in Category 5 had considerably higher blood pressure, 34% versus 19.4% for the other categories.

- *DeepFriedLastWeek*

  Generalization: *DeepFriedLastWeek* was divided into three categories (0), (1, 2, 3), and (4, 5, 6, 7). People in Category 0 were the most likely to have high blood pressure, with 28.7% of them having high blood pressure, versus 15.6% for (1, 2, 3) and 13.8% for (4, 5, 6, 7).

The generalizations made about each of the splits generated automatically for this data set provide food for thought about where further investigation should happen. Clearly, some of the information is what you would expect. For example, the older you are, the more likely you are to have high blood pressure, or the more physically active you are, the more likely you are to have lower blood pressure. Still, this data set presented some surprises, like the relationship of a person's height to their blood pressure.

### 6.5.2    Going to a Specific Split

If you want to go to a specific split, choose the *Go to Split* option from the Reshape menu. This will present a list of other splits that have been selected as the most influential.

The menu in Figure 6-5 will appear as shown on the next page. In our case, we select *smoking* from the menu and click on **OK.**

**Figure 6-5**   Selecting a split.

KnowledgeSEEKER decision trees are developed on the basis of statistical significance tests. Every time a potential split is calculated in KnowledgeSEEKER, a test of statistical significance is conducted to determine whether the effect that is captured by the partition (for example, a grouping of male and female heights) is reliable. The numbers you see on the right side of Figure 6-5 are representative of this statistical significance calculation. KnowledgeSEEKER relies on statistical theory and known probabilities of error to conduct these tests. This gives you more confidence in the results that are displayed in the decision tree.

### 6.5.3    Growing the Tree

The tree for smoking is only one level. We can grow the tree again. Choose the second-level node for regular smokers shown in Figure 6-6. (The second-level node named "regular" must be selected in order for this to work). Pull down the *Grow* menu and choose **Find Split**. You will see the screen shown in Figure 6-6.

KnowledgeSEEKER found that, among regular smokers, age is the most significant determinant of high blood pressure. Again, for regular smokers, age is a key indicator of whether you will have high blood pressure, with more than 56.7% of age 63–72 having high blood pressure versus 4.8% for people age 32–50.

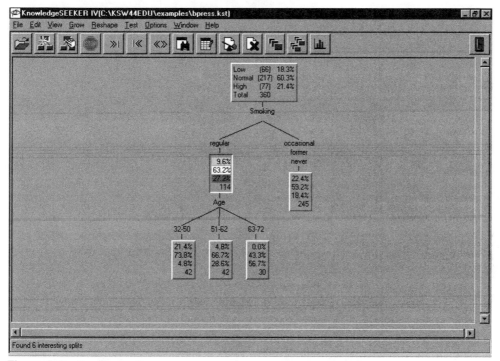

**Figure 6-6** Another split.

For regular smokers KnowledgeSEEKER found six splits in all.

The six splits KnowledgeSEEKER found for regular smokers are: *Age, Height, PorkLastWeek, DrinkPattern, Gender,* and *SaltConsumption.*

As an exercise, if you have loaded the CD-ROM included with this book, take a look at these splits and try to make some generalization about them.

More splits can be created. The tree can be built to as many levels as the data set (or memory constraints) will allow; however, the more levels you build, the less accurate the results will be. If there are several hundreds of variables, a tree can get quite complex.

### 6.5.4   Forcing a Split

Sometimes you will want to look at a variable that isn't automatically found. For example, I want to know how *PoultryLastWeek* affects high blood pressure. I can force this split, by pulling down the *Grow* menu and selecting **Force Split**.

You can see the variable list in Figure 6-7. Choose *PoultryLastWeek*, and press **OK**. For *PoultryLastWeek* there are eight values you can have: (0, 1, 2, 3, 4, 5, 6, 7). Sometimes it is easier to get significant values by grouping these values.

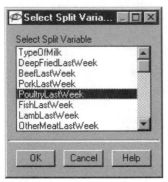

**Figure 6-7**   Forcing a split.

You will now see the Group Categories as shown in Figure 6-8.

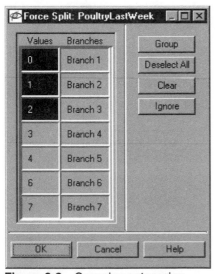

**Figure 6-8**   Grouping categories.

Select 0, 1, and 2 and press **Group**. This will group these three categories together. Select 3, 4, 5, 6, and 7 and press **Group**. In effect, you have defined two groups:

- Group 1 is [0, 1, 2] — having had poultry unknown or two or less times last week.
- Group 2 [3, 4, 5, 6, 7] — having had poultry three or more times last week.

Press **OK** and you will see the results of this split with the groupings you have created in Figure 6-9.

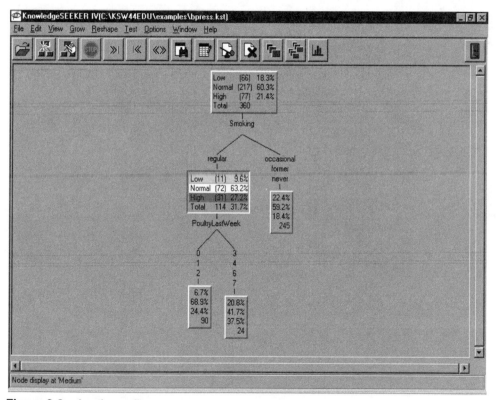

**Figure 6-9**  Another split.

In this case, the results were not conclusive. You might make a case that blood-pressure levels are less certain among regular smokers who eat more poultry than those who eat less poultry. However, when you get down to a sample size of 24, as shown on the bottom right leaf node of Figure 6-9, the results are speculative.

### 6.5.5    Validation

The results from one data set are interesting, but in data mining you always want to validate your results again. Angoss refers to other data sets as *Test Partitions*.

You can use another data set, the Test Partition, to verify the findings of the discovery. You can do so by choosing the menu in Figure 6-10 (although it is not available for the demo version).

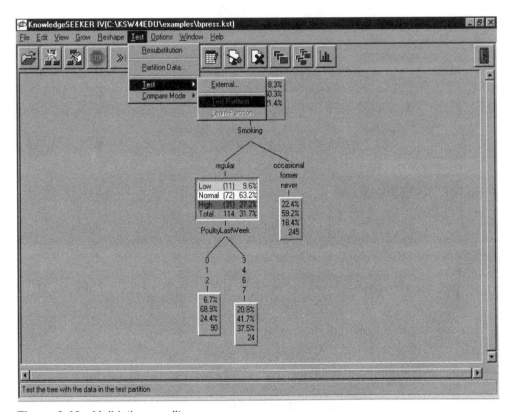

**Figure 6-10**    Validating a split.

### 6.5.6    Defining a New Scenario for a Study

We have just done a demo on finding candidate causes of high blood pressure. This was our dependent variable. Suppose you want to change what you are studying. For example, you want to study the differences in people who drink different amounts.

Choose *Edit* and select the **Change Dependent Variable** option from the menu.

You will see the variable list in Figure 6-11. Choose *DrinkPattern* and press **OK**. This effectively changes your *root node*. Your root node is now using the dependent variable, *DrinkPattern*, which has the values:

- Regular

- Occasional

- Former

- Never

Again, you can grow a new tree with *DrinkPattern* as the dependent variable. The mechanisms for using KnowledgeSEEKER remain the same, but the type of study we are doing changes dramatically. We are now studying drinking patterns and what affects this versus studying hypertension.

**Figure 6-11**  Changing dependent variables.

### 6.5.7  Growing a Tree Automatically

This chapter has demonstrated growing trees node by node. We can also automatically grow a tree. You can choose **Automatic** from the *Grow* menu. To stop this process, press the *Stop* icon (see Figure 6-12).

The process of identification of all the splits for the new root node is the same as for our previous example.

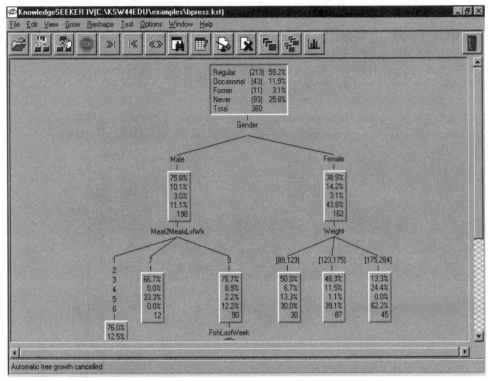

**Figure 6-12**   Growing a tree automatically.

### 6.5.8   Data Distribution

KnowledgeSEEKER has several ways to look at the layout of the data you are studying. First, you can view the raw data that you are mining. To do this, select the **View** menu and select **Data**. You will see a window like the one in Figure 6-13.

You can also look at the cross-tabular views of different data items in your set. To do this, choose the following icon:

Selecting this icon will open up the window in Figure 6-14.

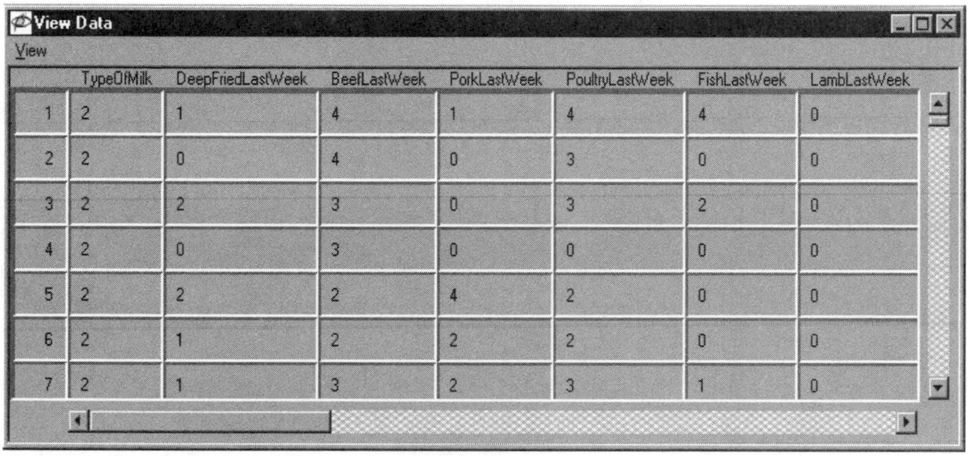


| | TypeOfMilk | DeepFriedLastWeek | BeefLastWeek | PorkLastWeek | PoultryLastWeek | FishLastWeek | LambLastWeek |
|---|---|---|---|---|---|---|---|
| 1 | 2 | 1 | 4 | 1 | 4 | 4 | 0 |
| 2 | 2 | 0 | 4 | 0 | 3 | 0 | 0 |
| 3 | 2 | 2 | 3 | 0 | 3 | 2 | 0 |
| 4 | 2 | 0 | 3 | 0 | 0 | 0 | 0 |
| 5 | 2 | 2 | 2 | 4 | 2 | 0 | 0 |
| 6 | 2 | 1 | 2 | 2 | 2 | 0 | 0 |
| 7 | 2 | 1 | 3 | 2 | 3 | 1 | 0 |

**Figure 6-13** A view of the hypertension data set.

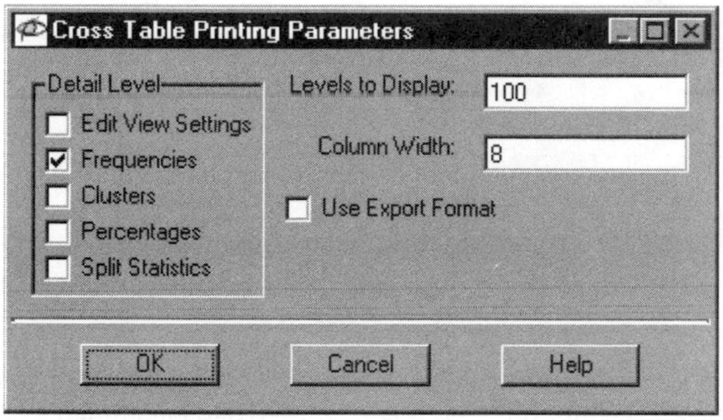


**Figure 6-14** Printing information on input fields.

If you leave the detail-level selection at frequencies and select the button **OK**, you will then see the window in Figure 6-15.

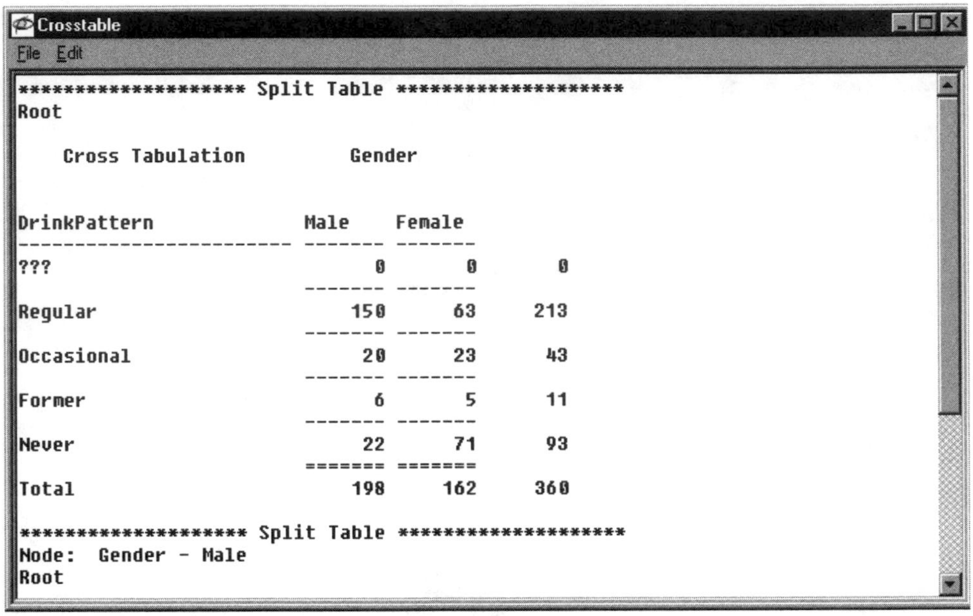

```
╔═══════════════════════════════════════════════════════════════════╗
║ 🖥 Crosstable                                              _ ▢ ✕  ║
║ File  Edit                                                         ║
╟───────────────────────────────────────────────────────────────────╢
║ ******************* Split Table *********************           ▲  ║
║ Root                                                               ║
║                                                                    ║
║    Cross Tabulation         Gender                                 ║
║                                                                    ║
║ DrinkPattern             Male    Female                            ║
║ ----------------------- ------- -------                            ║
║ ???                          0       0        0                    ║
║                         ------- -------                            ║
║ Regular                    150      63      213                    ║
║                         ------- -------                            ║
║ Occasional                  20      23       43                    ║
║                         ------- -------                            ║
║ Former                       6       5       11                    ║
║                         ------- -------                            ║
║ Never                       22      71       93                    ║
║                         ======= =======                            ║
║ Total                      198     162      360                    ║
║                                                                    ║
║ ******************* Split Table *********************           ▼  ║
║ Node:  Gender - Male                                               ║
║ Root                                                               ║
╚═══════════════════════════════════════════════════════════════════╝
```

**Figure 6-15**   A cross-tab report for the input Age, on hypertension.

## 6.6  Prediction

You now have a model that can be used for prediction. In other words, given a person's profile (are they a regular smoker, what's their age, how many times a week do they eat beef), KnowledgeSEEKER predicts the person's blood-pressure levels. The process of using decision trees for prediction is not automatic, but KnowledgeSEEKER allows you to save out all splits of variables to a file. The importance of each split is also calculated as a percentage. Using this information, it is possible to produce rules that will help in prediction. The *Node Detail* from the **Reshape** command gives you more information that can be used for predictions.

Decision-tree approaches have historically been used more for model understanding than for automating prediction, but they can be used for this purpose.

## 6.7  Summary

This chapter has shown a successful decision-tree-based analytical product, Knowledge-SEEKER.  While this product has many more features, this chapter discussed the general process of how it works.

A tool like this can be used across different industries. In fact, when you opened the blood pressure set, you may have noticed other data sets for banking, telecommunications, and insurance claims. Try them out. One benefit of a tool like the one shown here is that data will automatically be grouped in optimal ways. For example, the variable *Income* has been grouped into five groups: (3, 4, 5, 6, 7), (8, 9, 10), (11), (12, 13, 14,1 5), and (16–98). This grouping characteristic is especially valuable when you are looking at market-segmentation studies.

Creating decision trees for data sets does more than confirm what you might already know. It will help you discover brand-new insights, and will let you examine new trends and patterns.

# A Look at RightPoint DataCruncher

$\mathbf{T}$his chapter outlines the use of RightPoint's DataCruncher. A demonstration version of this product contained in the CD-ROM in the back of this book is used for the exercises.

The chapter is organized as follows:

- Section 7.1    Introduction
- Section 7.2    Data Preparation
- Section 7.3    Defining the Study
- Section 7.4    Read Your Data/Build a Discovery Model
- Section 7.5    Understanding the Model
- Section 7.6    Perform Prediction
- Section 7.7    Summary

## 7.1  Introduction

RightPoint Software, Inc., formerly DataMind Corporation, sells the DataCruncher data-mining tool as a module of RightPoint's Real-Time Marketing Suite for real-time marketing. Like several other companies mentioned in the first version of the book, RightPoint has taken its data-mining expertise and applied it to a specific application area, namely, to use data-mining models and business rules to deliver highly tailored 1:1 marketing messages to individuals as they interact with call centers, the web, email, fax, and other customer touchpoints. To get a more detailed description of RightPoint's real-time marketing application and how it applies data mining to an industry problem, refer to Chapter 8, "Industry Applications of Data Mining." This chapter specifically discusses the DataCruncher data-mining tool.

RightPoint DataCruncher is a client-server data-mining engine with the capacity to analyze large volumes of data found in today's warehouses. The DataCruncher has features including the ability to connect directly with many of today's leading relational database technologies, as well as data-mining *assistants,* to help build models for common marketing-oriented data-mining studies. RightPoint has added technology and algorithms that solve marketing problems.

The demonstration version of DataCruncher included in this book's CD-ROM has a limited functionality. It has two of the data-mining assistants: classification and clustering. The full version of RightPoint DataCruncher has assistants for performing classification, clustering, and association, as well as custom assistants for churn, cross-selling, direct mail, up-selling, product bundling, and customer segmentation.

To follow the data-mining study discussed in this chapter, install the demonstration version of RightPoint DataCruncher. Instructions for installation are in Appendix B.

### 7.1.1  RightPoint's Technology

Rightpoint has included a suite of data-mining algorithms with its product, as is the trend of all the leading commercially available data-mining tools. RightPoint makes use of neural network and statistical algorithms, as well several algorithms based on a unique approach to data mining, which RightPoint named the Agent Network Technology.

The Agent Network Technology was developed in France by Dr. Khai Min Pham early in 1990. This method of model building treats all data elements, or categories of defined data elements, as agents that are connected to each other in a significant way. The early developments of this technology are discussed in *Intelligent Hybrid Systems*, by S. Goonatilake and S. Khebal. In this book, the technology is described as a *polymorphic hybrid* approach, meaning it takes on the traits of different algorithms depending on how it is used.

The Agent Network Technology algorithm is:

- Extremely good at describing what factors are most influential in predicting an outcome capable of explaining reasons for predictions.
- Good at sorting the relevant from the irrelevant fields.
- Quick.
- Less memory-intensive than more traditional techniques like regression and neural networks.

RightPoint has also created a product called Real-Time Miner that dynamically creates models that can be understood by the DataCruncher. This is another module of their real-time marketing suite that allows users to keep track of information about offers that are accepted during marketing campaigns over the web or call center. The Real-Time Miner can then dynamically predict whether a particular offer is likely to be accepted by any customer at any specific time. The models are built on-the-fly, without the need for any historical data up front. As people call in through the call center or interact with the web, their responses are tracked and marketing offers are intelligently targeted to optimize success. This dynamic learning technology is an area of continued research.

### 7.1.2   How RightPoint Is Being Used

RightPoint's base data-mining technology is resold by Red Brick Systems (acquired by Informix Software) and is used by more than 50 large corporations, including AT&T, Norwest Bank, Franco-Belges Malting, ADP, and 360 Communications.

The RightPoint Real-Time Marketing Suite is used by many of the largest financial and telecommunication companies, including GTE, American Express, and Halifax Bank. Other companies that have announced reselling arrangements with RightPoint include Fair Isaac and Edify Corporation.

## 7.2   Data Preparation

The demonstration in this chapter can be used to improve customer retention. DataCruncher helps you understand the aspects of individual customer behavior that can lead to churn, or customer attrition. Specifically, this demonstration is a case study of a fictitious cellular service provider's efforts to identify the factors that influence churn, and understand their relative importance.

The data set used in this chapter is an example of detailed information about your current and churned customers. The sample data will provide you with this information for current and former cellular customers:

- Demographic information, such as age, occupation, residence.
- Subscription characteristics, such as duration and kind of services, and rate plan.
- Usage characteristics, such as call volume and charges, for both current and past periods.
- Churn specifics, such as when subscriptions terminated and why.

The data we will mine during this example reside in a file named churn.txt, which is installed by default in the Example directory under the DataCruncher installation directory. Take a look at the description of the fields in churn.txt that are provided in Table 7-1.

Notice that a significant proportion of the data describes both current and historical phone usage. This kind of data helps you detect trends in usage characteristics, in order to determine whether they might be indicators of churning.

AVG_LENGTH_CALLS_1-3M and AVG_LENGTH_CALLS_4-6M quantify the increase or decrease in call minutes since the last quarter and the quarter before it.

EXCESS_CHARGE_1-3M and EXCESS_CHARGE_4-6M quantify the increase or decrease in excess charges since the last quarter and the quarter before it.

Similar trends for peak minute usage and roaming call minutes are quantified by NBR_PEAK_MIN_1-3M, NBR_PEAK_MIN_4-6M, NBR_ROAM_CALLS_1-3M, and NBR_ROAM_CALLS_4-6M.

In the case of churned customers, the field values reflect conditions that existed at the time the customer left. For example, AVG_LENGTH_CALLS_0M is the average length of calls the month the customer churned. And AVG_LENGTH_CALLS_1-3M is the average length of calls made one through three months before the customer churned. In the case of non-churned customers, values such as these are relative to the current month.

Table 7-1 shows the elements.

**Table 7-1**　Data on Churn Management Campaign

| Column Name | Values | Explanation |
| --- | --- | --- |
| CUSTID | Integer, unique | Customer identification number |
| REGION | South, MidWest, South, NorthEast, West | Regions described by this cellular company |
| CITY | City names | Cities in the state of Colorado |
| MARITAL_STATUS | Single, Married, Widowed, Divorced | Marital status of customer |
| NBR_CHILDREN | Integer | Number of children |
| OCCUPATION | Professional,Skilled, Manager, Unskilled, Executive | Description of type of occupation |
| GENDER | Males, Female | Gender |
| HOME | Rent, Own | Did customer own or rent residence? |
| MO_EXPENSES | Integer | Monthly expenses of customer |
| MO_INCOME | Integer | Monthly income of customer |
| LENGTH_STAY | Vlow, Low, Medium, High, Very High | How long the customer has been with us, segmenting the duration into five ranges |

*(continued)*

**Table 7-1**   Data on Churn Management Campaign

| Column Name | Values | Explanation |
| --- | --- | --- |
| VISA_LIMIT | Vlow, Low, Medium, High, Very High | What is customer's credit limit, segmenting the values into five ranges |
| CUST_SEGMENT | A,B,C,D,E,F,G | Specific customer's segments, based on studies by cellular company |
| AVG_LENGTH_CALLS_4-6M | Vlow, Low, Medium, High, Very High | Average length of calls four to six months ago |
| AVG_LENGTH_CALLS_1-3M | Vlow, Low, Medium, High, Very High | Average length of calls one to three months ago |
| AVG_LENGTH_CALLS_OM | Vlow, Low, Medium, High, Very High | Average length of calls this month |
| LENGTH_STAY_OBL | Integer | How long is customer obligated to stay? |
| OBLIGATION_END | Integer | When is obligation over? Negative number indicates contractual obligation over by x days. |
| DAYS_PREFERRED | Integer | Number of days a preferred member |
| EXCESS_CHARGE_0M | Vlow, Low, Medium, High, Very High | How many excess charges has customer made this month? |
| EXCESS_CHARGE_1-3M | Vlow, Low, Medium, High, Very High | How many excess charges has customer made one to three months ago? |
| EXCESS_CHARGE_4-6M | Vlow, Low, Medium, High, Very High | How many excess charges has customer made four to six months ago? |
| MOBILE_TYPE | Car_Secure, Portable | Type of mobile phone |
| NBR_EXTRA_FEATURES | None, 1, 2_to_3, 4Plus | How many extra features does customer have? |
| RATE_PLAN | Standard, Business, Basic, Premium | Type of rate plan |
| CALL_WAIT | Yes, No | Does customer have call waiting? |
| CALL_ID | Yes, No | Does customer have caller id? |
| LONG_DIST_CAR | A, B, C | Who is long distance carrier? |
| MONTH_UPDATED | Integer | Date demographics last updated |

*(continued)*

**Table 7-1**  Data on Churn Management Campaign

| Column Name | Values | Explanation |
| --- | --- | --- |
| %_DEM_KNOWN | Integer | Percent demographic information known |
| MONTH_UPDATED | Integer | When was information last updated? |
| ACC_HIST_NON_CELL | Integer | Customer history on non-cellular products |
| CREDIT_RATE | Integer | Credit rating, one to 100 |
| NBR_PEAK_MIN | Integer | Number of peak minutes this month |
| NBR_PEAK_MIN_1-3M | Integer | Number of peak minutes one to three months ago |
| NBR_PEAK_MIN_4-6M | Integer | Number of peak minutes four to six months ago |
| NBR_ROAM_CALLS | Integer | Number of roaming calls this month |
| NBR_ROAM_CALLS_1-3M | Integer | Number of roaming calls one to three months ago |
| NBR_ROAM_CALLS_4-6M | Integer | Number of roaming calls four to six months ago |
| TOT_$_SPENT | Integer | Total dollars customer has spent with company |
| AVG_OCC_$ | Vlow, Low, Medium, High, Very High | Average OCC dollars spent |
| AVG_PEAK_$ | Vlow, Low, Medium, High, Very High | Average peak dollars spent |
| AVG_OFF_PEAK_$ | Vlow, Low, Medium, High, Very High | Average off-peak dollars spent |
| USAGE_DIF_1M | Integer | Change in usage levels over one month, a percentage |
| USAGE_DIF_2M | Integer | Change in usage levels over two months, a percentage |
| USAGE_DIF_3M | Integer | Change in usage levels over three months, a percentage |
| USAGE_DIF_4M | Integer | Change in usage levels over four months, a percentage |
| USAGE_DIF_5M | Integer | Change in usage levels over five months, a percentage |

*(continued)*

**Table 7-1**    Data on Churn Management Campaign

| Column Name | Values | Explanation |
|---|---|---|
| USAGE_DIF_6M | Integer | Change in usage levels over six months, a percentage |
| MAX_POS_INCR | Integer | Maximum increase in usage over six months, a percentage |
| MAX_NEG_INCR | Integer | Maximum decrease in usage over six months, a percentage |
| VARIANCE | Integer | Largest variance in activity levels over 6 months, a percentage |
| YR_END | 97, 98, 99 | Year customer closed account |
| MONTH_END | Jan, Feb, Mar, Apr, May, Jun, Jul, Aug, Sep, Oct, Nov, Dec | Month customer closed account |
| DAY_OF_WK | Mon, Tue, Wed, Th, Fri, Sat, Sun | Day of Week customer closed account |
| DAY_ENDED | Integer | What day, 1–365, did customer close? |
| REASON_CLOSED | Cost, Delinquent, Comp, Unknown, Service | Reason customer closed account |
| REASON_CLOSED1 | Comp, Not_Comp | If customer closed, was it for competitive reasons? |
| ACCOUNT_STATUS | Open, Closed | Of profitable customers, those that have remained active or closed during the last month |
| CLOSED | Y if closed; nothing otherwise | Flag for closed accounts |

The field *Account_Status* is the dependent variable to be used in this study. It indicates whether someone has kept their account open or closed over the last month.

This data set, like many data sets used in marketing campaigns, requires a better understanding of *derived fields*. Derived fields are those that do not exist in any database; instead, they are created by performing calculations using other data fields. For example, the field *Variance* defines the maximum variance, as a percentage, in the usage levels of a customer. This is not likely to be a field defined in a transactional system, but would be derived from a mathematical calculation using other fields. There is a fair amount of data preparation involved in creating this data set.

RightPoint will characterize some of the inputs in the data set as discrete, like *Avg_Peak_$*, which specifies the average peak dollars sent into ranges of low, medium, and high. It is possible to take number values and "bin" them into these ranges using DataCruncher, so that some of the data preparation is done by the tool.

## 7.3  Defining the Study

In this section, we will step through a process of defining an example of a churn-management campaign. You can follow along and do it yourself by installing RightPoint's software as explained in Appendix B.

### 7.3.1  Defining the Goal

In order to start using RightPoint, it is useful to define the goal of your study. The demonstration in this chapter profiles whether someone has responded to a direct-mail campaign. This goal can be stated as:

*Profile and predict the set of customers who are likely to churn.*

With its many competitive pressures, finding and retaining customers is of vital importance in the telecommunications industry. Many customers, sometimes 30% of them, churn even before the cost of recruiting them can be recovered. Acquiring new customers is significantly more costly than retaining existing customers. Reducing churn by even a few percentage points can result in significant savings.

When you mine your data, you not only discover the factors that have an important influence on churning, you also can use the prediction powers of the model to prevent your profitable customers from leaving. Data mining helps you predict which customers are likely to churn so that proactive measures can be taken to keep them, and it also helps you determine whether a potential new customer might be a churn risk.

### 7.3.2  Choosing a Dependent Variable

The field named ACCOUNT_STATUS is chosen as the dependent variable for this study. It contains values that indicate whether a customer is a current customer (OPEN) or a churned customer (CLOSED) as shown in Figure 7-1. All records you mine in churn studies should contain a churn indicator field. When you mine your records, DataCruncher will measure the influence of values in other fields on the churn indicator field, and you will discover which factors are most likely to be associated with customer loyalty and with churning.

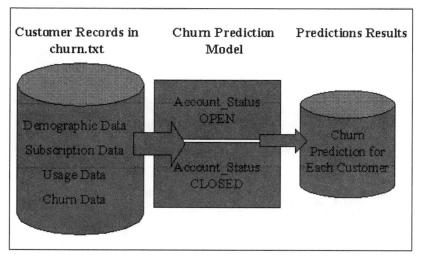

**Figure 7-1**   Choosing a dependent variable for a study.

To understand factors related to churn and predict which customers are high churn risks, a model is generated using the ACCOUNT_STATUS as the dependent variable. The generated churn prediction model predicts not only which customers are likely to churn but scores them to determine a way to rank, for example, the top 10% of those likely to churn.

### 7.3.3   Setting Up a Study

Do not limit yourself when selecting data for mining. Although data mining might reaffirm your knowledge, one of its benefits is discovering significant and previously unknown data interrelationships. Previously data, such as demographic and subscription data, were chosen to determine whether they have any impact on churning. No assumptions about the importance of these data for churn prediction were made. The data were chosen to assess their value in churn prediction. Initial studies will help you identify data that can be ignored in subsequent studies and suggest additional data that might be of interest.

After you have made a list of the kinds of information you think would be interesting to mine, decide how to obtain the data, and prepare the data for mining. For this tutorial, data preparation has already been conducted for you, resulting in the records in churn.txt. In truth, the data preparation can be the longest part of the data-mining cycle.

### 7.3.4    Starting RightPoint

After installing RightPoint as shown in Appendix B, you can automatically start up RightPoint DataCruncher by double-clicking on the icon with that name. When you start up, you will be asked to create or open a study.

1. Start DataCruncher Client as you would any Windows application, usually by using the Start menu. Select RightPoint from the Program list and click DataCruncher Client.

**Figure 7-2**    Starting up.

2. When the initial DataCruncher dialog box appears (see Figure 7-3) click Create New Study.

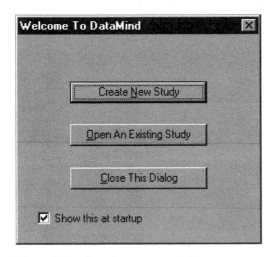

**Figure 7-3**    Creating a new study.

3. When the Create New Study dialog box appears, you will see the Figure 7-4. Click Classification Assistant.

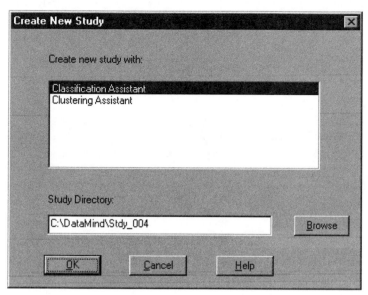

**Figure 7-4**   Using the Classification Assistant.

4. The Classification Assistant, which appears to the left of the Control Center, contains a series of commands used to progress through your study (see Figure 7-5).

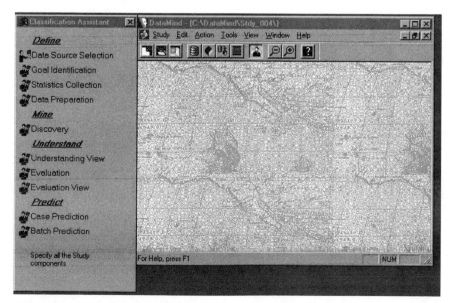

**Figure 7-5**   The DataCruncher main screen.

Notice also the icons that appear in front of each command. These icons provide you with information about which commands to use:

 Identifies the next command you are likely to use. The Assistant is holding a green flag.

 Identifies a command available for your use. The Assistant is holding a yellow flag.

 Identifies a command that is not available to use. The Assistant is holding a red flag.

 Identifies a command that has already been used. The arms of the Assistant are raised.

Take a moment to pass your cursor over the Classification Assistant's commands as shown in Figure 7-5, noticing how text explaining the effect of each command appears at the bottom of the Assistant.

The Control Center to the right of the Assistant provides you with several things:

• Across the top of the Control Center are several menus.

• Beneath the menus is the graphical toolbar. Pass your cursor over each icon in the toolbar to find out what each button does. Click the Save Study icon now to save your new study.

• The large area beneath the toolbar is a viewing area in which various images appear as you progress through your study, so you can visualize the elements in your study and the progress you have made.

• At the bottom of the viewing area is a status bar, where informational messages appear from time to time. You can press F1 when the Control Center is active to access online help topics. Click the assistant's menu, the informational area below it, or the Control Center itself, then press F1 to obtain information about any of these items. You can also use the Contents command on the Help menu to access online help topics. Try using one of these approaches for retrieving help to familiarize yourself with help information.

When you are using the various DataCruncher dialog boxes, click the Help button or press F1 to retrieve information describing the dialog box.

Now you are ready to use the Classification Assistant's Define commands to indicate the data source you want to mine and how you want to mine it.

### 7.3.5    Setting Up Data Specifications

Follow these steps to set up data specifications for your study:

1. Click Data Source Selection on the Assistant's menu.
2. The Table Definition dialog box that appears lets you specify a data source to mine. Because the sample data source we will use for this tutorial, churn.txt, is an ASCII file, leave ASCII selected.
3. Then, identify the name and location of the data source. By default, churn.txt resides in a directory named Example, under the DataCruncher installation directory, for example, C:\DataMind\Example\churn.txt.
4. Enter the data source information in the File Name field, or use the Browse button to browse for the file.
5. Notice that the Separator field contains Tab by default. Leave the Separator default setting as it is, since churn.txt is a tab-delimited file.
6. In the Fields Definition area, ensure that there is a check mark in the In First Row box, because the first row of churn.txt contains field names (see Figure 7-6).

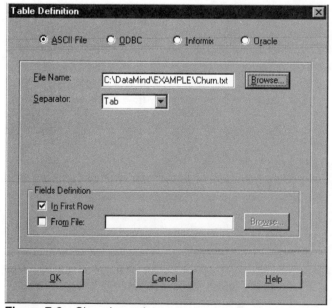

**Figure 7-6**   Choosing a data source.

7. The From File check box is used to identify a file called a header file, which we
   will use at a later time. For now, leave the From File box empty and click OK.

8. The next dialog box lets you specify a sample, or a percentage of data source
   records to mine, by specifying a number in the Samples field (see Figure 7-7).

   Leave the value of 100 in the Samples field. We will mine 100% of the records
   in churn.txt to generate a churn prediction model. Click OK to continue.

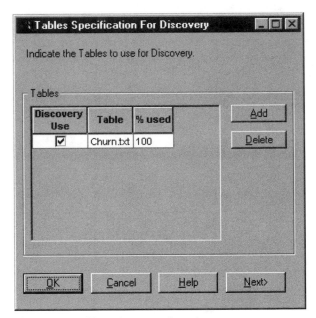

**Figure 7-7**  Choosing sampling size.

9. When you return to the Control Center you will notice three images (see Figure
   7-8).

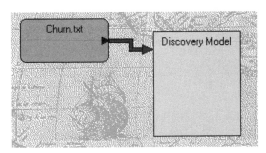

**Figure 7-8**  Study objects.

These images depict study objects. The Churn.txt image represents the data source you are mining. Data sources are **table** objects. The Discovery Model icon represents the prediction **model** you will soon generate. The arrow joining the data source and model represents a Discovery **task**. A task is a series of intermediate steps in the modeling process. DataCruncher conducts different kinds of tasks at different points in your study, as you will see. The Discovery task is the task you will soon run to generate the churn prediction model.

10. Click the churn.txt icon, then click your right mouse button. A popup menu appears, containing commands that operate on table objects. Click View to review the records in churn.txt as shown in Figure 7-9.

DataCruncher provides you with information about your study objects in what are known as views. The Table View simply lists the contents of a study table, in this case our data source. Click Close when you are finished exploring the records in churn.txt.

| | CUSTID | REGION | CITY | MARITAL_STATUS | NBR_CHILDRI |
|---|---|---|---|---|---|
| 1 | 1124 | NORTHEAST | COPE | Single | 4 |
| 2 | 1125 | NORTHEAST | COPE | Single | 4 |
| 3 | 1131 | NORTHEAST | KIM | Single | 1 |
| 4 | 1135 | NORTHEAST | KIM | Single | 1 |
| 5 | 1142 | WEST | HUGO | Married | 4 |
| 6 | 1143 | WEST | HUGO | Married | 4 |
| 7 | 1179 | NORTHEAST | DENVER | Single | 1 |
| 8 | 1180 | SOUTH | DENVER | Single | 1 |
| 9 | 1197 | NORTHEAST | STEAMBOAT SPRINGS | Single | |
| 10 | 1198 | NORTHEAST | STEAMBOAT SPRINGS | Single | |
| 11 | 1211 | NORTHEAST | MONTE VISTA | Married | 1 |
| 12 | 1212 | WEST | MONTE VISTA | Married | 1 |
| 13 | 1233 | NORTHEAST | LA JUNTA | Single | 2 |
| 14 | 1234 | NORTHEAST | LA JUNTA | Single | 2 |
| 15 | 1244 | NORTHEAST | GENOA | Single | 4 |
| 16 | 1245 | NORTHEAST | GENOA | Single | 4 |

**Figure 7-9**  The table view.

11. Now click Goal Identification on the Classification Assistant's menu. Recall that the churn indicator is the data source field that contains values indicating whether a customer has churned. In this case, the churn indicator field is ACCOUNT_STATUS, so pull down the Output Field list and click ACCOUNT_STATUS (see Figure 7-10).

    The churn indicator field is also known as an output field. An output field is the field that contains the values you want to be able to predict.

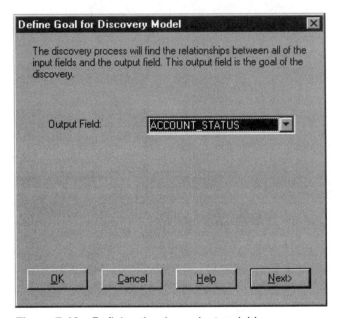

**Figure 7-10**   Defining the dependent variable.

12. Click OK, then click Customer Statistics Collection on the Assistant's menu. DataCruncher conducts a task known as a Statistics task, as you can see from the dialog box that appears briefly while the task is running. During this task, DataCruncher collects value information from churn.txt so that you can specify how you want the values mined. Default binning is also performed during the task.

13. When the Statistics task is finished, click Data Preparation on the Classification Assistant's menu. The main Fields Editor dialog box, the Field Properties dialog, appears. Although DataCruncher has several editors you can use to manage your study elements, the Fields Editor is often the only editor you will ever need to

use. The Fields Editor lets you set up field specifications that indicate how you want your data source values mined.

14. Maximize the Fields Editor dialog box so that all the information in it is readily visible. Notice that the table, or grid, that appears in the upper left contains a row for each column in churn.txt (see Figure 7-11).

| | Name | Type | Bins | Use |
|---|---|---|---|---|
| 1 | CUSTID | Number | Y | Input |
| 2 | REGION | String | - | Input |
| 3 | CITY | String | - | Ignored |
| 4 | MARITAL_STATUS | String | - | Input |
| 5 | NBR_CHILDREN | Number | N | Input |
| 6 | OCCUPATION | String | - | Input |
| 7 | GENDER | String | - | Input |
| 8 | HOME | String | - | Input |
| 9 | MO_EXPENSES | Number | Y | Input |
| 10 | MO_INCOME | Number | Y | Input |
| 11 | LENGTH_STAY | String | - | Input |
| 12 | VISA_LIMIT | String | - | Input |

**Figure 7-11** Data definition.

The **Name** column contains the data-source column name, known as a study field.

The **Type** column indicates whether the field contains values that are numbers or strings (collections of alphanumeric characters).

The **Bins** column indicates whether numeric values have been binned. Recall that your default binning is set up so that values in fields containing more than 20 unique values are binned in 5 equidistributed bins.

The **Use** column indicates how a field is to be mined. Currently, this column contains either "Input," "Output," or "Ignored." Input indicates that you want to mine a field's data. Output indicates the one field used as the dependent variable (in this case ACCOUNT_STATUS). Ignored indicates you want to ignore values in a field while mining. By default, DataCruncher ignores fields containing more than 100 unique values, as the CITY field indicates. The reason DataCruncher initially ignores fields with more than 100 values is because too many unique field/value pairs will make the process of understanding the model complex, and including these fields is better left to the user's discretion (you can easily change the default, which we do in this study for the CITY field).

15. CUSTID is currently a used, binned field. We will make CUSTID an identifier field instead of a used field. Identifier fields uniquely identify individual records in the data you mine. The values in identifier fields are ignored when a model is generated, but are useful for mapping prediction results back to individual records. To make CUSTID an identifier field, click in the CUSTID row, then pull down the Use list and select Identifier (see Figure 7-12).

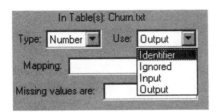

**Figure 7-12** Identifiers.

DataCruncher has binned CUSTID values because there are over 20 of them. Because you want to retain unique individual values, we will unbin CUSTID. Simply remove the check from the Bins box in the binning area to unbin CUS-TID as shown in Figure 7-13.

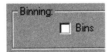

**Figure 7-13** Turning off binning.

16. Change CITY from an ignored field to a used field by clicking in its row, then selecting Used from the Use pull-down list. For our churn study, we are interested in whether subscribers who live in particular cities are likely to churn, so we will mine the values in CITY.

17. Now click the MARITAL_STATUS row and look at the display of this field's values on the right (see Figure 7-14).

| | Value | # Records | % Records |
|---|---|---|---|
| 1 | -Missing- | 6 | 1.37% |
| 2 | Married | 263 | 60.18% |
| 3 | Single | 139 | 31.81% |
| 4 | Widowed | 29 | 6.64% |

**Figure 7-14** Missing values.

Notice that six records contain no value in the MARITAL_STATUS field. By default, DataCruncher ignores missing values when generating a model. If you are interested in determining the importance of missing values, you can specify a value to use for missing values. Enter "Missing" in the "Missing values are" field so that the six missing values are mined together as a group (see Figure 7-15).

**Figure 7-15**  Defining default for missing values.

18. Also specify "Missing" for these fields:
NBR_CHILDREN,
EXCESS_CHARGE_0M,
EXCESS_CHARGE_1-3M, and
EXCESS_CHARGE_4-6M.

19. Click the MO_EXPENSES row and briefly review its bins (see Figure 7-16).

| | Label | Low | High | Width | # Records | % Records |
|---|---|---|---|---|---|---|
| 1 | [514,884] | 514 | 884 | 370 | 87 | 19.91% |
| 2 | (884,1158] | 884 | 1158 | 274 | 87 | 19.91% |
| 3 | (1158,1884] | 1158 | 1884 | 726 | 88 | 20.14% |
| 4 | (1884,2685] | 1884 | 2685 | 801 | 87 | 19.91% |
| 5 | (2685,11152] | 2685 | 11152 | 8467 | 88 | 20.14% |

**Figure 7-16**  Choosing a binning strategy.

The Label column tells you the range of values in each bin. In Figure 7-16 the range [514, 884] inludes all numbers in the range of 514 to 884, including the numbers 514 and 884 themselves. The range (884, 1158] includes all the numbers from 884 to 1158, excluding 884. The "(" character specifies that 884 was excluded. If you wanted to, you could change the bin labels to other descriptions, such as "High" and "Low," but for this study we will retain the bin ranges as labels.

20. Scroll down to the end of the fields list and make the following fields ignored fields: YR_END, MONTH_END, DAY_OF_WK, DAY_ENDED, REASON_CLOSED, REASON_CLOSED1, and CLOSED, as shown in Figure 7-17. These fields contain information only for customers who have churned.

In this study, we want to compare churned and current customers, so these fields are not of interest. Also, make the field CLOSED as Ignored, because this field contains only one value.

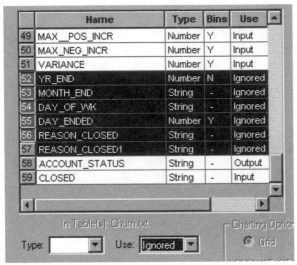

**Figure 7-17**   Ignoring fields.

21. Now spend a few minutes reviewing more of the values in your study fields. First click in the VISA_LIMIT row. Notice that the value "middle levelF" appears in one of the records. Typographical errors such as this one are easy to detect using the Fields Editor. For this study, we will not correct this value, but in a real data mining study, you would want to ensure that the data you mine is as clean as you can make it so your results are as reliable as they can be.

22. Now click the REGION row, then click Bars in the Charting Options area to review the values in bar chart form (see Figure 7-18).

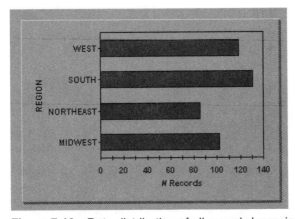

**Figure 7-18**   Data distribution of all records by region.

23. To review the distribution of REGION values for only churned customers, pull down the list in the Charting Options area and select CLOSED (see Figure 7-19).

**Figure 7-19** Data distributions for specific outcomes.

Notice that more than half of the churned customers subscribed to cellular services in the NORTHEAST region (see Figure 7-20).

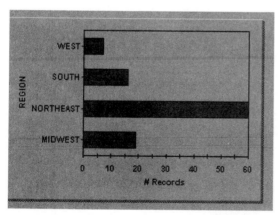

**Figure 7-20** Data distribution for REGION field, illustrating the distribution of churned customers by region.

24. Now contrast values for churned and current customers in these fields: CUST_SEG and USAGE_DIFF_1M through USAGE_DIFF_6M. Although the exact predictive importance of the values in your study fields will not be known until you generate a model, you have already identified some potentially interesting relationships.

25. Continue to explore the values in churn.txt as long as you like. When you are done, click Close to leave the Fields Editor and proceed with your study.

## 7.4  Read Your Data/Build a Discovery Model

The discovery process is put in motion by a mouse click.

Before we generate our first model, we will save the field specifications we just set up in a header file so that they can be reused in other studies. Click the churn.txt icon, then the right mouse button. On the popup menu, click Save Fields. In the dialog box that appears, enter the name churn1.fld for your header file, then click Save. Later, you will see how easy it is to use the header file in another study to re-use field specifications.

You can also start the discovery process with the icon below.

**Figure 7-21**  Running the discovery process.

Click Discovery to generate a churn-prediction model.

DataCruncher runs the Discovery task, which generates a Discovery model. Because the sample data source contains relatively few records (437) with relatively few columns, model generation takes only a few seconds.

The length of the discovery process depends on the number of input parameters, output categories, the number of rows of data, and the number of unique values within the data.

A spooler is started to read the data and build a model for you. This spooler runs in the background. For large volumes of data, the RightPoint DataCruncher is used to build models. In the case of the DataCruncher product, it actually runs on an NT or UNIX server in the background.

RightPoint's Agent Network Technology is used in the discovery process. In the full product version this is augmented by statistics and a neural network algorithm.

## 7.5  Understanding the Model

The discovery process will result in the generation of a model. After the model has been generated, click Understanding View to review information about your model. Once again, DataCruncher runs a task, this time the Understanding task. When the task has finished, the Understanding View window appears, as shown in Figure 7-22.

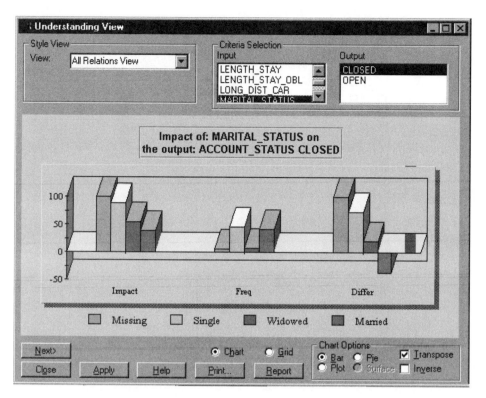

**Figure 7-22**   Understanding View window, illustrating the influence of MARITAL_STATUS on whether someone had churned (ACCOUNT_STATUS *Closed*).

1. Click on the "Grid" radio button as shown in Figure 7-22. In the Criteria Selection window, for Input Select REGION. Click Apply.

   Scroll through the rows and notice how few records are contained in the REGION WEST. The **frequency** (Freq) value tells you the percent of records for churned (CLOSED) and current (OPEN) customers that are associated with a city. The number of records is indicated by the occurrence (Occur) column. Only seven records, or 6.86% of churned customer records, contain the value WEST in the REGION column.

   Now notice the **impact** values. Impact is a metric that tells you the predictive importance of a field value. Impact values range from 0 to 100. For studies with two outcomes (in this case OPEN and CLOSED) impact values over 60 or 70 accompany predictive criteria. In this case, the maximum impact of 100 signals very predictive values. An impact of 50 is neutral; it has no predictive value.

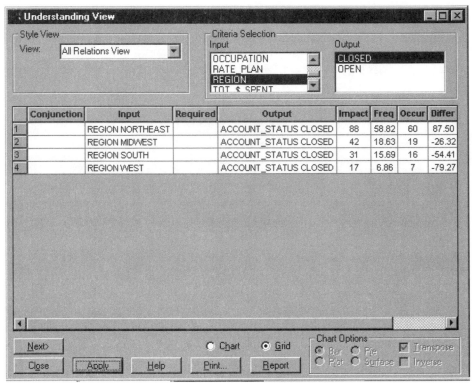

**Figure 7-23**  REGION's impact on ACCOUNT_STATUS CLOSED.

Impacts of 0 to 30 indicate a strong negative influence; for example, custom-ers in the West region are unlikely to churn. While all the churn.txt records for customers who live in Idaho Springs are for churned customers, there are too few records for Idaho Springs to conclude its actual predictive importance. You would want to mine more records for individuals from region West before draw-ing conclusions about its predictive value.

A frequently asked question for those who look at this for the first time is:

### How do you know if an input is correlated to an output?

The relative importance an input has on an output is determined by two col-umns, frequency and impact. High frequency and high impact together indicate a strong correlation between the output and the input criteria. In the example given above, REGION NORTHEAST has both a high impact (88) and a high frequency (58.82), so it could be said there is a strong relationship. In statistics there is a metric referred to as *correlation*. This metric is also calculated in the full version of the product and would also show this relationship.

Click the Advanced Understanding View Window so you can obtain more information about the LENGTH_STAY field. Select LENGTH_STAY in the Input list, and click Apply (see Figure 7-24).

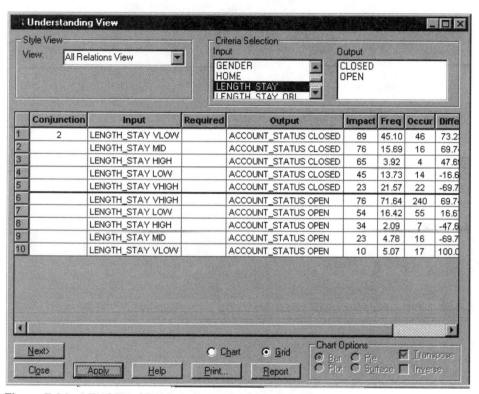

**Figure 7-24**  LENGTH_STAY's impact on ACCOUNT_STATUS.

As shown in Figure 7-24, almost half the customers who churned were very-short-term subscribers (LENGTH_STAY VLOW), while almost three-quarters of the current customers are very-long-term customers.

2. Notice the number 2 in the Conjunction column for very-short-term churned customers, indicating LENGTH_STAY VLOW is part of a conjunction. A conjunction is a group of two or more input criteria that *together* influence an output criterion. Whenever criteria in a conjunction occur in records containing a particular output criterion, they always occur *together*. To review the entire conjunc-

tion, select Conjunctions from the pull-down list in the Style View area, deselect LENGTH_STAY in the Input list by clicking it, and click Apply (see Figure 7-25).

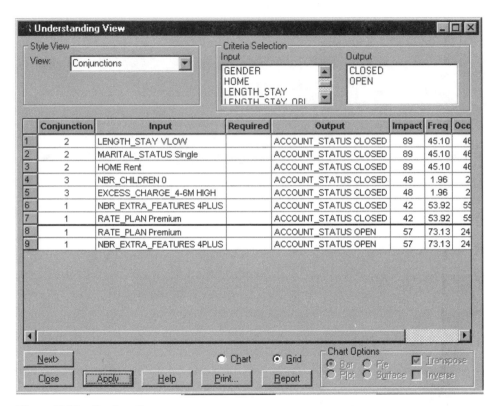

**Figure 7-25**   Conjunctions.

LENGTH_STAY VLOW is co-joined in conjunction 2 with MARITAL_STATUS Single and HOME Rent. Almost half of the former customers were single individuals who rented a residence and had been very-short-term customers. Contrast conjunction 2 with conjunction 1, which is present in a significant proportion of both current and churned customer records. Unlike conjunction 2, conjunction 1 is not important. Its criteria are redundant. Any customer who has a Premium rate plan is automatically entitled to four extra features. In addition, the impacts associated with conjunction 1 for both output criteria are not very impressive.

3. Now return to the Understanding View window. Notice that there are several USAGE_DIFF values high on the criteria list. Click USAGE_DIFF_4M (11,12) and review its relative impact on the two output values. Increased phone usage from four months earlier strongly characterizes current customers (see Figure 7-26).

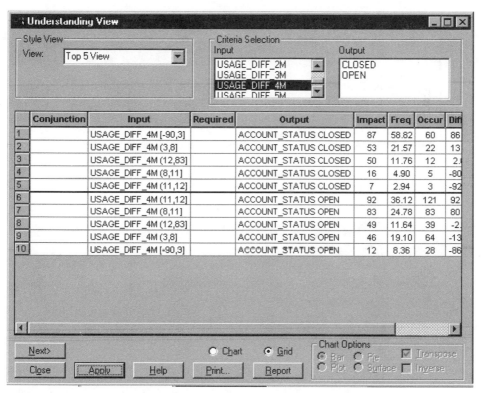

**Figure 7-26** USAGE_DIFF_4M's impact on ACCOUNT_STATUS.

Contrast this finding with USAGE_DIFF_4M (-90,3), a value indicating a drop in usage during the same period: Churned customers were much more likely to exhibit a decrease in phone usage.

Now, return to the Advanced Understanding View window to obtain a consolidated picture of all the USAGE_DIFF criteria. In the Input list, select USAGE_DIFF_1M. Scroll down and click USAGE_DIFF_6M while holding down the Shift key. Click CLOSED in the Output list, select the All Relations View from the View list, then click Apply. Click the Field column heading to sort the rows by field name. When there are fewer than 300 rows, you can click a column heading in the Advanced Understanding View to sort rows using values in a column.

Notice that for all the periods, churned customers demonstrated a significant drop in cellular usage, making USAGE_DIFF a very important field for churn prediction:

|                          | Impact | Frequency |
|--------------------------|--------|-----------|
| USAGE_DIFF_1M (-87,-9)   | 77     | 41.18     |
| USAGE_DIFF 2M (-92,-7)   | 76     | 40.20     |
| USAGE_DIFF 3M (-89,-7)   | 75     | 39.22     |
| USAGE_DIFF 4M (-90,3)    | 87     | 58.82     |
| USAGE_DIFF 5M (-92,-9)   | 77     | 41.18     |
| USAGE_DIFF 6M (-100,2)   | 82     | 50.98     |

4. Click NBR_CHILDREN in the Input list, de-select CLOSED in the Output list, then click Apply (see Figure 7-27)

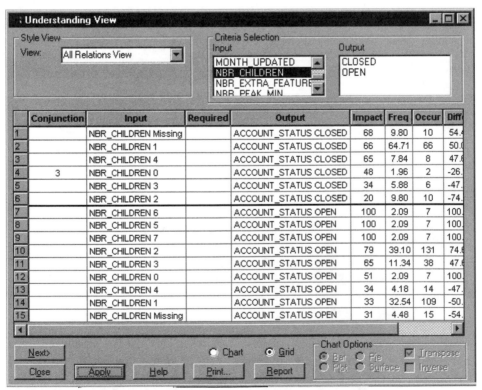

**Figure 7-27**  NBR_CHILDREN's impact on ACCOUNT_STATUS.

As shown in Figure 7-27, notice that NBR_CHILDREN Missing has a high impact value, 68, for churned customers. Almost 10% of the records for churned customers contain no value in the NBR_CHILDREN field. You are able to detect this information because you specified the value "Missing" when you set up your field specifications earlier in the study. Because missing values in this case appear to be important, you would want to explore reasons for them. If you found that values were not typically recorded when a customer had no children, you might want to specify a missing value of 0, then regenerate the model.

5. Once again, return to the Understanding View window to find out more about this field. Select MO_EXPENSES in the Input list, then click Apply (see Figure 7-28).

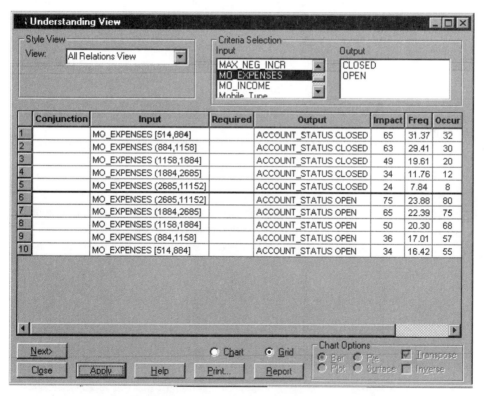

**Figure 7-28**   MO_EXPENSES's impact on ACCOUNT_STATUS.

Two of the bins, containing lower-expense values, are primarily associated with churned customers. Two other bins, which describe customers with higher expenses, are primarily associated with current customers. The middle bin is not useful for predicting either churned or current customers.

**HTML Reports.**    DataCruncher has a Report button on almost all the generated views you have been generating. DataCruncher can generate each of these reports into HTML format for viewing through an Internet browser. The reports are organized by pre-defined sections, like Field Ranking, Understanding View, Data Distribution summaries, and Evaluation Views. You can add other sections as you wish, but hsi is a convenient way to share the findings of this tool with others.

### 7.5.1   Evaluation

To quantify the value of your model for prediction, you use the Churn Assistant's Evaluate commands. Click Close in the Understanding View window to proceed with evaluation.

The evaluation process runs a data set against your discovery model in order to see if the model created during discovery is accurate. Evaluation compares generated results against known outcomes. The evaluation process runs the data set against the discovery model in order to see if the model created during discovery is accurate.

1. Click Evaluation on the Assistant's menu. In the dialog box that appears, ensure that churn.txt is checked and that you use 100% of its records to evaluate the model. Click OK to run the Evaluation task.

   Although we will evaluate the model using the same records we used to gener-ate the model, you may evaluate a model using different records. The approach we are taking tells you how accurate the model is for the records in churn.txt. Out-of-sample testing is done to avoid *overfitting* the model to the given data set as discussed in the earlier chapters. There is a point where a model can too accu-rately predict the outcome of the data being used to create the model, at the expense of recognizing trends that will be most useful in the future. This is referred to as overfitting.

   During the Evaluation task, DataCruncher uses your model to predict the out-put criterion for each record in churn.txt. Then the predicted criteria are com-pared with the actual output criteria in churn.txt.

2. When the Evaluation task is finished, review the results by clicking Evaluation Results on the Classification Assistant's menu (see Figure 7-29).

As shown in Figure 7-29, the Evaluation View indicates that our model successfully predicted ACCOUNT_STATUS CLOSED 96.08% of the time. It successfully predicted ACCOUNT_STATUS OPEN 97.61% of the time.

Prediction success rates as high as these are not likely to occur so quickly in a real data-mining study, if at all. Most likely, this high prediction rate is due to "in-sample" test-ing. If you had set aside 25–50% of your data as a test sample and had not used it for building the model, the test results would have been more realistic. The data in churn.txt has been derived to make this tutorial quick and simple. So, do not be alarmed if you experience much lower success rates with your own early models.

A model that is 76% accurate may actually be a very good model, or at least the best model that the available data permits you to generate. On the other hand, you may improve a model's prediction accuracy by many percentage points by varying your field specifications, especially your binning, or even the data you mine. For example, binning the monetary values in MO_EXPENSES into seven groups rather than five might have changed the accuracy of you model. Creating the most accurate model can involve much trial and error.

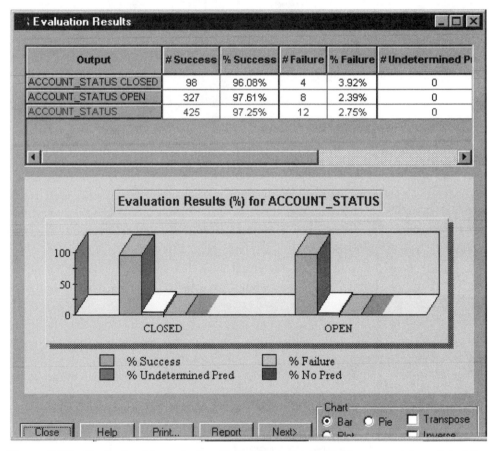

**Figure 7-29**  Evaluation View window, illustrating how effectively our model predicted the right outcome (OPEN and CLOSED) compared to the known results.

### 7.5.2    Refining the Model

Even though our model is a very good one, there is always room for an additional study to refine it. There are many ways to improve the prediction success rate of the model for churned customers.

For example, close the Evaluation View to review additional information available to you about your model's prediction accuracy. As shown in Figure 7-30, when you conducted the Evaluation task, several new images appeared on your Control Center.

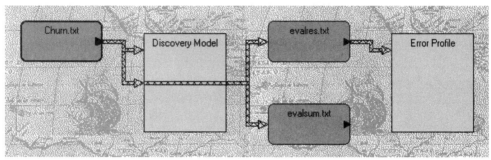

**Figure 7-30**   Evaluation objects.

The table named eval_res.txt contains prediction scores for each of the records used for evaluation. During the Evaluation task, DataCruncher mines the records in eval_res.txt and generates a model. The generated model, the Error Profile model, can help you understand how input criteria might adversely affect the ability of a model to predict an output criterion.

The demonstration version of this product has disabled the full capability of this error profiling; however, if you use the production version, it is possible to change the accuracy of the model using the error-profile model.

The full version of DataCruncher improves our model's ability to predict customers who might churn. Again, you must be careful about overfitting due to in-sample testing and validation. An improved model predicted 100% of the churned customers, compared to 96.08% for our previous model, and had a 98.96% overall accuracy (a feat this author has only ever achieved using demonstration data).

As you have seen, improving a model is an iterative process. You generate and evaluate a series of models, modifying field specifications or even the data you mine to try to improve the predictive capability of your model.

As long as it is feasible, continue the iterative model improvement process until you have produced a model that is likely to be successful for the optimal percentage of the time in predicting the output criteria. DataCruncher makes it easy to generate and regenerate models once you have prepared your data for mining.

Here are several factors that affect your ability to optimize a model:

- The **complexity of the data** you mine. Data sources with hundreds of columns that contain a large number of unique values are, of course, complex. Models generated using complex data generally produce lower prediction successes. Group complex data so that the number of unique values is smaller, as we did in churn.txt. If you have done all you can do to reduce the complexity of your data and your model's accuracy doesn't appreciably change, you may have arrived at the best model.

- The **complexity of the problem** you are trying to solve. A complex problem has many dimensions that change rapidly over time. Churn is an excellent example of a complex problem. Factors leading to churn change rapidly as technological and competitive forces continue to multiply and evolve. Churn models need to be updated continuously, probably at least once a month, so that they are adjusted for changing conditions. When you update a model, mine the same records with updated values or mine a different set of records containing fresh data.

- The **time and resources** you have to improve the model. The money you spend trying to prevent churn should not exceed the money you save because of diminished churn. Nonetheless, generating an initial churn-prediction model will take longer than keeping it up to date over time. Once data has been prepared and consolidated and a method established for keeping it up to date, regenerating models takes relatively little time.

- The **output criteria** for which the model must be accurate. Many models are more accurate for one output criteria than for others. Pick the output criterion of greatest importance (ACCOUNT_STATUS CLOSED, in our case), and focus on optimizing the predictive capabilities for only that criterion.

- Whether you can identify ways to improve the model for a particular **subset of your records**. If you have spent considerable amount of time and effort trying to optimize a model that can predict an outcome for a large, heterogeneous population, consider focusing instead on optimizing the model for a promising subset of the population. In our case study, for example, REGION NORTHEAST has a high impact for churned customers, and almost 60% of the customers who churned subscribed to services in that region. You could prepare a data source containing records for customers associated with only the Northeast region, and invest further model refinement efforts on understanding and predicting churn in this region.

For now, we will conclude that our latest model is good enough to use for predicting which current customers might churn.

### 7.5.3    Conducting a Cost Benefit Analysis

DataCruncher can help you assess some of the cost and benefit trade-offs involved in using your model to identify individuals to target in a customer-retention campaign.

Although the demonstration version does not have this window, we can do a Cost Benefit Analysis View on the Churn Assistant's menu. The Cost Benefit Analysis View lets you evaluate costs and profits associated with preventing current customers from churning.

The graphical image in the view is known as a lift chart (see Figure 7-31).

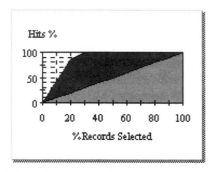

**Figure 7-31**    The "lift" chart.

The diagonal line in Figure 7-31 depicts churn prevention without using a churn-prediction model. To prevent 80% of your customers from churning, you would have to approach and entice 80% of your customers, because you have no model that tells you which customers are most likely to churn.

The area above the diagonal line depicts the situation when you use your model to detect which customers to approach. Using your model, to approach 80% of your customers likely to churn you would only have to contact 20% of your customers, the 20% your model tells you are most likely to churn.

The information in the lift chart is based on the information shown to its left (see Figure 7-32).

The value in the Output field, CLOSED, is the output criterion used to generate the lift chart. There are 437 records in your Evaluation data source (churn.txt), 102 of which contain the output value CLOSED.

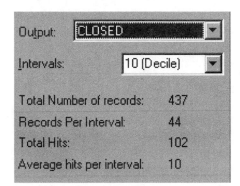

**Figure 7-32** Statistics on ACCOUNT_STATUS CLOSED.

The Intervals field lets you view information about CLOSED records in groups. Right now, 10 (Decile) is selected, so there are 10 rows in the grid. Each row represents 10% of the records containing ACCOUNT_STATUS CLOSED in churn.txt (see Figure 7-33).

| | Interval | | | Cumulative | | |
|---|---|---|---|---|---|---|
| | Score | Hits | % | Hits | % | % of total |
| 1 | 270.00 | 43 | 98.4 | 43 | 98.4 | 42.2 |
| 2 | 70.00 | 43 | 98.4 | 86 | 98.4 | 84.3 |
| 3 | -110.00 | 16 | 36.6 | 102 | 77.8 | 100.0 |
| 4 | -180.00 | 0 | 0.0 | 102 | 58.4 | 100.0 |
| 5 | -230.00 | 0 | 0.0 | 102 | 46.7 | 100.0 |
| 6 | -280.00 | 0 | 0.0 | 102 | 38.9 | 100.0 |
| 7 | -320.00 | 0 | 0.0 | 102 | 33.3 | 100.0 |
| 8 | -360.00 | 0 | 0.0 | 102 | 29.2 | 100.0 |
| 9 | -410.00 | 0 | 0.0 | 102 | 25.9 | 100.0 |

**Figure 7-33** Analyzing lift.

Take a look at the Interval columns in the first row in the grid, or the first decile. This decile contains prediction scores for ACCOUNT_STATUS CLOSED of 320 and higher. There are 43 customers in this score range who have churned (Hits); these customers represent 98.4% of records in the first decile. Now look at the Cumulative information. The 43 customers represent 42.2% of all the churned customers in churn.txt.

Contrast the information for the first decile with that for the third decile. In the third decile, about 37%, or 16, of the customers churned. The cumulative data indicates that 102 records in the first three deciles contain ACCOUNT_STATUS CLOSED and that all the records containing this output criterion appear in the first three deciles (% of total = 100). Therefore, if you were to approach all customers likely to churn, you would approach those having ACCOUNT_STATUS CLOSED prediction scores of −110 and greater, 102 customers in this example.

The area to the right of the lift chart lets you enter values to help you determine churn campaign cost/profit trade-offs associated with contacting different numbers of customers likely to churn. For this example, assume that you will offer customers likely to churn a 10% discount on a $100 item. You would specify the following values in the Cost area, shown in Figure 7-34.

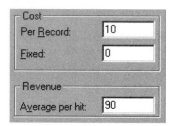

**Figure 7-34**  Cost analysis.

Figure 7-35 shows you the cost/profit trade-offs.

| | Interval | | | Cumulative | | | Analysis | | | Cumulative | | |
|---|---|---|---|---|---|---|---|---|---|---|---|---|
| | Score | Hits | % | Hits | % | % of total | Cost | Revenue | Profit | Cost | Revenue | Profit |
| 1 | 270.00 | 43 | 98.4 | 43 | 98.4 | 42.2 | 440.00 | 3870.00 | 3430.00 | 440.00 | 3870.00 | 3430.00 |
| 2 | 70.00 | 43 | 98.4 | 86 | 98.4 | 84.3 | 440.00 | 3870.00 | 3430.00 | 880.00 | 7740.00 | 6860.00 |
| 3 | -110.00 | 16 | 36.6 | 102 | 77.8 | 100.0 | 440.00 | 1440.00 | 1000.00 | 1320.00 | 9180.00 | 7860.00 |
| 4 | -180.00 | 0 | 0.0 | 102 | 58.4 | 100.0 | 440.00 | 0.00 | -440.00 | 1760.00 | 9180.00 | 7420.00 |
| 5 | -230.00 | 0 | 0.0 | 102 | 46.7 | 100.0 | 440.00 | 0.00 | -440.00 | 2200.00 | 9180.00 | 6980.00 |
| 6 | -280.00 | 0 | 0.0 | 102 | 38.9 | 100.0 | 440.00 | 0.00 | -440.00 | 2640.00 | 9180.00 | 6540.00 |
| 7 | -320.00 | 0 | 0.0 | 102 | 33.3 | 100.0 | 440.00 | 0.00 | -440.00 | 3080.00 | 9180.00 | 6100.00 |
| 8 | -360.00 | 0 | 0.0 | 102 | 29.2 | 100.0 | 440.00 | 0.00 | -440.00 | 3520.00 | 9180.00 | 5660.00 |
| 9 | -410.00 | 0 | 0.0 | 102 | 25.9 | 100.0 | 440.00 | 0.00 | -440.00 | 3960.00 | 9180.00 | 5220.00 |

**Figure 7-35**  Cost/profit analysis.

The cumulative profit values are shown in the rightmost column. Locate the largest value: $7,860 as shown on the righthand side of Figure 7-35. Now notice that a prediction score of –110 appears in the first column of that row. You would have to contact every customer likely to churn whose prediction score is –110 and greater to potentially realize a $7,860 profit, but you would approach 100% of the customers likely to churn, or 102 customers in this case. Notice that the cost associated with this profit is $1,320.

Were you to approach only 85% of those likely to churn, your cost would be significantly less, $880, but your profit would also be less, $6,860. You would have to decide whether the additional potential profit warranted the additional cost.

## 7.6  Perform Prediction

RightPoint also performs prediction. The same impact scores that were calculated for model understanding are used for prediction. There are two forms of prediction with RightPoint: case and batch prediction. *Case prediction* uses your discovery model to interactively predict an outcome on a specific case. *Batch prediction* reads a series of cases and performs prediction without user interaction.

The Prediction Process is the process whereby new data sets are run against the model we have created.

### 7.6.1  Conducting What-If Analyses

DataCruncher provides you with a facility for predicting whether one particular individual, hypothetical or real, that exhibits a particular set of criteria might be a churn candidate:

1. Click Case Prediction on the Classification Assistant's menu.
2. The Case Prediction screen appears. The Criteria Selection area lets you specify individual criteria. Simply click in the Value column for a particular field, and select one of the values. In this case, enter the following:

   - MARITAL_STATUS = Married
   - NUMBER_CHILDREN = 0
   - HOME = Rent
   - LENGTH_STAY = MID
   - VISA_LIMIT = very high
   - CUST_SEG = C
   - EXCESS_CHARGE = LOW

For this example, the predicted outcome is that this customer will remain loyal, with a predicted score of 498, as shown in Figure 7-36.

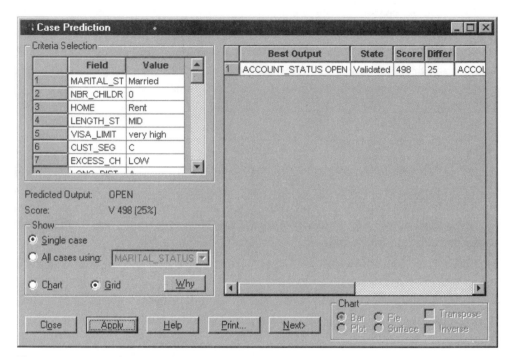

**Figure 7-36**   The Case Prediction window.

3. It is possible to examine why this prediction was made. Click on Why, as shown in Figure 7-37.

The screen in Figure 7-37 is displayed. This particular example predicted the customer's account will remain open for the reasons listed above. The primary reason was that their customer segmentation, or CUST_SEG field, was C. This segment had an *impact* of 77 on the outcome that the customer would stay.

| Example | Output | Input | Conjunction | Impact | Require |
|---|---|---|---|---|---|
| 1 | ACCOUNT_STATUS OPEN | CUST_SEG C | | 77 | |
| 1 | ACCOUNT_STATUS OPEN | LONG_DIST_CAR A | | 61 | |
| 1 | ACCOUNT_STATUS OPEN | MARITAL_STATUS Married | | 61 | |
| 1 | ACCOUNT_STATUS OPEN | VISA_LIMIT very high | | 61 | |
| 1 | ACCOUNT_STATUS OPEN | EXCESS_CHARGE_1-3M Missing | | 59 | |
| 1 | ACCOUNT_STATUS OPEN | NBR_CHILDREN 0 | | 51 | |
| 1 | ACCOUNT_STATUS OPEN | EXCESS_CHARGE_0M Missing | | 47 | |
| 1 | ACCOUNT_STATUS OPEN | EXCESS_CHARGE_4-6M LOW | | 30 | |
| 1 | ACCOUNT_STATUS OPEN | HOME Rent | | 24 | |
| 1 | ACCOUNT_STATUS OPEN | LENGTH_STAY MID | | 23 | |
| 1 | ACCOUNT_STATUS CLOSED | MARITAL_STATUS Single | 2 | 269 | |
| 1 | ACCOUNT_STATUS CLOSED | HOME Rent | 2 | 269 | |
| 1 | ACCOUNT_STATUS CLOSED | LENGTH_STAY VLOW | 2 | 269 | |
| 1 | ACCOUNT_STATUS CLOSED | NBR_CHILDREN 0 | 2 | 95 | |

**Figure 7-37**   Why was this prediction made?

## 7.6.2    Conducting Batch Prediction

While using case prediction helps you understand the effect of specific groups of criteria on churning, the primary power of your churn-prediction model is its ability to make predictions for a collection, or a batch, of customer records.

1. Close the Case Prediction screen.
2. Click Batch Prediction on the Classification Assistant's menu. When the Tables dialog box appears, select 100% of the records in churn.txt as your Prediction sample. In a real study, you would probably make predictions using a different set of records. For example, models based on data from January through June might be used for prediction on July records. Click OK. (See Figure 7-38).
3. DataCruncher runs the Prediction task and puts prediction results in a table named pred_res.txt. Click the pred_res.txt icon and use its pop-up menu (by clicking on the right mouse button while this object is selected) to display a Table View so you can review its contents. Scroll to the bottom of the table, noticing that it contains 102 records. These are the records for customers you would approach with retention incentives, using the CUSTID field value to map prediction results to actual customers.

   The file predres.tst has appended to the very end of the rows the prediction outcomes and the scores associated with each outcome. For example, while there might be a score of 519 for outcome ACCOUNT_STATUS Open, there might be a score of 434 for outcome ACCOUNT_STATUS Stay; therefore, we predict that this customer will remain with us with a high margin of confidence, or 75 points difference between them.

For each row this report shows the best-case prediction, the score, the margin of victory, the challenger prediction, and the challenger prediction score. If there were more than two outcomes being predicted, a score would be calculated for each of them. The row information is also stored in the resulting prediction file and can be used, as in the lift chart example, to rank each row by the prediction made and the confidence in each prediction.

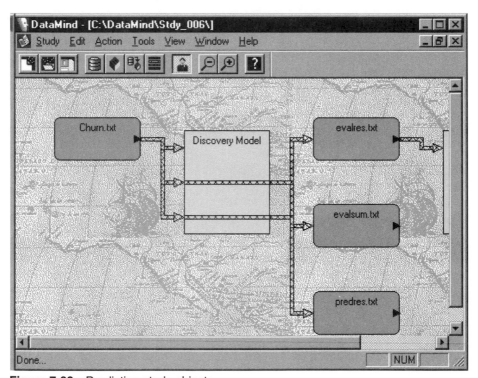

**Figure 7-38**  Prediction study objects.

## 7.7  Summary

This chapter covered the basics of how to use the RightPoint DataCruncher product. The example model built in this study examined customer retention, which is a business problem of major consequence to large corporations. Although the look and feel of this tool differs greatly from KnowledgeSEEKER, discussed in the last chapter, the process used was similar. We defined a study, built a model, understood the model, and then used it for predictive purposes. The next chapter explores in more detail how the data-mining tools discussed in the last chapters are used with industry-specific applications.

# Industry Focus

Chapters 8 and 9 focus on specific industry uses of data mining. In Chapter 8, industry examples are provided for banking and finance, retail, healthcare, and telecommunications. Chapter 9 looks at how data warehouses provide a methodology for helping to perform data-mining studies within each of these industries.

# Industry Applications of Data Mining

$\mathbf{T}$his chapter contains examples of how data mining is used in banking/finance, retailing, healthcare, and telecommunications. The purpose of this chapter is to give the user some ideas of the types of activities in which data mining is already being used and what companies are using them.

The chapter is organized as follows:

## 8.1  Data-Mining Applications in Banking and Finance

Data mining has been used extensively in the banking and financial markets. In the banking industry, data mining is heavily used to model and predict credit fraud, to evaluate risk, to perform trend analysis, and to analyze profitability, as well as to help with direct marketing campaigns.

In the financial markets, neural networks have been used in stock-price forecasting, in option trading, in bond rating, in portfolio management, in commodity price prediction, in mergers and acquisitions, as well as in forecasting financial disasters.

Several of the financial companies who use neural networks and have been referenced on the Internet are Daiwa Securities, NEC Corporation, Carl & Associates, LBS Capital Management, Walkrich Investment Advisors, and O'Sullivan Brothers Investments. The number of investment companies that data mine is much more extensive than this, but they are not willing to be referenced.

One interesting book in the area of global finance is *Neural Networks in the Capital Markets*, edited by Apostolos-Paul Refenes. The book explores equity applications, foreign exchange applications, bond applications, and macroeconomic and corporate performance. Most of the contributed chapters are from university professors, a group whose publishing in the areas of economic and capital market forecasting is most impressive; however, there are government and industry contributions from Citibank N.A., Daimler Benz AG, County NatWest Investment Management, and NeuroDollars.

### 8.1.1   Stock Forecasting

There are many software applications on the market that use data-mining techniques for stock prediction. One such application used for stock prediction is shown in Figure 8-1.

**Figure 8-1**   Stock forecasting.

NETPROPHET by Neural Applications Corporation is a stock-prediction application that makes use of neural networks. The two lines shown in the graph in Figure 8-1 represent the real and the predicted stock values.

In banking, the most widespread use of data mining is in the area of fraud detection. HNC's Falcon product specifically addresses this area. HNC comments that credit fraud detection is now in place to monitor more than 160 million payment-card accounts this year. They also claim a healthy return on investment. While fraud is decreasing, applications for payment card accounts are rising as much as 50% a year.

The widespread use of data mining in banking has not been unnoticed. In 1996, *Bank Systems & Technology* commented: "Data mining is the most important application in financial services in 1996."

Finding banking companies who use data mining is not easy, given their proclivity for silence. The following list of financial companies that use data mining required some digging into SEC reports from data mining vendors that are made available to the public. The list includes: Bank of America, First USA Bank, Headlands Mortgage Company, FCC National Bank, Federal Home Loan Mortgage Corporation, Wells Fargo Bank, Nations-Banc Services, Mellon Bank N.A., Advanta Mortgage Corporation, Chemical Bank, Chevy Chase Bank, U.S. Bancorp, and USAA Federal Savings Bank. Again it is reasonable to assume that most large banks are performing some sort of data mining, although many have policies not to discuss it.

### 8.1.2  Cross-Selling and Customer Loyalty in the Banking Industry

Most major financial institutions have statistics and data-mining groups. In fact, banks like Wells Fargo, Bank of America, Fleet Bank, and others have been the subject of many articles about their sophisticated data mining, and modeling of their customers' behavior. The next question to ask is: how well do financial institutions know their customers? A study published in DM News and conducted by Deluxe Corporation found that 43% of consumers surveyed said their financial service provider does not know their specific needs well at all; 60% said the offers they received were not relevant to their needs; and 39% said they did not receive offers at all.

The study by Deluxe Corporation demonstrates a significant problem with data mining: the inability to leverage data-mining studies into actionable results. For example, while a bank may know that customers meeting certain criteria are likely to close their accounts, it is another matter to figure out a strategy to do something about it. One vendor that has developed a suite of products designed at integrating predictive technologies with customer interaction points is RightPoint software. Other vendors are working on the same problem, particularly on the web, where predicting what a customer will best respond to is critical. Web banking companies like Security First and BroadVision, among others, are also trying to incorporate one-to-one marketing, using predictive technologies, to their banking sites.

The RightPoint Real-Time Marketing Suite takes data-mining models and leverages them within real-time interactions with customers. The RightPoint Real-Time Marketing Suite is designed to create, manage, and deliver 1:1 marketing campaigns for high-touch industries (such as banking, telecommunications, and retail sales) that rely on direct customer interaction to conduct business. For these and similar businesses, it is essential to ensure that each customer interaction seizes the opportunity to increase customer satisfaction, loyalty, and revenue-generation potential. Predictive models are used to evaluate the right marketing message to be delivered to customers. Dynamic learning technology also builds predictive models on the fly and calculates probabilities of acceptance, indicating which offers are being accepted by which types of customers. (See collaborative filtering as discussed in Chapter 4, for a discussion of one dynamic learning technology) These predictive models can also be used in conjunction with business rules to provide the right offer at the right time.

One aspect of pinpointing market opportunities is identifying high-value customers. In his book, *All Consumers are Not Created Equal*, author Garth Hallberg cites MediaMark Research, Inc. findings that about one-third of customers account for 68% of all purchases. Traditionally, marketers have focused on segmenting and courting high-value consumers. Where marketers have fallen short is in taking that understanding of high-value customers and using this information to predict the qualities that would raise the value of mid-level consumers, opening a large (and largely untapped) market opportunity.

Real-time marketing focuses on executing one-to-one campaigns that utilize predictive technologies to capture a sense of personalization. The idea is that by tailoring marketing options to consumers, companies get a better response rate for their campaigns.

Equally important, businesses now have an effective outlet for building loyalty and brand value, by tapping into customers' demands for personalized service, and their desire to escape the hassle of researching different service offerings. For example, a mortgage customer may tell the lending bank about an existing auto loan. An agent of the bank can add this information to the customer's profile, and present back a pre-approved refinance of the auto loan. This will save the customer money by consolidating the existing mortgage and auto loan with one bank. If the bank can calculate the savings on the fly, the customer can see a clear benefit.

### Halifax Bank Using Real-Time Marketing

Halifax PLC, the second largest bank in the United Kingdom, has chosen its RightPoint Real-Time Marketing Suite as the foundation for a customer relationship initiative. RightPoint will enable Halifax customer service representatives to mobilize vital information about a customer and determine which campaigns, products or services to offer at the point of customer contact.

Halifax's direct customer service center receives more than 20 million customer calls per year and employs 800 customer service representatives. With the call center increasingly becoming the customer interaction center, a customer's decision to do business with a company is often based on whether a company is aware of that customer's preferences and acts upon them accordingly. Using RightPoint, Halifax representatives will have a valuable tool for reliably predicting and delivering on the requirements of their customers in real-time, thereby increasing customer satisfaction and loyalty, and attaining an important competitive advantage.

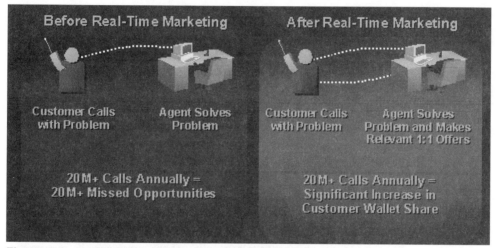

**Figure 8-2**   Halifax Bank engaging in real-time marketing.

"Our direct channel is playing an ever-increasing role in delivering customer contact, with call volumes predicted to grow to more than 50 million calls per year over the next three years," says Dick Spelman, director of distribution at Halifax. "We need to ensure that we can harness customer data at the point of contact so that a customized service is delivered in real-time. This is what the RightPoint solution will deliver to our agents. The other parallel challenge that call centers face is generating sales income. Rather than add more agents and use questionable handover techniques, RightPoint offers us the potential to convert inbound service calls into profitable sales. If organizations don't tackle the revenue-generation aspect of their call-center activities, they will not be able to afford the current unbridled growth in service traffic.

"RightPoint gives Halifax the ability to leverage each and every customer interaction and make one-to-one marketing a reality," Spelman continues. "By capitalizing on the untapped revenue potential present during each customer interaction, Halifax will be able to grow the lifetime value of its customers while also reaching out and building stronger relationships. Halifax is looking to see a significant increase in response rates to campaigns that will ultimately help increase its market share in this highly competitive industry."

### Delivering Predictive Technologies in a Real-Time Environment

An analyst may have built a data-mining model that can predict that 30% of mortgage customers meeting a certain set of criteria would agree to taking out auto loans with you if you could make a compelling offer. The challenge is to take this knowledge and:

- Deliver it to customer-contact points.
- Put it in combination with business rules.
- Leverage information you may have gathered during customer interaction.
- Provide an immediate feedback loop on the effectiveness of an active marketing campaign.
- Allow marketers to fine-tune their campaigns on the fly.

By combining these capabilities in a closed-loop system, businesses have the ability to react quickly to market conditions and significantly improve customer-response rates.

Looking further into the architecture of any real-time marketing software solution, there should be three primary components: a tool for targeting marketing campaigns, a campaign server, and a suite of applications for moving the campaigns out to various customer touch points.

Figure 8-3 shows the components of this system that are required to deliver predictive technologies in a real-time environment:

- Predictive models for mass marketing, represented in the left-hand oval.
- Customer information, which may include transactional data, a customer marketing database, and information that the customer just gave you while interacting with you (represented in the right-hand oval).
- A predictive engine capable of delivering the predictions in real time (seconds on web or call center).
- Business rules, which state when to use which predictive models (i.e. this model is only used when the person calling in has a family, has over $30,000 with us, and has not been pitched a product before).
- A feedback loop of responses that will monitor the success of the technology as well as allow marketers to dynamically learn from it.

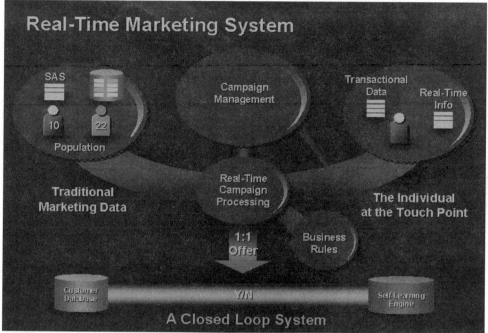

**Figure 8-3** Using predictive technologies with a real-time marketing system.

The real-time campaign marketing tool is used by marketers to collect and capture market specifications for new campaigns. Because segmentation is at least half the effort of any marketing campaign, an important function of this tool is providing pinpoint accuracy when segmenting target markets. Campaign marketing tools with embedded data-mining technology provide advanced pattern recognition for high accuracy and predictive capabilities that enable marketers to proactively plan campaigns. Another important feature is the ability to support incremental updates, so that any time a customer's profile changes — for example, marital status — that data can be automatically factored into a marketer's customer segmentation. This ensures that customers are targeted to the appropriate campaigns at all times.

A campaign server administers and monitors active campaigns to enable one-to-one marketing. As customer information comes in from one of the touch point applications, the server should be able to take this up-to-date information and make on-the-fly predictions about the marketing campaigns that will be the most effective; for example, in building that customer's loyalty or obtaining additional revenue through up-selling and cross-selling. The campaign server then sends the appropriate campaigns up to the touch point application. Ideally, the campaign server will also store the results of active marketing campaigns, allowing marketers to evaluate their effectiveness and make any necessary adjustments in real-time.

Finally, touch point applications actually deliver marketing campaigns to the user. These applications transparently call down to the campaign server with the customer information, and then present the most appropriate marketing offer(s). For example, a touch point application for the call center will reside on each call center agent's computer and "pop up" up-selling or cross-selling opportunities on the fly, presenting the agent with a script. Similarly, when a consumer visits the Web site and types in an ID, the Web touch point application can present screens with offers or information of particular interest to that person.

Businesses cannot afford to wait months, or even weeks, to evaluate the effectiveness of a marketing campaign. Central to real-time marketing is having a closed-loop system that allows marketers to easily review the effectiveness of active marketing campaigns and then immediately adjust the campaign if it's not performing as expected. The ability to fine-tune a marketing campaign in a matter of days allows marketers to maximize response rates and focus resources on the highest value campaigns.

Emerging enterprise software for incorporating data mining technology with real-time marketing will play a central role in the ability of businesses to build both their brand value and the value of their customers. By providing pinpoint segmentation, companies can now conduct personalized, one-to-one customer marketing on a broad scale. Powerful capabilities for updating and reviewing campaign-related information on the fly means that marketers are serving today's customer needs, not yesterday's. It also means that businesses have a feedback loop for evaluating marketing campaigns and immediately adjusting them for greater effectiveness. The ability to extend marketing campaigns in real time across multiple touch points provides companies with unprecedented customer outreach. Most importantly, companies can now conduct effective, proactive marketing campaigns for the first time.

## 8.2  Data-Mining Applications in Retail

Slim margins have pushed retailers into embracing data warehousing earlier than other industries. Retailers have seen improved decision-support processes lead directly to improved efficiency in inventory management and financial forecasting. The early adoption of data warehousing by retailers has given them a better opportunity to take advantage of data mining. Large retail chains and grocery stores store vast amounts of point-of-sale data that is information rich. In the forefront of the applications that have been adopted in retail are direct marketing applications.

Chapter 5 used the example of a direct-mail campaign to show the usefulness of data mining in retail-marketing activities. The direct-mail industry is an area where data mining, or data modeling, is widely used. Almost every type of retailer, including catalogers, consumer retail chains, grocers, publishers, business-to-business marketers, and packaged goods manufacturers, uses direct marketing. There are many vertical applications that support direct-marketing campaigns, such as HNC's Marksman product. The claim could be made that every Fortune 500 company today has used data mining in a direct marketing campaign, usually through outsourcing lists to third parties like Harte-Hanks or The Polk Company.

Direct marketers are often concerned about customer segmentation, which is a clustering problem in data mining. Many vendors offer customer segmentation packages, like the one shown in Figure 8-4.

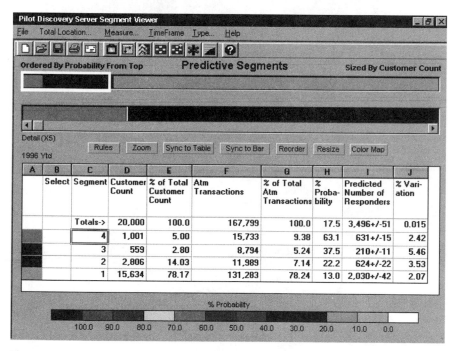

**Figure 8-4**  Customer segmentation software. Courtesy of Pilot Software.

Pilot Software also uses the customer segmentation to help in direct-mailing campaigns, as shown in Figure 8-5.

IBM has used data mining for several retailers to analyze shopping patterns within stores based on point of sale (POS) information. For example, one retail company with $2 billion in revenue, 300,000 UPC codes, and 129 stores in 15 states found some interesting results after analyzing its sales information. A store executive comments: "We found that people who were coming into the shop gravitated to the left-hand side of the store for promotional items and were not necessarily shopping the whole store." Such information is used to change promotional activity and provide a better understanding of how to lay out a store in order to optimize sales.

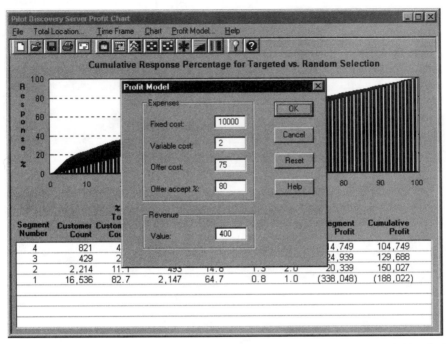

**Figure 8-5**   An application for a direct marketing campaign. Courtesy of Pilot Software.

**Other Types of Retail Data-Mining Studies**   Retailers are interested in many different types of data-mining studies. In the area of marketing, retailers are interested in creating data-mining models to answer questions like:

- How much are customers likely to spend over long periods of time?
- What is the frequency of customer purchasing behavior?
- What are the best types of advertisements to reach certain segments?
- What advertising mediums are most effective at reaching customers?
- What is the optimal timing at which to send mailers?

Merchandisers are beginning to profile issues such as:

- What types of customers are buying specific products?

- What determines the best product mix to sell on a regional level?
- What are the latest product trends?
- When is a merchandise department saturated?
- What are the times when a customer is most likely to buy?
- What types of products can be sold together?

In discussing customer profitability, customers may wish to build models to answer questions like:

- How does a retailer retain profitable customers?
- What are the significant customer segments that buy products?

Customer identification is critical to successful retail organizations, and is likely to become more so. Data mining helps model and identify the traits of profitable customers and reveal the "hidden" relationship that standard query processes have not already found. For further reading on the area of customer management, one interesting work is the book *The One-to-One Future* by D. Peppers and M. Rogers.

### 8.2.1   An Example of Data Mining for Property Valuation

One application of data mining in real estate is the AREAS Property Valuation product from HNC Software, which performs property valuation as shown in Figure 8-6.

While some would not categorize the real estate market as a retail industry, the concept of using data mining to predict property valuations can be directly applied to any product or commodity. For example, the proper valuations of antique furniture, used cars, or clothing apparel could be predicted in the same manner.

Another application of data mining in the airline industry is a customer retention management package by SABRE Decision Technologies™. SABRE is a leader in working with the airline industry to use data warehousing to increase profitability, and make better business decisions.

Some companies that use data mining in retail, and that have been referenced in articles or by data-mining companies, are Victoria's Secret, National Car Rental, JOCKEY International, Marriott Ownership, the Reader's Digest, and WalMart. In Chapter 2, a sample figure from MapInfo Corporation shows a visualization application for locating optimal site locations for businesses.

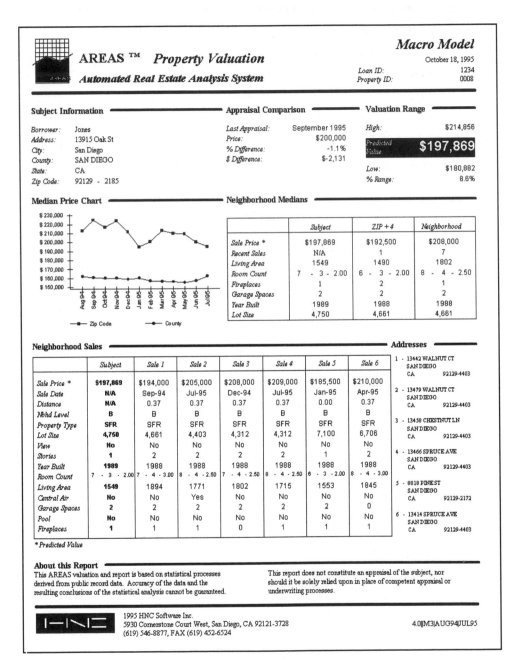

**Figure 8-6**   A data-mining application for property valuation from HNC Software, Inc.

### 8.2.2    An Example of Analyzing Customer Profitability in Retail

In the previous chapters we addressed methodologies that extract information from transactional data to produce "product-focused," actionable recommendations. In this section, we describe a methodology where the actionables are "customer-focused." This is an area in which Dovetail Solutions has significant expertise. Dovetail Solutions' methodology is the Value, Activity, and Loyalty™ Method, or VAL™ for short. VAL™ uses transactional data to extract information about customer activity, churn rate, and expected future purchases.

Customer value is not only determined by past revenues, but also by the customer's expected future purchasing behavior. This can be measured by customer activity and expected lifetime. Activity gauges the likelihood that a customer will purchase again, while lifetime measures how long a customer is expected to remain active. This would allow a retailer to measure the overall "health" of its customer base by determining profitability and "churn" rate. In turn, retailers could use these findings to determine customer acquisition goals needed to meet future revenue or profitability objectives.

Retail customers rarely ever tell a store that they have stopped shopping there (have become "inactive"). Therefore, it is highly advantageous for a store to know how many "active" customers reside in its customer base, how much sales revenue is expected from them, and what the customer churn or attrition rate is.

A common method of measuring churn rates is by looking at rules of thumb based on recency. For example, if a customer has not shopped for a long hiatus, say for the past year, she is considered inactive. While intuitive, this rule of thumb is overly simplistic in that it ignores differences in purchasing behavior across customer segments and individuals. For example, suppose that a customer shops twice a month. If this frequent shopper became inactive eight months ago, we may still count her as "active" because her last purchase is within the arbitrarily specified hiatus of one year. However, given her purchase habits, it is unlikely that this customer is still active. Likewise, infrequent shoppers might be incorrectly classified as inactive when in fact they are still active.

However, there is usually not enough data on individual customers to be able to adequately extract their purchasing patterns. The VAL methodology addresses this limitation by pooling the entire customer base to robustly estimate individual customer behavior based on limited individual purchase history. The underlying mathematical description of the overall customer population is based on "hazard rate" types of models, extracted from analogous processes in the natural sciences. This is validated by many studies that have shown that customer purchase patterns follow trends and regularities that can be accurately described using these types of models. An interesting reference, and one that influenced this discussion, is *Repeat Buying: Facts, Theory and Applications*, by A.S.C. Ehrenberg (Oxford University Press, 1988).

The VAL method uses transactional data to measure the probability that any given customer is active (the activity), gauges how many active customers reside in the customer database, determines the customer-base churn or attrition rate, and forecasts revenues from the currently active customers. It also extracts useful bellwether information, such as average customer lifetime (how long customers are expected to remain active), and average repurchase rates. This methodology is superior to the classic RFM (Recency, Frequency, and Monetary) analysis because it is forward-looking, as opposed to backward-looking, and produces more actionable results.

For example, segmenting the customer base by activity and value can suggest marketing strategies to stimulate those customers who are marginally active, but who have high expected value. Churn rates in conjunction with revenue forecasts can be used to determine what customer acquisition rate is required to meet revenue or profitability goals. Churn rates over time can also be used to identify and counteract seasonal periods that might trigger inactivity.

Transactional data can be a very valuable asset to retailers because of the actionable information it can generate if it is analyzed and mined carefully. With today's computing power and affordability, mining transactional data is no longer reserved for the large retailers. Mid-size and small retailers can now routinely collect and analyze transactional data. Moreover, there is less need to rely on outside vendors of panel data, since much of the information can be obtained directly from in-house transactional data. Market Basket Analysis, Assortment Optimization (discussed in earlier chapters), and the Value, Activity, and Loyalty methodology are examples of techniques that generate both product-focused and customer-focused actionables.

## 8.3  Data-Mining Applications in Healthcare

Chapter 3 discussed types of studies that can be done in the healthcare industry, as well as data-preparation issues. With the amount of information and issues in the healthcare industry, not to mention the information from medical research, biotechs, and the pharmaceutical industry, the types of studies listed in Chapter 3 are only the tip of the iceberg for data-mining opportunities.

Data mining has been used extensively in the medical industry already. For example, NeuroMedical Systems used neural networks to perform a pap smear diagnostic aid. Vysis uses neural networks to perform protein analysis for drug development. The University of Rochester Cancer Center and the Oxford Transplant Center use KnowledgeSEEKER, a decision tree technology, to help with their research. The Southern California Spinal Disorders Hospital uses Information Discovery to data mine. Information Discovery quotes one doctor as saying" "Today alone, I came up with a diagnosis for a patient who did not even have to go through a physical exam."

### 8.3.1   Uses of Data Visualization in the Medical Industry

Data visualization is one area that has built interest in the medical field. Belmont Research's CrossGraphs product has been used in many different applications. For example, Figure 8-7 shows a diagram for studying healthcare costs.

The graph shows the average cost-per-patient for fee-for-services patients, HMO patients, and other patients. For the categories 14 and 112, costs for "other" payer types varies widely.

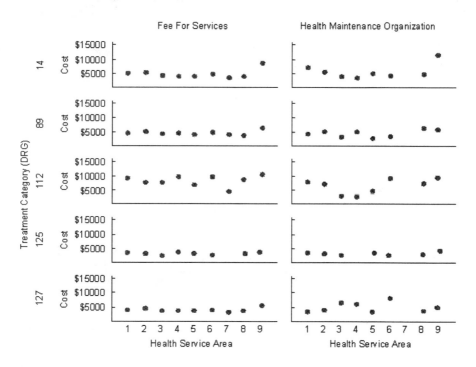

**Figure 8-7**   Average cost per patient by health service area, treatment category (DRG), and payer type (Belmont Research).

Another example, shown in Figure 8-8, is an array of graphs that show, side-by-side, a story of antibacterial activity of Cefdinir over time.

Figure 8-8 is useful for comparing the efficacy rates of different antibacterial pathogens over time. In this case, the antimicrobial agent, Cefdinir, is being studied against other agents for an eight-hour period.

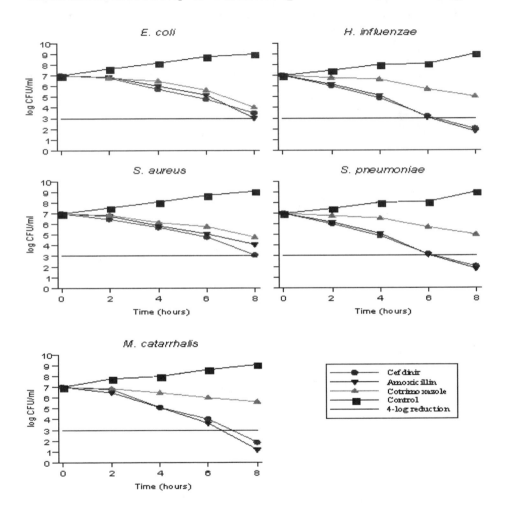

**Figure 8-8**   Efficacy of several antibacterial drugs over time (Belmont Research, Inc.).

Another example of a very useful application of data visualization is from MapInfo, using mapping technology to show patient location in order to deliver better service, as shown in Figure 8-9.

## 8.4    Data-Mining Applications in Telecommunications

In recent years, the telecommunications industry has undergone one of the most dramatic makeovers of any industry. The U.S. Telecommunications Act of 1996 allowed Regional Bell Operating Companies (RBOCS) to enter the long-distance market and offer "cable-like" services. The European Liberalization of Telecommunications Services, effective January 1, 1998, liberalized telecommunications services in Europe, and offers full competition among participating European nations. Sixty-eight nations liberalized their telecommunications market on January 1, 1998 to coincide with the European commitment based on the World Trade Organization's Telecommunications Agreement.

Not only has there been massive deregulation, but in the United States, there has been a sell-off by the FCC of airwaves to companies pioneering new ways to communicate. The cellular industry is rapidly taking on a life of its own.

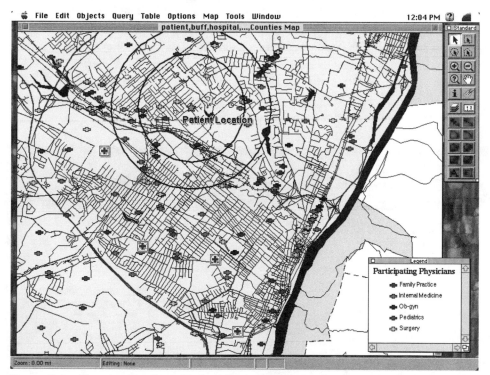

**Figure 8-9**    Mapping locations of physicians, patients, and patient care facilities.

With the hyper-competitive nature of this industry, a need to understand customers, to keep them, and to model effective ways to market new products to these customers is driving a demand for data mining in telecommunications where no demand existed in distant memory.

Companies like AT&T®, GTE Telecommunications®, and AirTouch® Communications have announced the use of data mining. American Management Systems® (AMS) Mobile Communications Industry Group has taken an active interest in data mining as well. AMS and AT&T offer consulting services around data mining, as do GTE and Cincinnati Bell Information Services®, among others.

Coral Systems® of Longmont, Colorado is a company that incorporates data-mining techniques in their FraudBuster™ product, which tracks known types of fraud by modeling subscriber usage patterns and predicting when a carrier is suspected of fraud. There are several companies looking at cellular fraud for telecommunications, including Lightbridge® and GTE.

Several other companies offer products to combat customer churn. For example, RightPoint Corporation focuses on data-mining issues in the telecommunications industry and, in particular, customer retention or churn. Industry experts have pointed out that the cellular telephone market experiences a 30% churn rate in the United States. A report by Digital Equipment Corporation®, produced by Evan Davies and Hossein Pakraven in September 1995, quantifies the cost of customer churn. In their report, they estimate that the cost of acquiring new customers is as high as $400 for each new subscriber.

Data visualization is another area with many strategic uses in telecommunications. Figure 8-10 shows a map, created by Empower Geographics® using MapInfo's technology, showing problem areas for a wireless telecommunications network.

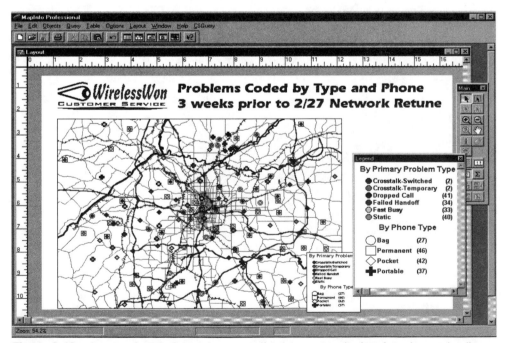

**Figure 8-10**   A map of a wireless telecommunications network pinpoints dropped calls.

### 8.4.1 Types of Studies in Telecommunications

The telecommunications industry is interested in answering a wide variety of questions with the help of data mining. For example:

- How does one recognize and predict when cellular fraud occurs?
- How does one retain customers and keep them loyal when competitors offer special offers and reduced rates?
- Which customers are most likely to churn?
- What characteristics make a customer likely to be profitable or unprofitable?
- How does one predict whether customers will buy additional products like cellular service, call waiting, or basic services?
- What are the factors that influence customers to call more at certain times?
- What characteristics indicate high-risk investments, such as investing in new fiber-optic lines?
- What products and services yield the highest amount of profit?
- What characteristics differentiate our products from those of our competitors?
- What set of characteristics indicates companies or customers who will increase their line usage?

## 8.5 Summary

This chapter covered industry examples of data mining in banking and finance, retail, healthcare, and telecommunications. While this is certainly not an inclusive list of all data mining activities, it does provide examples of how data mining is employed today. Chapter 8 will discuss specific data-mining studies for these industries, and will attempt to describe many of the data-preparation issues involved in performing these studies. More experienced users of data mining acknowledge that accumulation and preparation of data are the biggest hurdles to beginning the process of data mining.

# CHAPTER 9

# Enabling Data Mining Through Data Warehouses

The biggest challenge business analysts face in using data mining is how to extract, integrate, cleanse, and prepare data to solve their most pressing business problems. This issue is a formidable one and can take up the bulk of the time in the data-mining process. This chapter will discuss how data mining is enabled through the use of data warehousing.

The purpose of this chapter is not to provide a crash course in data-warehouse design, but to introduce examples of data warehouses and how they would be used for data mining. While data warehouses do not always have to be in place for data mining to occur, they do present a methodology for data integration and preparation. For a more in-depth discussion of data warehousing, I would recommend *The Data Warehouse Toolkit* by Ralph Kimball.

This chapter is organized as follows:

- Section 9.1    Introduction
- Section 9.2    A Data-Warehouse Example in Banking and Finance
- Section 9.3    A Data-Warehouse Example in Retail
- Section 9.4    A Data-Warehouse Example in Healthcare
- Section 9.5    A Data-Warehouse Example in Telecommunications
- Section 9.6    Summary

## 9.1  Introduction

Before discussing examples of data warehouses for use in data mining, it is important to
be aware of the process of preparing data for decision-support systems. Ultimately, it is the
process of data integration, cleansing, and preparation used in deploying data warehouses
that makes data warehouses so valuable to data mining. The most common issue companies face when looking at data mining is that the information is not all in one place. Consider Figure 9-1, which shows how data resides at many different levels and in many
different organizations within a company.

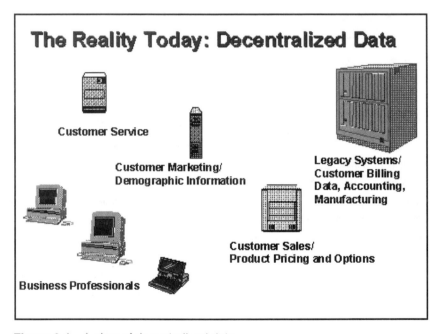

**Figure 9-1**    A view of decentralized data.

The first step in creating an environment for data mining is to integrate all data
sources as shown in Figure 9-2. Comprehensive business decisions require an integrated
data repository.

The steps involved in preparing data actually extend beyond the data warehouse
itself. Below is a brief sketch of this data preparation process for decision support, as well
as a brief mention of some of the companies that offer solutions to make the process easier. A brief mention is also made of *data marts*, currently a popular concept offering
smaller, targeted data warehouses, usually at a lower overhead cost.

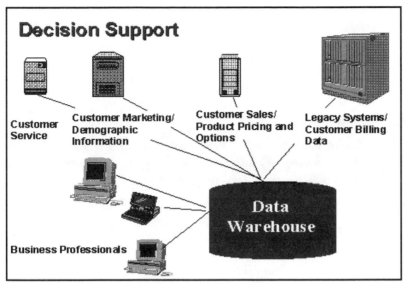

**Figure 9-2**  Creating a centralized data warehouse.

### 9.1.1   Data Acquisition

The first step to any decision-support system is acquiring data to put into that decision-support system. Since data may be in many forms and often reside on legacy systems that do not have easy-to-understand formats, many companies make a living extracting, transforming, and transporting data for the creation of decision-support systems. These companies include the following: (All products are trademarks or registered trademarks of their respective companies.)

- Carleton Corporation
- Electronic Data Systems Corporation
- Evolutionary Technologies International, Inc.
- Informatica Corporation
- Platinum Technology, Inc.
- Prism Solutions, Inc.

### 9.1.2   Data Refinement

Once data has been acquired for a decision-support system, there are often many steps involved in cleaning that data. Among other things, there may be data that are typed incorrectly, out of date, redundant, or simply incorrect. Again, there are several vendors who offer data-refinement tools. These vendors include:

- Acxiom Corporation
- Electronic Data Systems Corporation
- Harte-Hanks Data Technologies
- Platinum Technology, Inc.
- Prism Solutions, Inc.

### 9.1.3    Data Warehouse Design

During the process of acquiring and refining data, a data warehouse must be designed. Again, there are many vendors who offer tools to facilitate this process. Vendors who automate the process of building entity-level diagrams for databases include:

- Bachman Software & Services
- Evergreen Software Tools, Inc.
- LBMS, Inc.
- LogicWorks, Inc.
- Popkin Software & Systems, Inc.
- Sybase, Inc.

### 9.1.4    Data Warehouse and DataMart Implementation

Many vendors offer databases for data warehousing. There is also a newer market emerging for smaller data warehouses, or *data marts*. Vendors involved in data-warehouse and data-mart implementation include:

- Broadbase Information Systems, Inc.
- Informix Software, Inc.
- IBM Corporation
- Oracle Corporation
- Sagent Technologies, Inc.
- Sybase, Inc.
- NCR Corporation

## 9.2  A Data-Warehouse Example in Banking and Finance

The following data-mining example uses a sample database that monitors households that have accounts with a bank. When compared to an actual bank, the data structure used is quite simplistic, but it does help to present the issues surrounding the preparation of data-mining studies. The data model stores transactional data as well as information that would be more fitting to a data warehouse. Since this is the case, it is helpful to first discuss the issues of having a transaction database system versus a data warehouse. Most banks today just have a transaction system, but the trend is to move towards integrating their data into a data warehouse for decision support.

### 9.2.1   A Transactional Database System versus a Data Warehouse

Most Database Management Systems (DBMS) today are transactional, which means they are optimized for inserting and updating information and not for decision support.

Relational systems in banks handle transactions like ATM deposits, inquiries, and withdrawals, which can process millions of transactions per day. They are designed to be fast and to hold a minimal amount of information. If our fictitious bank had four years of data for 1 million customers who averaged 100 transactions a year, and each of those transactions needed 20 data fields to record necessary information, one table alone could require hundreds of gigabytes of data. There is a limit to what a transactional system can handle, although it is getting higher every year.

When a decision-support analyst wants to extract information from transactional data, that analyst may want to summarize data from the account or derive new data. For example, when looking at credit fraud, it may be valuable to look at the number of credit transactions a customer performs in an hour. This information is not directly stored in a transactional system but is attainable.

Data warehouses are designed specifically for decision support, and will usually add many fields of information that transactional systems do not have. In fact, a data warehouse might integrate multiple transactional database systems.

Data mining is often viewed as a follow-up to data warehousing because of the necessity to integrate and derive new information that transactional systems do not provide.

Having said that, this sample data model includes transactional data purposely to help distinguish types of information valuable for data-mining studies, and types of information not valuable for data mining.

### 9.2.2   The Sample Data Model

The data diagram in Figure 9-3 represents data stored by our fictitious bank.

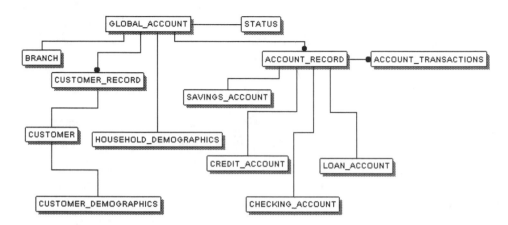

**Figure 9-3**   A simple data diagram for a bank.


Below is a list of fields within the entities described in the data diagram in Figure 9-3.

**Global Account Record.**   Figure 9-4 is the global account record for customers. A global account is an identification of a customer, or group of customers, who hold one or more different accounts with a bank. One account can have a primary and secondary account holder, and one customer can have different types of accounts as well.


GLOBAL_ACCOUNT

| Global_Acc_ID |
|---|
| Address |
| City |
| State |
| Zip |
| Branch_ID |

**Figure 9-4**   Global account.


**Customer Record/Customer.**   The CUSTOMER_RECORD table links one or more customers with a global account. There could be more than one person who has account privileges, but there is only one primary account holder. The *primary* field in the customer table indicates (yes or no) if the customer is the primary account holder. The CUSTOMER table in Figure 9-5 specifies the customer's name and Social Security Number.

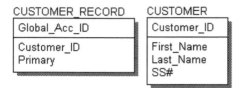

**Figure 9-5**   Customer information.

**Demographic Information.**   Demographic information can be stored for the household as well as for each customer. Information providers, like those listed in Chapter 3, can provide a great deal of demographic information, as shown in Figure 9-6. Some data warehouses have hundreds of fields on just demographic information.

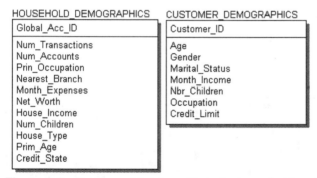

**Figure 9-6**   Demographic information at a household and customer level.

**Branch Information.**   Figure 9-7 shows the location and summary information on branches and ATM sites. Such information is useful in determining the most convenient sites for customers as well as trends in customer usage.

**Account Information.**   Figure 9-8 shows the tables for the different accounts. In this model, the table, *ACCOUNT_RECORD*, is a master table that stores all accounts tied to a global account identifier. A global account may have several accounts. For each account, there is another view that can pull up a snapshot of account information based on the date and time requested. The information for each individual account consists of summary information from monthly transactions, and in this model, is created as a view that is generated from the table ACCOUNT_TRANSACTIONS to avoid the tremendous amount of space that would be needed to store this information.

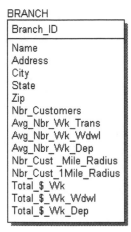

**Figure 9-7**  Location and summary information of branches and ATMs.

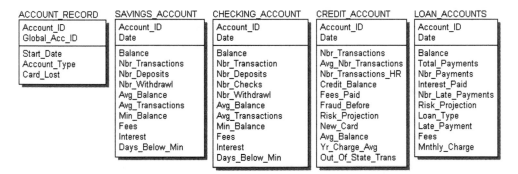

**Figure 9-8**  Account summary information.

**Account Transaction Information.**  The table ACCOUNT_TRANSACTIONS, shown in Figure 9-9, holds information on every deposit, withdrawal, balance inquiry, loan payment, credit charge, and any other bank transaction. This table is necessarily huge. While it is possible to data-mine transactional data, summary data is very useful. The *transaction type* field in this example specifies an ATM, mail, electronic, branch, or credit transaction. The *transaction subtype* field specifies the nature of the transaction, i.e., deposit, withdrawal, inquiry, etc.

ACCOUNT_TRANSACTIONS

| Transaction_ID |
| --- |
| Account_ID<br>Date<br>Transaction_Type<br>Transaction _Subtype<br>Fees<br>$_Deposit<br>$_Withdrawl<br>Indicator<br>Description<br>Branch_ID<br>Location |

**Figure 9-9**   Transaction information.

**Status Information.**   The following table has the status information of an account. This information is used directly for decision support and includes items like an indicator of whether customers have an account with another bank, an indicator of what types of services they have used with this bank in the past, an indicator of whether they have left this bank or are still a customer, or indicators of what types of difficulties (like foreclosure and late payments) this customer might have had.

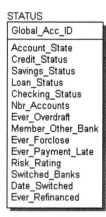

STATUS

| Global_Acc_ID |
| --- |
| Account_State<br>Credit_Status<br>Savings_Status<br>Loan_Status<br>Checking_Status<br>Nbr_Accounts<br>Ever_Overdraft<br>Member_Other_Bank<br>Ever_Forclose<br>Ever_Payment_Late<br>Risk_Rating<br>Switched_Banks<br>Date_Switched<br>Ever_Refinanced |

**Figure 9-10**   Status information.

### 9.2.3   An Example of a Credit-Fraud Study

Credit issuers are very concerned about the ability to forecast when a credit-card transaction is fraudulent. There are systems in place today that check credit transactions and provide an indication of whether to allow a credit charge or not. Using the data model shown in Section 9.2.2, we can build a model that could help predict a potentially fraudulent transaction.

**Preparing the Data for a Credit-Fraud Model.**    The table shown in Figure 9-9, ACCOUNT_TRANSACTION, has a field, *Transaction Type*, that indicates whether or not the transaction was a credit-card charge. It is possible to extract information on the transaction by using a query tool or formulating an SQL statement to extract the information requested. SQL, or Structured Query Language, is the standard for interacting with relational databases. For example, an SQL statement to get transaction information on only credit charges from a Oracle relational database would be:

```
SELECT * FROM TRANSACTION_RECORD WHERE TRANSACTION_TYPE = 'CREDIT'
```

In preparing data for credit-fraud models, banks include more than just the transactional information itself. For example, in the table *Credit Card Account,* there are several fields that could be useful in predicting whether a credit-card transaction is fraudulent, like *Nbr Transactions*, *Avg Nbr Transactions*, *Nbr Transactions Hr*, *New Card*, *Fraud Before,* or *Out of State Trans.* The field *Nbr_Transactions* shows the monthly total for transactions for a customer. The table ACCOUNT_TRANSACTIONS is also useful in determining credit fraud, since it contains a field, *Indicator,* which indicates if a card associated with this account has been reported lost.

There are three tables of information in our example that can be used to create this study. In essence, information for this study is extracted as shown in Figure 9-11.

The question many people struggle with when trying to prepare the data to build a model is:

### How do I get the information in the right form?

There are three ways to approach preparing the data for this study:

1. Use a query tool to extract the information from a relational database and put it into the right form. Tools from vendors like Brio, Business Objects, and Cognos will easily create tables like the one in Figure 9-11. This approach will limit the number of records extracted from the data warehouse because the data is being downloaded to a client computer.
2. Create a *view* within a relational database to represent the virtual data to be mined.
3. Construct an SQL statement to get data in the right form.

Ideally, data-mining tools should automatically transform raw data into a form it can manage. As of this writing, that is not the case. Red Brick is the first relational vendor to integrate data mining directly with a relational database; query and OLAP vendors are integrating data mining with their tools, but data mining has, until recently, been done largely on flat files that require a good deal of preparation.

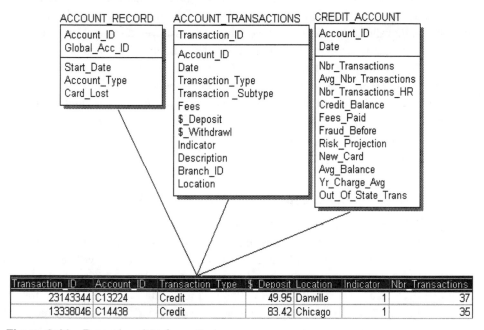

**Figure 9-11**   Preparing data for a study.

For this model, several data fields could be derived from existing columns that might be useful. For example, it may be interesting to examine whether more credit fraud occurs on Tuesdays than on Wednesdays. To do so, deriving a field to specify day-of-the-week is necessary in most data mining tools. The *Trx_Timestamp* field could be used to derive many fields, like d*ay_of_week, day_of_month, hour_of_day, month, year, week_of_year*, and so forth. Views, query tools, and SQL statements will all allow the creation of new derived fields, but this falls into the category of data preparation and is usually not automated by data-mining vendors today.

**Classification Versus Clustering for the Credit-Fraud Model.**   The   table ACCOUNT_TRANSACTIONS has the field *Indicator*, which indicates whether or not a transaction is valid. This field is determined after a transaction is validated and is modified as fraud is verified. The field can be used as a dependent variable for modeling the characteristics that make some transactions more likely to be fraudulent than others. This is a traditional *classification* study.

Sometimes there may be no historical data. For example, *Indicator* may be blank because there is no historical information on which transactions are fraudulent. In this case, fraud detection may be started by *clustering* data. Since fraudulent charges will usually have unique characteristics — for example, many charges made in a very short time, which is more common of new cards — clustering data should provide groupings that are more likely to be valid and more likely to be fraud. The discovered groups can be labeled, with some investigation, as more likely to be fraudulent and more likely to not be fraudulent. In the absence of historical data on fraudulent records, clustering alone can't tell you whether a group is more or less likely to be fraudulent; however, clustering is useful in telling you about similar and dissimilar groupings and, if one claim is fraudulent, similar claims are more likely to be suspect. Once the findings are verified, the *Indicator* field can be updated by flagging the discovered clusters, and now a classification model for credit fraud can be built.

### 9.2.4    An Example of a Retention-Management Study

Banks are always interested in understanding how to keep their customers loyal. It is much more costly to attract a new customer than it is to keep an existing one. Industry analysts are starting to define customer lifecycles and the needs a customer will have through each stage of life. Early on, a customer may be interested in college loans and home loans. Later in the cycle, a customer will be more interested in saving for retirement and investment opportunities. Surprisingly, building models to understand customer retention and customer lifecycles is new to many institutions, and the banking industry is not alone.

**Preparing the Data.**    The sample database in Figure 9-3 has many data elements that could be of interest in creating a customer-retention model. The HOUSEHOLD_STATUS table is important because it contains information on whether a customer is loyal or has left for a competitor. The actual fields in this sample are *Switched_Banks* and *Date_Switched* field.

In this example, customer and household demographic information is clearly useful. Branch information may also be useful. One branch may be better at attracting and keeping customers than another. Account information is also of benefit. It may be that having multiple accounts indicates that a customer will be more loyal. And finally, transaction information is useful in retention models. If a customer slows down substantially using a bank's services, or if information on ATM transactions through this bank's teller machines show a customer using another bank's account, these are sure signs a customer is gravitating to a competitor.

The creation of a data table for building this model will involve joining information from all the tables.

**Time Dependency in Customer Retention.**  The database model in Figure 9-3 shows account records as summaries for a specific period. For example, it will provide the number of account transactions in March. A customer-retention model usually has a table that shows a progression of account activity over time. If a model is being built to study the likelihood someone will drop an account in July, then the account activity for January, February, March, April, May, and June may be fields in the data set for this model as shown in Figure 9-12.

| Nbr Trans Jan | Nbr Trans Feb | Nbr Trans Mar | Nbr Trans Apr | Nbr Trans May | Nbr Trans Jun | Nbr Trans Jul | Left in Aug |
|---|---|---|---|---|---|---|---|
| 20 | 19 | 14 | 14 | 15 | 8 | 7 | Y |
| 19 | 16 | 15 | 22 | 14 | 19 | 18 | N |
| 15 | 20 | 20 | 4 | 4 | 2 | 1 | Y |
| 9 | 8 | 11 | 7 | 9 | 3 | 7 | N |

**Figure 9-12**  A time-dependent data set for customer retention.

The field *Nbr_Trans_May* in Figure 9-12 is the total number of transactions, but our data model in Figure 9-3 calculates number of transactions by account. *Nbr_Trans_May* would be the sum of the total number of transactions for checking and savings accounts. Also, the data model in Figure 9-3 does not have a table with fields for number of savings account and checking account transactions for January, February, March, and so forth. It does have an account-record table with number of transactions and a period associated with it; so, in order to prepare columns like the one in Figure 9-12, multiple instances of account records have to be used. An example of the actual SQL to perform this type of data preparation is shown below. The example shows monthly transactions for checking and savings accounts as well as demographic information on customers. The information stored in the table could be expanded greatly, but as an example, this is overkill.

```
CREATE TABLE MINE_CUST_RETENTION (
Global_Acc_ID                   INTEGER,
Nbr_S_Trans_6mnths_ago          INTEGER,
Nbr_C_Trans_6mnths_ago          INTEGER,
Nbr_S_Trans_5mnths_ago          INTEGER,
Nbr_C_Trans_5mnths_ago          INTEGER,
Nbr_S_Trans_4mnths_ago          INTEGER,
Nbr_C_Trans_4mnths_ago          INTEGER,
Nbr_S_Trans_3mnths_ago          INTEGER,
Nbr_C_Trans_3mnths_ago          INTEGER,
Nbr_S_Trans_2mnths_ago          INTEGER,
```

```
Nbr_C_Trans_2mnths_ago        INTEGER,
Nbr_S_Trans_1mnths_ago        INTEGER,
Nbr_C_Trans_1mnths_ago        INTEGER,
City                          VARCHAR (30),
State                         VARCHAR (30),
Net_Worth                     INTEGER,
House_Income                  INTEGER,
Num_Children                  INTEGER,
Prim_Age                      INTEGER,
Num_Accounts                  INTEGER,
Nearest_Branch                INTEGER,
Left_This_Month               INTEGER)


INSERT INTO MINE_CUST_RETENTION
(Global_Acc_ID
,Nbr_S_Trans_6months_ago
,Nbr_C_Trans_6months_ago
,Nbr_S_Trans_5months_ago
,Nbr_C_Trans_5months_ago
,Nbr_S_Trans_4months_ago
,Nbr_C_Trans_4months_ago
,Nbr_S_Trans_3months_ago
,Nbr_C_Trans_3months_ago
,Nbr_S_Trans_2months_ago
,Nbr_C_Trans_2months_ago
,Nbr_S_Trans_1months_ago
,Nbr_C_Trans_1months_ago
, City
, State
, Net_Worth
, House_Income
, Num_Children
, Prim_Age
, Num_Accounts
, Nearest_Branch
, Left_This_Month
)
SELECT Global_Account.Global_Acc_ID,sum(case when AccountType=
      'Savings' and Transaction_Date between date '1997-01-01'
and
          date '1997-01-31'
      then 1
      else 0
      end),
    sum(case when AccountType='Checking' and Transaction_Date
          between date '1997-01-01' and date '1997-01-31'
```

```
                    then 1
                    else 0
                    end),
                sum(case when AccountType='Savings' and Transaction_Date
                        between date '1997-02-01' and date '1997-02-28'
                    then 1
                    else 0
                    end),
                sum(case when AccountType='Checking' and Transaction_Date
                        between date '1997-02-01' and date '1997-02-28'
                    then 1
                    else 0
                    end),
                sum(case when AccountType='Savings' and Transaction_Date
            between
                        date '1997-03-01' and date '1997-03-31'
                    then 1
                    else 0
                    end),
                sum(case when AccountType='Checking' and Transaction_Date
                        between date '1997-03-01' and date '1997-03-31'
                    then 1
                    else 0
                    end),
                sum(case when AccountType='Savings' and Transaction_Date
            between
                        date '1997-04-01' and date '1997-04-30'
                    then 1
                    else 0
                    end),
                sum(case when AccountType='Checking' and Transaction_Date
                        between date '1997-04-01' and date '1997-04-30'
                    then 1
                    else 0
                    end),
                sum(case when AccountType='Savings' and Transaction_Date
            between
                        date '1997-05-01' and date '1997-05-31'
                    then 1
                    else 0
                    end),
                sum(case when AccountType='Checking' and Transaction_Date
                        between date '1997-05-01' and date '1997-05-31'
                    then 1
                    else 0
                    end),
                sum(case when AccountType='Savings' and Transaction_Date
```

```
between
        date '1997-06-01' and date '1997-06-30'
    then 1
    else 0
    end),
    sum(case when AccountType='Checking' and Transaction_Date
        between date '1997-06-01' and date '1997-06-30'
    then 1
    else 0
    end),
    Global_Account.City,
    Global_Account.State,
    Household_Demographics.Net_Worth,
    Household_Demographics.House_Income,
    Household_Demographics.Num_Children,
    Household_Demographics.Prim_Age,
    Household_Demographics.Num_Accounts,
    Household_Demographics.Nearest_Branch,
    case when Status.Switched_Banks = 1 and Sta-
tus.Date_Switched
        between date'1997-07-01' and date'1997-07-31'
    then 1 else 0 end as Left_This_Month
FROM Global_Account, Household_Demographics, Status,
    Account_Record, Account_Transaction
WHERE Global_Acount.Global_Acc_ID=
    Household_Demographics.Global_Acc_ID
    and Global_Acount.Global_Acc_ID=Staus.Global_Acc_ID
    and
Global_Acount.Global_Acc_ID=Account_Record.Global_Acc_ID
    and
Account_Record.Account_ID=Account_Transaction.Account_ID
GROUP BY Global_Account.City, Global_Account.State,
    Household_Demographics.Net_Worth,
    Household_Demographics.House_Income,
    Household_Demographics.Num_Children,
    Household_Demographics.Prim_Age,
    Household_Demographics.Num_Accounts,
    Household_Demographics.Nearest_Branch,
    Left_This_Month
```

The dependent variable for this study is the *Left_This_Month* field that is created from information on the *Switched_Banks* and *Date_Switched* fields.

Additionally, the actual number of transactions per month may not be as interesting as the percent change in number of transactions from month to month. Again, this would require the derivation of another set of columns to calculate the change in number of transactions.

Because customer retention is time dependent, the model that would be used in July would change in August: you would add July account activity to the August model that you didn't have a month earlier. The time dependency of this model clearly demonstrates that data mining is a process. Data-mining models are being updated on an ongoing basis as trends and patterns change over time.

**Clustering in Customer Retention.**   Using clustering techniques for customer retention is useful. By creating groupings of similar customers, it may be possible to identify certain segments that are more likely to leave a bank.

### 9.2.5   Data-Trends Analysis

Another type of data-mining activity is discovering trends. Trend analysis can be an additional activity on top of another data-mining process. For example, if you are studying customer retention, you may build a model in August and a model in September. By comparing the models for each month, it is possible to note the most significant changes are from month to month. This may help you discover seasonal changes or just unexpected changes as a business environment evolves.

Another way to perform trend analysis is to use a time field as the dependent variable. For example, with the data model in Figure 9-3, you could mine all existing account records by quarter. For every account, there would be four records: an account record summary for spring, summer, winter, and fall. A study like this may show changes in items like number of transactions, transaction amounts, or fees from season to season. Another example would be to change the time from a season to a day in a week. This model would discover changes in account behavior based on the day of the week.

## 9.3  A Data-Warehouse Example in Retail

The sample model used in this study is a point-of-sale (POS) model for a retail chain. When a customer buys a product or series of products at a register, that information is stored in a transactional system. The transactional system is likely to hold other information, such as when the purchase happened, where it happened, what types of promotions were involved, as well as who bought the product. This information can be used to perform many types of studies, several of which are discussed here.

Examples of data structures for data warehousing common in the retail market are examined in *The Data Warehouse Toolkit*, a book by Ralph Kimball. This book provides numerous in-depth data-modeling examples, including a model for a grocery store, an inventory warehouse, a shipment system, a value-chain organization, and a subscription business.

### 9.3.1    The Sample Data Model

Figure 9-13 diagrams a data structure for a retail organization logging customers' transactions at their outlets in several malls across the U.S.

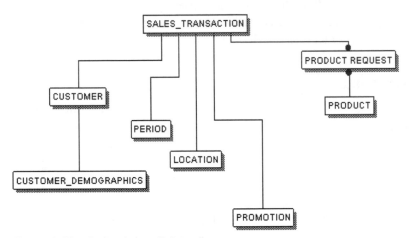

**Figure 9-13**   A simple retail-data diagram.

The descriptions of the different entities shown in Figure 9-13 follow.

**Sales Transaction Information.**   The sales transaction is the primary table for this database. For every sale, a transaction, location, time, and customer identifier are stored, along with the total price and the number of products purchased. Transaction information excluding products purchased is stored in the SALES_TRANSACTION table.

Because any number of products can be purchased for a transaction, there is a second table, PRODUCT REQUEST, that stores a new row of data for every product purchased.

All products purchased are linked to the SALES_TRANSACTION table through the *Transaction ID* field (see Figure 9-14).

**Customer Information.**   The CUSTOMER table is a list of all the customers who are known to purchase at this retail outlet. For the customers that are known, customer demographic information has been purchased through third-party sources, and company demographic information has been purchased through third-party sources; see CUSTOMER_DEMOGRAPHIC table (Figure 9-15).

**Figure 9-14** Point-of-sale record.

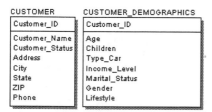

**Figure 9-15** Customer information.

**Period.** While the *Date* field in the SALES_TRANSACTION table lists the specific time a purchase was made, it is useful in data mining to break the time in a PERIOD table as shown in Figure 9-16.

**Figure 9-16** Information based on the time of purchase.

**Location Dimension.** This LOCATION table stores information containing the region, store, and sales representative involved in the sale, as shown in Figure 9-17.

**Figure 9-17** Location where merchandise is purchased.

**Promotion Information.**   The PROMOTION table stores information on the type of promotion, where the promotion was advertised, and the type of discount offered with the promotion, if there was any.

**Figure 9-18**   Promotion information.

**Product Information.**   The PRODUCT table stores information on a product indicated by its *stock keeping unit* (SKU). Information includes name, standard price, shelf placement, package size, category, and brand. The number of descriptive elements on a product is potentially much greater than this. In retail chains, there can be tens of thousands of products and they are changing all the time as products, are upgraded and their SKUs change.

**Figure 9-19**   Product information.

### 9.3.2   What Types of Customers are Buying Different Types of Products

In this example, assume we are looking at customer purchases of plastic containers for storage. There are several brands of plastic containers that the store carries: STOR_N'TOTE, PAK_AWAY, and DR_PACK. Each of the containers comes in 4-gallon, 7-gallon, 9-gallon, and 20-gallon sizes. There are 12 SKU numbers arbitrarily made up, one for each brand/size combination. The PRODUCT table has the fields *Category, Brand*, *Size,* and *SKU.* They have the elements:

*Category*:   Plastic Containers
*Brand*:       STOR_N'TOTE, PAK_AWAY, and DR_PACK
*Size*:         4_GAL, 7_GAL, 9_GAL, and 20_GAL
*SKU*:         11055, 11056, 11057, 11058, 11155, 11156, 11157, 11158, 11255,
               11256, 11257, 11258

The goal of this study is to determine what customers are buying the different brands and sizes of plastic containers. Retailers want to know what combinations of product (in this case, containers) should be offered at different locations (in this case, at each of several outlet malls). It is not necessarily the case that 20-gallon PAK_AWAY containers will sell as well to customers from one location as those from another location.

**Preparing the Data Set.**    This example creates a table MINE_PRODUCT, which integrates all the product and product request information for all records with a matching SKU for the products to be examined.

The SQL shown in this example can be used to profile other products by simply replacing the SKU numbers of the plastic containers with other products.

```
CREATE TABLE MINE_PRODUCT
Transaction_ID       INTEGER,
SKU                  INTEGER,
PRICE                REAL,
Promotion_ID         INTEGER,
Trans_Date           DATE,
Total_Price          REAL,
Nbr_Products         INTEGER,
Cust_ID              INTEGER,
Location_ID          INTEGER,
State                VARCHAR (4),
City                 VARCHAR (30),
Age                  INTEGER,
Children             INTEGER,
Type_Car             VARCHAR (30),
Income_Level         INTEGER,
Marital_Status       VARCHAR (30),
Gender               VARCHAR (4),
Lifestyle            VARCHAR (30),
Day_Of_Week          INTEGER,
Day_Of_Yr            INTEGER,
Hr_Of_Day            INTEGER,
Week_Of_Yr           INTEGER,
Month                VARCHAR (4),
Holiday              INTEGER,
Sales_Rep            VARCHAR (30),
```

```
Store                   VARCHAR (30),
Region                  VARCHAR (20),
Promotion_Type          VARCHAR (20),
Medium_Used             VARCHAR (20),
Discount_Offered        VARCHAR (20),
Product_Price           VARCHAR (20),
Shelf_Placement         VARCHAR (20),
Package_Size            VARCHAR (20),
Category                VARCHAR (30),
Brand                   VARCHAR (20))


INSERT INTO MINE_PRODUCT
SELECT (Transaction_ID, PRODUCT.Sku, Price, Comment,
Product_Type, Product_Name, Product_Description,
Product_Standard_Price, Shelf_Placement, Brand, Category,
Package_Size, Trans_Date, Total_Price, Nbr_Products, City,
State, Age, Children, Type_Car, Income_Level, Marital_Status,
Gender, Lifestyle, Sales_Rep, Store, Region, Promotion_Type,
Medium_Used, Discount_Offered, Day_Of_Week, Day_Of_Yr,
Hr_Of_Day, Week_Of_Year, Month, Holiday)

FROM PRODUCT_REQUEST, PRODUCT, SALES_TRANSACTION, CUSTOMER,
CUSTOMER_DEMOGRAPHIC, LOCATION, PROMOTION, PERIOD

WHERE PRODUCT.SKU is [11055, 11056, 11057, 11058, 11155, 11156,
11157, 11158, 11255, 11256, 11257, 11258]

   AND PRODUCT.SKU=PRODUCT_REQUEST.SKU
   AND PRODUCT_RREQUEST.SKU = SALES_TRANSACTION.SKU
   AND PRODUCT_REQUEST.TRANSACTION_ID =
       SALES_TRANSACTION.TRANSACTION_ID
   AND PRODUCT_REQUEST.PROMOTION_ID = PROMOTION.PROMOTION_ID
   AND SALES_TRANSACTION.LOCATION_ID = LOCATION.LOCATION_ID
   AND SALES_TRANSACTION.TRANS_DATE = PERIOD.TRANS_DATE
   AND SALES_TRANSACTION.CUSTOMER_ID = CUSTOMER.CUSTOMER_ID
   AND CUSTOMER.CUSTOMER_ID =
CUSTOMER_DEMOGRAPHICS.CUSTOMER_ID
```

This query provides a table MINE_PRODUCT that is ready to mine! It should be noted that this is not necessarily the optimal way to perform this operation.

**Choosing a Dependent Variable for the Study.**    To look at influencing factors on the different plastic containers' brand and size, the *SKU* field could be used as the dependent variable. To eliminate the effect of brand, the *Package_Size* field could be used similarly to eliminate the effect of package size on the study, and the *Brand* field could be used as the dependent variable.

This study will tell you the relevance of customer information on the type of brand, but since data on the promotion, location, and time have also been provided in the data set, the study will also indicate their influence on the purchase of the 12 different products.

**Clustering Approach.**   Instead of using standard classification studies, a clustering approach can be taken to see if there are significant groupings of customers who have purchased containers in general. This type of study would help one understand profiles of individuals looking to buy containers.

### 9.3.3   An Example of Regional Studies and Others

The table, MINE_PRODUCT, can be used to study many other things. Simply by changing the dependent variable of the study, the emphasis of the model changes. For example, if the dependent variable was changed to the field *Region,* the study would examine the relationship of customer characteristics, time periods, product decisions, and promotions on the region where a particular container was bought.

Another approach would be to change the dependent variable of the study to *Day_Of_Wk.* In this case, the study would focus on what factors are more common to the day of week.

As an exercise, examine the fields created in the table, MINE_PRODUCT, and see what type of model would be created if you made each specific field a dependent variable.

## 9.4   A Data-Warehouse Example in Healthcare

The sample healthcare data discussed in Table 2-1 in Chapter 2 had to be derived from somewhere. There is information in this table that discusses patient information, procedures performed, physician information, facility information, medications used, and objective findings during examinations of a patient. The data warehouse in this section provides a starting point from which such a table of information could be created.

### 9.4.1   The Example Data Model

Figure 9-20 shows a data-model diagram for the healthcare example.

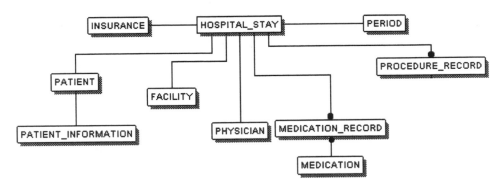

**Figure 9-20**   A data diagram for healthcare.

The descriptions of the different entities in Figure 9-20 follow.

**Hospital Stay.**   The HOSPITAL_STAY table is the central table of this data-warehouse design. For each hospital stay, there is information on the time, the patient, the insurance, the physician, the facility, the procedures, and the medication, which are pointed to with identifiers. The cost of the stay, length of stay, and overall recovery time are also stored.

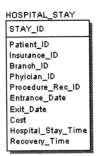

**Figure 9-21**   Table for hospital stay.

**Patient Information.**   The PATIENT table is a list of all the patients for this hospital, including their name, phone, and address. The PATIENT_INFORMATION table includes medical history and descriptive information about a patient. The amount of information on a patient would actually be much larger than what is represented in Figure 9-22.

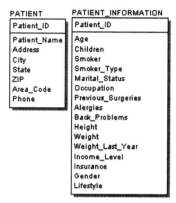

**Figure 9-22**   Patient information.

**Facility and Physician.**   The FACILITY and PHYSICIAN tables store information about the hospital branch where a patient stayed, as well as information on the attend-
ing physician. These tables would usually have much more data than is represented in
Figure 9-23.

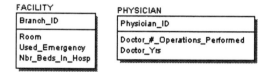

**Figure 9-23**   Facility and physician information.

**Procedure Record.**   The PROCEDURE_RECORD table tracks all operations and
procedures performed on a patient during a hospital stay, as shown in Figure 9-24.

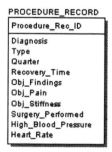

**Figure 9-24**   Procedure record.

**Medication Record/Medications.** The MEDICATIONS_RECORD table tracks all medicines prescribed to a patient, and the dosages used during a hospital stay. The information on medications is pointed to with the *medication_ID* field and is stored in the MEDICATION table (see Figure 9-25).

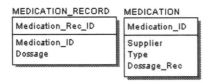

**Figure 9-25**   Medication prescribed to patient.

**Period.** The PERIOD table stores the date of a procedure in several different time representations, as shown in Figure 9-26.

**Figure 9-26**   The period table.

**Insurance.** The INSURANCE table specifies what type of insurance a patient uses during a hospital stay, as shown in Figure 9-27.

**Figure 9-27**   Insurance information.

### 9.4.2   A Look at Sample Studies in Healthcare

In order to create a table like the one in Table 2-2, discussed in Chapter 2, a view can be created in the relational database storing this sample model. The code to do this would look like the code below.

The SQL is involved, and a six-way join of tables is required, but it does return the desired view of information.

```
CREATE VIEW MINING_VIEW AS SELECT Recovery_Time,
Hospital_Stay, Age, Smoker, Smoker_Type, Marital_Status,
Occupation, Insurance, Pain_Reliever_Used, Doctor_Yrs,
Doctor_#_Operations_Performed, Nbr_Beds_In_Hosp,
Systolic_Pressure, Diastolic_Pressure, Allergies,
Previous_Surgeries, Back_Problems, Month, Obj_Pain,
Obj_Stiffness, Area_Code, Height, Weight,
Weight_Last_Year FROM HOSPITAL_STAY a, PATIENT b,
PATIENT_INFORMATION c, FACILITY d, PHYSICIAN e, PERIOD f,
PROCEDURE_RECORD g, WHERE a.Patient_ID = b.Patient_ID and
a.Patient_ID = c.Patient_ID and a.Facility_ID = d.Facility_ID
and a.Physician_ID = e.Physician_ID and a.Entrance_Date =
f.Tran_Date and a.Procedure_Rec_ID = g.Procedure_Rec_ID
```

Another reason data mining is used with data warehouses is that data warehouses are usually optimized to handle joins of this complexity. Transactional databases may have a huge performance hit in trying to accomplish this join.

**Choosing a Dependent Variable for the Study.**   Section 2.4 discussed defining a study to model recovery times of patients. In this case, the dependent variable is the field *Recovery_Time*. Any number of variables can be used as the dependent variable for the data view created above. Below are two examples of studies.

Selecting the field *Smoker*, with values "Yes" and "No" as the dependent variable, changes the focus of the study to model the differences between smokers and non-smokers.

Selecting the field *Doctor_Yrs* as the dependent variable shifts the focus to the differences in the surgeries performed when a doctor is more or less experienced. In this study, the data is numeric and might possibly be binned (i.e., 0–2 years, 2–5 years, and 5 or more years).

### 9.4.3   A Discussion on Adding Credit Data to Our Example

One of the areas where data mining adds tremendous value is when disparate databases are integrated and information is then mined. It is not obvious that a person's credit information would have any bearing on their ability to recover from a hospital stay, but by adding this information to the view MINING_VIEW (shown in Section 9.4.2), one could easily find out if there is a connection. The reason a seemingly random data source is discussed here is that a *Wall Street Journal* article discussed a relationship that an insurance company found between someone's credit rating and their likelihood to be a good driver. Again, the connection is not always obvious, but it is interesting to try such studies if they can be managed.

## 9.5 A Data-Warehouse Example in Telecommunications

The following is an example data model and discussion of sample data-mining models concerning promotions and competitive marketing in the cellular-phone industry. Competitive information is not always easy to find. An article in *Wireless Week* entitled *Carriers Mum on Market Stats* (6/24/96) discusses the lack of competitive information. They quote several industry spokepersons about the secretiveness of information. For example, a spokeswoman for U.S. West NewVector Group commented: "We are reluctant to enable our competitors to find out market numbers." A spokeswoman for BellSouth Cellular Corporation comments: "We never give out market-share information — only our subscriber numbers in aggregate." A spokeswoman for Ameritech Cellular Services commented: "What is the point of releasing [market] information?" The trend towards secrecy is widely practiced in cellular services.

The question to ask then is:

*"How is data mining performed when the information is available?"*

In the cellular market, only about 15% of the population used a wireless phone as of mid-1996, and none of the competitors in the market have complete, accurate information on their competition.

Hopefully, this example will argue that even with an absence of completely accurate information, *data mining is a process*, and you have to start somewhere. If models are built to describe a competitive landscape, over time a company will be able to fill in critical information that will help create a more accurate picture. The alternative is not attractive.

### 9.5.1   The Sample Data Model

Figure 9-28 shows a simplified data schematic for a cellular provider tracking promotions on a rational level. It has a table for competitive market-share information in a given area.

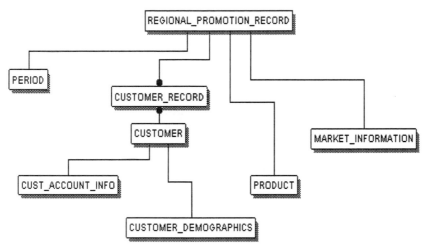

**Figure 9-28** A simple diagram for the telecommunication industry.

Given the diagram in Figure 9-28, following is a listing of types of fields you might find for each of the tables in this schematic.

**Regional Promotion Record.** The table REGIONAL_PROMOTION_RECORD shows regional promotions. The promotions being tracked are those where a customer will respond in some way if engaged.

REGIONAL_PROMOTION_RECORD

| Region_Promo_ID |
| --- |
| Period_ID |
| Market_ID |
| Product_ID |
| Region |
| Medium |
| Cash_Incentive |
| Competitive_Promo_Level |
| Promotion_Type |

**Figure 9-29** Regional promotion record.

**Customer Record.** The CUSTOMER_RECORD table shown in Figure 9-30 is a table tracking the customers who are sent a regional promotion. If the customer responds to a marketing campaign, there is a field *Responded* to track it. The CUSTOMER table is a current list of all customers.

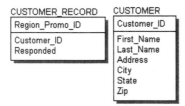

**Figure 9-30**   Household information.


**Customer Demographics/Customer_Status.**   Figure 9-31 stores customer-demographic information as well as customer status information based on their usage patterns, and information on their current activity with the company.

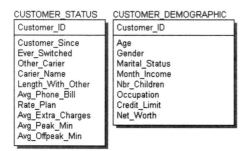

**Figure 9-31**   Promotional information.


**Market Information.**   Figure 9-32 lists market information that we want to collect for an account. The information provided specifies market information that can be gathered, such as the number of potential customers in a regional market, the number of actual customers in a market, this company's market share, and estimates of competitors' market shares. This model assumes two competitors, Carrier 1 and Carrier 2. The other information to be collected is market share on the regional level. Because information is not definite on market-share numbers, fields for minimum and maximum market share are provided.

MARKET_INFORMATION

| Market_ID |
| --- |
| Reg_Mkt_Share |
| %Incr_Mkt_Share_Region |
| Reg_Mkt_Share_Car1_Min |
| Reg_Mkt_Share_Car1_Max |
| Reg_Mkt_Share_Car2_Min |
| Reg_Mkt_Share_Car2_Max |
| Nbr_Potential_Cust_Mkt |
| Nbr_Actual_Cust_Mkt |

**Figure 9-32**  Market-share information.

**Product Information.**   Figure 9-33 shows fields describing information on the product, such as product name, category, and a competitive pricing metric.

PRODUCT

| Product_ID |
| --- |
| Product_Name |
| Product_Category |
| Comp_Price_Metric |

**Figure 9-33**  Product information.

**Period.**   Figure 9-34 breaks down the data of a promotion into different time fields, such as day of the week and hour of the day.

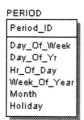

PERIOD

| Period_ID |
| --- |
| Day_Of_Week |
| Day_Of_Yr |
| Hr_Of_Day |
| Week_Of_Year |
| Month |
| Holiday |

**Figure 9-34**  Time dimension.

### 9.5.2   Data Collection

Because market-share information is not readily available, some detective work is necessary before a data set that can be mined can be created. The MARKET_INFORMATION table needs to be filled in. One suggestion is to start by collecting data on a regional level. For example, we might track competitive data in the Denver metropolitan area.

Market-share information for the cellular company itself should be easy enough to create. Similarly, it is possible to purchase a listing of all the potential customers in metropolitan areas: whatever customers in the target list, who are not customers of this cellular company, could be categorized as other market share, either untapped or competitor's customers.

According to an article in *Wireless Week* entitled "Study Reveals Digital Fallacy" (11/11/96), "most cellular-phone users are executives, sales staff, and administrative personnel . . . the largest percentages of users are 30- to 39-year-olds with annual incomes of $100,000 or more." It might be necessary to start with a "customer list" that includes only the most likely people to use cellular phones (which can always be expanded as a data model becomes more accurate).

The toughest part of getting market-share information at a regional level is knowing the other competitor's market share. Some assumptions could be made about the minimum and maximum market-share rates. This could be accomplished by survey techniques as well as by tracking in this regional area, all the customers who change from another service to this company's, and all those customers who move to another competitor. Over time, some general numbers can be gathered.

The same process can be used to gather information on a product level. All the data does not need to be in place before mining can take place. The process of model-building needs to start at some point, and, over time, the models will get better as business is better understood.

### 9.5.3   Creating the Data Set

The tables in this SQL example all have the *Account_ID* as an identifier. This makes the creation of a data set much easier.

```
CREATE VIEW MINING_VIEW AS
SELECT Promotion_ID, Month, City, State, Area_Code, Responded,
Promotion_Type, Medium, Principal_Occupation, Region,
Month_Expenses, Net_Worth, Avg_Phone_Bill, House_Income,
Num_Children, House_Type, Principal_Age, Credit_State, Age,
Gender, Marital_Status, Month_Income, Nbr_Children, Occupa-
tion, Credit_Limit, Customer_Since, Rate_Plan, Ever_Switched,
Other_Carrier, Carrier_Name, Length_With_Other, Reg_Mkt_Share,
%Incr_Mkt_Share_Region, Reg_Mkt_Share_Car1_Min,
Reg_Mkt_Share_Car1_Max, Reg_Mkt_Share_Car2_Min,
Reg_Mkt_Share_Car2_Max, Product_Name, Product_Category,
Comp_Price_Metric

FROM REGIONAL_PROMOTION_RECORD a, CUSTOMER_RECORD b, CUSTOMER
c, CUSTOMER_STATUS d, CUSTOMER_DEMOGRAPHIC e,
```

```
MARKET_INFORMATION f, PRODUCT g, PERIOD h

WHERE a.Region_Promo_ID IN ['101','102','103'] and b.Responded
= "Yes"

    and a.Region_Promo_ID = b.Region_Promo_ID
    and b.Customer_ID = c.Customer_ID
    and c.Customer_ID = d.Customer_ID
    and c.Customer_ID = e.Customer_ID
    and a.Market_ID = f.Market_ID
    and a.Product_ID = g.Product_ID
    and a.Period_ID = h.Period_ID
```

### An Alternative Structure for the Example

The example above used the *Responded* field from the table CUSTOMER_RECORD. The problem with this example is that it tracks responders, but not the list of those to whom a promotional was sent.

Alternatively, one could maintain two tables: PROMO_SENT_TO and PROMO_RESPONDED_TO and derive a view called CUSTOMER_RECORD. This is a more flexible solution and tracks responders and non-reponders, whereas the previous solution tracked only responders.

```
CREATE TABLE Promo_Sent_To
( Customer_IDdatatype NOT NULL
, Promo_IDdatatypeNOT NULL
)

CREATE TABLE Promo_Responded_To
( Customer_IDdatatype NOT NULL
, Promo _IDdatatypeNOT NULL
, RespondedCHARACTER(3) DEFAULT NULL
)
CREATE VIEW Customer_Record AS
SELECT Promo_Sent_To.Customer_ID, Promo_Sent_To.Promo_ID,
Promo_Responded_To.Responded
FROM Promo_Sent_To LEFT OUTER JOIN Promo_Responded_To using
Customer_ID, Promo_ID
```

### 9.5.4   An Example Study on Product/Market Share Analysis

We have gathered a data set of customers who were sent promotions in several regions, taking a random sampling of cellular users of competitive basic cellular rate plans. The promotions have the identifiers 101, 102, and 103. Demographic, market share, and promotional information on each of the customers responding to one of these three promotions has been gathered. The view created in Section 9.5.3, MINING_VIEW, contains this information. The study is meant to look at the differences in characteristics of those that responded to one of the three promotions. The *Region_Promo_ID* field then becomes the dependent variable. The created view has been limited to only the promotions 101, 102, and 103.

### 9.5.5    An Example Study of a Regional Market Analysis

The same data set as described in Section 9.5.4 could be used to perform a regional/ market study by setting the dependent variable to represent one of the regions where sampling took place. This is specified by the *Region* field in the REGIONAL_PROMOTION_RECORD table. In this case, the most important criteria for each region will be examined.

Some of the fields used in a study like this one might not be useful. For example, you might expect a certain promotion to figure prominently in one region because it was a regional promotion. Still, this study will show regional differences clearly.

## 9.6  Summary

This chapter introduces the process of creating data warehouses to enable data-mining studies in different industries. The chapter discussed a few studies that examine studies on customer retention, product comparisons, promotional activities, and the recovery-time of patients. The type of studies used in each of the four data warehouse examples purposely vary. Moreover, studies like customer retention readily cross over between industries.

One fallacy of data mining is that all data must be in place before mining can take place. The process of model building needs to start at some point, and, over time, the models will get better as business is better understood. Data mining used in this way is not bent on finding the million dollar piece of information, but in building the foundation to model how your business operations are doing. The central point this chapter makes is that data mining is best performed when integrated data repositories are created. The example data warehouses integrated several types of data not commonly placed together in transaction-based databases.

Data mining is a process. New models are built as data is updated The number of studies that can be built with data mining is limitless.

# Data-Mining Vendors

$\mathbf{A}$ppendix A provides the addresses of a number of software vendors. Not only are data-mining companies listed, but useful Web sites are provided, along with information access providers, query tool, EIS and data warehousing vendors. They are listed in the following order:

- Section A.1  Data-Mining Players
- Section A.2  Visualization Tools
- Section A.3  Useful Web Sites
- Section A.4  Information Access Providers
- Section A.5  Data-Warehousing Vendors

## A.1  Data-Mining Players

**Angoss Software International LTC. (KnowledgeSEEKER, KnowledgeSTUDIO)**
34 St. Patrick Street, Suite 200
Toronto, Ontario, Canada, M5T 1V1
(416) 593-1122
Web: http://www.angoss.com

**Attar Software USA (XpertRule Miner)**
Two Deerfoot Trail on Partridge Hill
Harvard, MA 01451
(508) 456-3946
Web: http://www.attar.com

**Business Objects, Inc. (BusinessMiner)**
2870 Zanker Road
San Jose, CA 95134
(408) 953-6000
Web: http://www.businessobjects.com

**Cognos Corporation (Scenario)**
3755 Riverside Drive
P.O. Box 9707, Station T
Ottawan, ON Canada K1G 4K9
(613) 738-1440
Web: http://www.cognos.com

**Dovetail Solutions ("Value, Activity, and Loyalty Technique," Product Triangulation, Conjoint Value)**
2261 Market Street, #457
San Francisco, CA 94114
(510) 583-0831
Web: http://www.dovetailsol.com

**HNC Software Inc. (wide range of data mining solutions)**
5930 Cornerstone Court West
San Diego, California 92121-3728
619-546-8877
Web: http://www.hnc.com

**IBM Corporation (Intelligent Miner for Data, Intelligent Miner for Text)**
Old Orchard Road
Armonk, NY 10504
(914) 765-1900
Web: http://www.ibm.com

**Information Discovery, Inc. (The Data Mining Suite,
The Knowledge Access Suite)**
703B Pier Avenue, Suite 169
Hermosa Beach, CA 90254
(310) 937-3600
Web: http://www.datamining.com

**ISoft (AC2, Alice d'ISoft)**
Chemin de Moulon
F-91190 Gif sur Yvette
33-1 69 35 3737
Web: http://www.alice-soft.com

**NeoVista Solutions, Inc. (Retail Decision Suite, SmartCRM, Decision Series)**
10710 N. Tantau Ave
Cupertino, CA 95014
(408) 777-2929
Web: http://www.neovista.com

**Neural Applications Corp. (NetProphet, Aegis)**
2600 Crosspark Rd.
Coralville, IA 52241
(319) 626-5000
Web: http://www.neural.com

**Oracle Corporation (Darwin)**
500 Oracle Parkway
Redwood Shores, CA 94065
(650) 506-7000
Web: http://www.oracle.com and http://www.think.com

**RightPoint Software (DataCruncher)**
2121 S. El Camino Real, Suite 1200
San Mateo, CA 94403
(415) 287-2000
Web: http://www.rightpoint.com

**Silicon Graphics Computer Systems (MineSet)**
2011 N. Shoreline Blvd.
Mountain View, CA 94043
(415) 960-1980
Web: http://www.sgi.com

**SPSS, Inc. (SPSS Clementine)**
232 S. Wacker Drive, 11th Floor
Chicago, IL 60606
(800) 543-2185
Web: http://www.spss.com

**SAS Institute Inc. (Enterprise Miner)**
SAS Campus Dr.
Cary, NC 27513-2414
(916) 677-8000
Web: http://www.sas.com

**Trajecta (dbProphet)**
611 S. Congress, Suite 420
Austin, TX 78704
(512) 250-2242
Web: http://www.trajecta.com

**Unica Technologies, Inc. (Model 1)**
55 Old Bedford Rd.
Lincoln, MA 01773
(781) 259-5900
Web: http://www.unica-usa.com

**Wizsoft Inc. (WizRule, WizWhy)**
3 Beit Hillel Street
Tel Aviv, Israel 67017
(972) 3-5631948
Web: http://www.wizsoft.com

## A.2  Visualization Tools

**Advanced Visual Systems (AVS/Express)**
300 Fifth Ave.
Waltham, MA 02154
(617) 890-4300
Web: http://www.avs.com

**Alta Analytics, Inc. (NetMap)**
929 Eastwind Drive, Suite 203
Westerville, Ohio 43081
(800) 638-6277
Web: http://www.ALTAnalytics.com

**Belmont Research, Inc. (CrossGraphs)**
84 Sherman St.
Cambridge, MA 02140
(617) 868-6878
Web: http://www.belmont.com

**Environmental Systems Research Institute, Inc.
(MapObjects, ARC/INFO, Arc GIS, Spatial Database Engine)**
380 New York St.
Redlands, CA 92373
(909) 793-2853
Web: http://www.esri.com

**MapInfo Corp. (MapInfo, SpatialWare)**
1 Global View
Troy, NY 12180
(518) 285-6000
Web: http://www.mapinfo.com

**Silicon Graphics Computer Systems (MineSet)**
2011 N. Shoreline Blvd.
Mountain View, CA 94043
(415) 960-1980
Web: http://www.sgi.com

## A.3  Useful Web Sites

**Knowledge Discovery Mine**
Web: http://www.kdnuggets.com

**StatLib (Sample data sets)**
Web: http://lib.stat.cmu.edu/datasets

**U.S. Census Bureau**
Web: http://www.census.gov

**Edgar**
Web: http://www.edgar-online.com

**SGI Source (MLC++)**
Web: http://www.sgi.com/Technology/mlc/

**Getting Marketing Information**
Web: http://www.marketingtools.com

**Source Code for C4.5 Decision Tree Algorithm**
Web: http://ftp.cs.su.oz.au/pub/ml/ (patches)

**Source Code for OC1, a Decision Tree Algorithm**
Web: http://www.cs.jhu.edu/

## A.4  Information Access Providers

**ACNielsen**
177 Broad Street
Stamford, CT 06901
(203) 961-3000
Web: http://www.acnielsen.com

**Acxiom Corporation**
301 Industrial Blvd.
Conway, AR 72032
(800) 922-9466
Web: http://www.acxiom.com

**CACI Marketing Systems**
1100 Glebe Road
Arlington, Virginia 22201
(703) 841-7800
Web: http://www.caci.com

**CorpTech**
12 Alfred Street, Suite 200
Woburn, MA 01801
(800) 454-3647
Web: http://www.corptech.com

**Claritas**
1525 Wilson Blvd., Suite 1000
Arlington, VA 22209
(703) 812-2700
Web: http:/www.claritas.com

**Equifax, Inc.**
1600 Peachtree St. NW
Atlanta, GA 30302
(404) 885-8000
Web: http://www.equifax.com

**Harte-Hanks Data Technologies**
PO Box 269
San Antonio, TX 78291
(212) 829-9000
Web: http://www.harte-hanks.com

**Healthdemographics**
4901 Morena Blvd., Suite 701
San Diego, CA 92117
(800) 590-4545
Web: http://www.healthdemographics.com

**Polk & Co.**
1621 18th St.
Denver, CO 80202
(303) 292-5000
Web: http://www.polk.com

**TRW Information Systems & Services**
1900 Richmond Road
Cleveland, OH 44124
(216) 291-7000
Web: http://www.trw.com
(800) 952-8779

## A.5  Data-Warehousing Vendors

**NCR (Teradata)**
1700 S. Patterson Blvd.
Dayton, OH 45479
(513) 445-5000

**Carleton Corp. (Passport)**
8 New England Executive Park
Burlington, MA 01803
(617) 272-4310

**Evolutionary Technologies, Inc. (Extract Tool Suite)**
4301 Westbank Drive
Austin, TX 78746
(512) 327-6994

**IBM Corp. (IBM DB2 Parallel Edition)**
Old Orchard Rd.
Armonk, NY 10504
(800) 426-3333

**Informix Software, Inc. (INFORMIX-OnLine Dynamic Server)**
4100 Bohannon Drive
Menlo Park, CA 94025
(415) 926-6300

**Oracle Corporation (Parallel Query Option)**
500 Oracle Parkway
Redwood Shores, CA 94086
(800) 633-0583

**Prism Solutions, Inc. (Prism Warehouse Manager)**
1000 Hamlin Court
Sunnyvale, CA 94089
(408) 752-1888

# Installing Demo Software

T his appendix steps through the installation of the exercises and the software products discussed in Chapters 6 and 7.

This appendix is organized as follows:

- Section  B.1  Installing Angoss KnowledgeSEEKER Demo
- Section  B.2  Installing RightPoint DataCruncher
- Section  B.3  Getting Help

## B.1  Installing Angoss KnowledgeSEEKER Demo

The KnowledgeSEEKER Demo runs on Windows 95 and Windows NT. The requirements are:

- 12MB RAM for Windows 95
- 4MB free hard-disk space

For this demo release, a data set for hypertension has been automatically loaded. You will not have the ability to load any other sample data sets. A few of the advanced features have also been grayed out.

We are now ready to install KnowledgeSEEKER, using the included CD-ROM. To do this, follow these steps:

1. Start Microsoft Windows 95 on your PC.
2. Put the CD in your CD-ROM drive. Normally, this is Drive D, but it may be different for you.
3. Choose **Run** from the **Start** menu in the Windows 95 toolbar.
4. Enter *D:\KSeeker\ksedu44.exe* in the Run dialog box and click **OK.**
5. Follow the dialog boxes as you are asked the name of the directories where you want to install the components. The KSW44EDU names appear in the dialog box as C:\ksw43.
6. To start, you will find a program group, KnowledgeSEEKER IV, under the **Programs** section from **Start**.

## B.2  Installing the RightPoint DataCruncher Demo

The RightPoint (formerly DataMind) DataCruncher Demo runs on Windows 95 and Windows NT. It has several limitations, such as the number of columns allowed.

---

**NOTE**: The DataMind demo now requires a password for installing, which is "genius." The requirements for installing this demo are:

- 16MB RAM for Windows 95 and Windows NT
- 6MB free hard-disk space

---

We are now ready to install DataMind, using the included CD-ROM. To do this, follow these steps:

1. Start Microsoft Windows 95 or NT on your PC.
2. Put the CD in your CD-ROM drive. Normally, this is Drive D, but it may be different for you.
3. Choose **Run** from the **Start** menu in the Windows 95 toolbar.
4. Enter *D:\DataMind\disk1\Setup* in the Run dialog box and click **OK.**
   Follow the dialog boxes as you are asked the name of the directories where you want to install the components.
5. You will be prompted for a password to use this demonstration. The password is "genius."

6. The default directory names appear in the dialog box as C:\DataMind.
7. To start, you will find a program group, DataMind, under the **Programs** section from **Start**.

# References

T he following is a list of references used in this book. It also provides a good list of other books that can help you learn more about data mining.

1. Breiman, L., Fredman, J., Olshen, R.A., and Stone, C.J. *Classification and Regression Trees*. Monterey, CA: Wadsworth & Brooks, 1984.
2. Chester, M. *Neural Networks: A Tutorial*. Englewood Cliffs, NJ: Prentice Hall, 1993.
3. Fayyad, U.M.; Piatestsky-Shapiro G.; Smyth D.; and Uthurusamy R. *Advances in Knowledge Discovery and Data Mining*. Cambridge, MA: AAAI Press/MIT Press, 1996.
4. Groth, R. and Gerber, D. *Hands-On SQL: The Language, Querying, Reporting, and the Marketplace*. Upper Saddle River, NJ: Prentice Hall PTR, 1997.
5. Kimball, R. *The Data Warehouse Toolkit, Practical Techniques for Building Dimensional Data Warehouses*. New York, NY: John Wiley & Sons, Inc., 1996 .
6. Michalewicz, Z. *Genetic Algorithms + Data Structures = Evolution Programs*. New York: Springer-Verlag, 1994.
7. Quinnlan, J. *C4.5: Programs for Machine Learning*. Redwood City, CA: Morgan Kaufmann, 1988.

8. Refenes, A. *Neural Networks in the Capital Markets*. New York, NY: John Wiley & Sons, Inc., 1995.

9. Welstead, S.T. *Neural Network and Fuzzy Logic Applications in C/C++*. New York, NY: John Wiley & Sons, Inc., 1994.

# Index

US West, data-mining case study, 9–11

# LICENSE AGREEMENT AND LIMITED WARRANTY

READ THE FOLLOWING TERMS AND CONDITIONS CAREFULLY BEFORE OPENING THIS DISK PACKAGE. THIS LEGAL DOCUMENT IS AN AGREEMENT BETWEEN YOU AND PRENTICE-HALL, INC. (THE "COMPANY"). BY OPENING THIS SEALED DISK PACKAGE, YOU ARE AGREEING TO BE BOUND BY THESE TERMS AND CONDITIONS. IF YOU DO NOT AGREE WITH THESE TERMS AND CONDITIONS, DO NOT OPEN THE DISK PACKAGE. PROMPTLY RETURN THE UNOPENED DISK PACKAGE AND ALL ACCOMPANYING ITEMS TO THE PLACE YOU OBTAINED THEM FOR A FULL REFUND OF ANY SUMS YOU HAVE PAID.

1.　　**GRANT OF LICENSE:** In consideration of your payment of the license fee, which is part of the price you paid for this product, and your agreement to abide by the terms and conditions of this Agreement, the Company grants to you a nonexclusive right to use and display the copy of the enclosed software program (hereinafter the "SOFT-WARE") on a single computer (i.e., with a single CPU) at a single location so long as you comply with the terms of this Agreement. The Company reserves all rights not expressly granted to you under this Agreement.

2.　　**OWNERSHIP OF SOFTWARE:** You own only the magnetic or physical media (the enclosed disks) on which the SOFTWARE is recorded or fixed, but the Company retains all the rights, title, and ownership to the SOFT-WARE recorded on the original disk copy(ies) and all subsequent copies of the SOFTWARE, regardless of the form or media on which the original or other copies may exist. This license is not a sale of the original SOFTWARE or any copy to you.

3.　　**COPY RESTRICTIONS:** This SOFTWARE and the accompanying printed materials and user manual (the "Documentation") are the subject of copyright. You may not copy the Documentation or the SOFTWARE, except that you may make a single copy of the SOFTWARE for backup or archival purposes only. You may be held legally responsible for any copying or copyright infringement which is caused or encouraged by your failure to abide by the terms of this restriction.

4.　　**USE RESTRICTIONS:** You may not network the SOFTWARE or otherwise use it on more than one computer or computer terminal at the same time. You may physically transfer the SOFTWARE from one computer to another provided that the SOFTWARE is used on only one computer at a time. You may not distribute copies of the SOFTWARE or Documentation to others. You may not reverse engineer, disassemble, decompile, modify, adapt, translate, or create derivative works based on the SOFTWARE or the Documentation without the prior written consent of the Company.

5.　　**TRANSFER RESTRICTIONS:** The enclosed SOFTWARE is licensed only to you and may not be transferred to any one else without the prior written consent of the Company. Any unauthorized transfer of the SOFT-WARE shall result in the immediate termination of this Agreement.

6.　　**TERMINATION:** This license is effective until terminated. This license will terminate automatically without notice from the Company and become null and void if you fail to comply with any provisions or limitations of this license. Upon termination, you shall destroy the Documentation and all copies of the SOFTWARE. All provisions of this Agreement as to warranties, limitation of liability, remedies or damages, and our ownership rights shall survive termination.

7.　　**MISCELLANEOUS:** This Agreement shall be construed in accordance with the laws of the United States of America and the State of New York and shall benefit the Company, its affiliates, and assignees.

8.　　**LIMITED WARRANTY AND DISCLAIMER OF WARRANTY:** The Company warrants that the SOFTWARE, when properly used in accordance with the Documentation, will operate in substantial conformity with the description of the SOFTWARE set forth in the Documentation. The Company does not warrant that the SOFT-

WARE will meet your requirements or that the operation of the SOFTWARE will be uninterrupted or error-free. The Company warrants that the media on which the SOFTWARE is delivered shall be free from defects in materials and workmanship under normal use for a period of thirty (30) days from the date of your purchase. Your only remedy and the Company's only obligation under these limited warranties is, at the Company's option, return of the warranted item for a refund of any amounts paid by you or replacement of the item. Any replacement of SOFTWARE or media under the warranties shall not extend the original warranty period. The limited warranty set forth above shall not apply to any SOFTWARE which the Company determines in good faith has been subject to misuse, neglect, improper installation, repair, alteration, or damage by you. EXCEPT FOR THE EXPRESSED WARRANTIES SET FORTH ABOVE, THE COMPANY DISCLAIMS ALL WARRANTIES, EXPRESS OR IMPLIED, INCLUDING WITHOUT LIMITATION, THE IMPLIED WARRANTIES OF MERCHANTABILITY AND FITNESS FOR A PARTICULAR PURPOSE. EXCEPT FOR THE EXPRESS WARRANTY SET FORTH ABOVE, THE COMPANY DOES NOT WARRANT, GUARANTEE, OR MAKE ANY REPRESENTATION REGARDING THE USE OR THE RESULTS OF THE USE OF THE SOFTWARE IN TERMS OF ITS CORRECTNESS, ACCURACY, RELIABILITY, CURRENTNESS, OR OTHERWISE.

IN NO EVENT, SHALL THE COMPANY OR ITS EMPLOYEES, AGENTS, SUPPLIERS, OR CONTRACTORS BE LIABLE FOR ANY INCIDENTAL, INDIRECT, SPECIAL, OR CONSEQUENTIAL DAMAGES ARISING OUT OF OR IN CONNECTION WITH THE LICENSE GRANTED UNDER THIS AGREEMENT, OR FOR LOSS OF USE, LOSS OF DATA, LOSS OF INCOME OR PROFIT, OR OTHER LOSSES, SUSTAINED AS A RESULT OF INJURY TO ANY PERSON, OR LOSS OF OR DAMAGE TO PROPERTY, OR CLAIMS OF THIRD PARTIES, EVEN IF THE COMPANY OR AN AUTHORIZED REPRESENTATIVE OF THE COMPANY HAS BEEN ADVISED OF THE POSSIBILITY OF SUCH DAMAGES. IN NO EVENT SHALL LIABILITY OF THE COMPANY FOR DAMAGES WITH RESPECT TO THE SOFTWARE EXCEED THE AMOUNTS ACTUALLY PAID BY YOU, IF ANY, FOR THE SOFTWARE.

SOME JURISDICTIONS DO NOT ALLOW THE LIMITATION OF IMPLIED WARRANTIES OR LIABILITY FOR INCIDENTAL, INDIRECT, SPECIAL, OR CONSEQUENTIAL DAMAGES, SO THE ABOVE LIMITATIONS MAY NOT ALWAYS APPLY. THE WARRANTIES IN THIS AGREEMENT GIVE YOU SPECIFIC LEGAL RIGHTS AND YOU MAY ALSO HAVE OTHER RIGHTS WHICH VARY IN ACCORDANCE WITH LOCAL LAW.

### ACKNOWLEDGMENT

YOU ACKNOWLEDGE THAT YOU HAVE READ THIS AGREEMENT, UNDERSTAND IT, AND AGREE TO BE BOUND BY ITS TERMS AND CONDITIONS. YOU ALSO AGREE THAT THIS AGREEMENT IS THE COMPLETE AND EXCLUSIVE STATEMENT OF THE AGREEMENT BETWEEN YOU AND THE COMPANY AND SUPERSEDES ALL PROPOSALS OR PRIOR AGREEMENTS, ORAL, OR WRITTEN, AND ANY OTHER COMMUNICATIONS BETWEEN YOU AND THE COMPANY OR ANY REPRESENTATIVE OF THE COMPANY RELATING TO THE SUBJECT MATTER OF THIS AGREEMENT.

Should you have any questions concerning this Agreement or if you wish to contact the Company for any reason, please contact in writing at the address below.

Robin Short
Prentice Hall PTR
One Lake Street
Upper Saddle River, New Jersey 07458

# About the CD-ROM

## CONTENTS

The CD included with this book includes white papers, utilities, and scripts. The CD is intended to complement the book by offering additional information such as architecture white papers, product features, and performance tuning tips. The CD also includes SQL scripts that can be used to monitor database performance.

## SYSTEM REQUIREMENTS

The file types are noted in each README file per section. You may need a PostScript viewer (.ps files) such as pageview on Solaris, a browser (.html files), Acrobat Reader (.pdf files), Microsoft PowerPoint (.ppt files), Microsoft Word (.doc files), and a text editor (.txt or .sql files). The CD is organized into the following directories:

- hp: HP white papers and bulletins
- nca: Network Computing Architecture white papers
- oracle: Oracle white papers
- scripts: Performance monitoring scripts (SQL)
- sequent: Sequent white papers and utilities
- sun: Sun white papers, bulletins, and scripts
- veritas: Veritas white papers

## TECHNICAL SUPPORT

The CD does not include software. Therefore, technical support is not provided by Prentice Hall nor the author. If, however, you feel that your CD is damaged, please contact Prentice Hall for a replacement: disc_exchange@prenhall.com.